Reading Like a Lawyer

Reading Like a Lawyer

Mastering the Art of Reading Law Like an Expert

THIRD EDITION

Ruth Ann McKinney

CAROLINA ACADEMIC PRESS
Durham, North Carolina

Library of Congress Cataloging-in-Publication Data

Names: McKinney, Ruth Ann, 1951– author.
Title: Reading like a lawyer : mastering the art of reading law like an expert / by Ruth Ann McKinney.
Description: Third edition. | Durham, NC : Carolina Academic Press, LLC, [2022] | Includes bibliographical references and index.
Identifiers: LCCN 2022008158 (print) | LCCN 2022008159 (ebook) | ISBN 9781531024864 (paperback) | ISBN 9781531024871 (ebook)
Subjects: LCSH: Law students—United States—Handbooks, manuals, etc. | Law—Study and teaching—United States. | Reading comprehension.
Classification: LCC KF283 .M398 2022 (print) | LCC KF283 (ebook) | DDC 340.071/173—dc23/eng/20220526
LC record available at https://lccn.loc.gov/2022008158
LC ebook record available at https://lccn.loc.gov/2022008159

Carolina Academic Press
700 Kent Street
Durham, North Carolina 27701
(919) 489-7486
www.cap-press.com

Printed in the United States of America

To my parents, who taught me to love reading;

To the students, faculty, and staff of the University of North Carolina School of Law, where I learned to love reading law;

and

To Ray, who reminds me to play.

CONTENTS

INTRODUCTION

Exceptional law students, and exceptional lawyers, are expert readers. From the first semester of law school, fledgling lawyers commonly read hundreds of pages of dense, challenging law in a week, and thousands of pages in a semester. Later, in practice, lawyers read statutes, cases, and administrative regulations every day, decoding the words in the texts and reaching behind the words to the many possible meanings that could be attributed to the law they're reading.

Law students—and lawyers—who read law well are getting something from their reading that is not shared by those who read law less proficiently. Starting with the first days of class, what law students understand about the reading process itself has a major impact on how they read their assignments. How they read their assignments determines what they are able to get from those cases and statutes, what they are able to bring to class discussions and take from class discussions, and—ultimately—what they are able to learn for exams. How they read in law school, in turn, directs the path of their reading in the profession.

Practicing lawyers who have developed sound reading practices in law school approach their analytical work with confidence, secure in the knowledge that they can read the law powerfully, passionately, and accurately. Put succinctly, these lawyers read with conviction, knowing they are reading like an expert.

The good news is that the ability to read law like an expert is not a gift that you're either born with or lack from birth. Students and practitioners have not been separated into the sheep and the goats prior to entering law school, relegated forever to green pastures or rocky cliffs. Rather, reading law like an expert is a skill that can be acquired by everyone with the curiosity, determination, and flexibility to adapt their prior reading skills to this new setting—and these skills can be acquired *at any time*. Once acquired and whenever acquired, the skill of reading law like an expert brings cascading rewards, enriching the reader's understanding of existing law and enhancing the reader's ability to create new paths to the law of the future.

The purpose of this book is to teach you what the experts already know: how to read law-related material as efficiently, effectively, and powerfully as possible. **Each chapter includes Practice Exercises at the end** so that you can apply what you are learning. After you've tried your hand at those exercises, you can **check the accompanying website (caplaw.com/rll)** to see some of the ideas I had as I wrote those questions.

The book is divided into three parts:

Part I (Building a Strong Foundation) introduces you to background information you need to know about the study and practice of law to get in the reading game. If you are confident that you already understand the fundamentals of legal logic and the structure of law school, you may choose to go directly to Part II.

Part II (Mastering Reading in a Law School Casebook) focuses on casebook reading, the kind of reading that dominates the first years of law school. This second section introduces seven specific reading strategies, captured in the acronym E.M.P.O.W.E.R., that are common to all expert reading, and explores how law students can apply these strategies in the context of their casebook reading.

Part III (Moving Beyond the Casebook) explores how students and practitioners can read statutes and unedited cases accurately, confidently, and efficiently. This third section also explores how expert readers process important information when reading on a screen, including tips for how not to get distracted when reading complex legal material online.

At the end of the book, there are four appendices: Appendix A gives you a chance to test your baseline reading speed; Appendix B introduces a case-reading checklist that beginning students can use to develop healthy casebook reading habits; Appendix C introduces an advanced case-reading checklist to help successful students speed up their reading once they've developed sound habits. Appendix D offers a reading list for those who would like to explore the topic of legal reading in greater depth.

At their core, both law study and law practice are dependent on reading. If you learn to read law efficiently and effectively, you will be well on your way to achieving excellence in the study and practice of law. It is my hope that what you learn from this book will help get you started on the right page.

PART I

Building a Strong Foundation

CHAPTER 1

Reading Right

The Key to Success in Law School

The study of law is intriguing, inspiring countless works of fiction and enhancing movie careers for actors ranging from Gregory Peck to Reese Witherspoon. All this attention stems partly from the novelty of law study, a form of education that is infamous for being different from other forms of professional training, and partly from the inherent drama that surrounds the stories of human conflict that characterize law.

For students entering law school, the study of law moves quickly from the realm of the dramatic into the stark reality of their daily lives. For some law students, the reality of law study turns out to be far less captivating than they had imagined it would be. For others, the original excitement associated with law study never wears off.

The difference lies—at least in part—in whether the student eventually decodes the mystery of law school and engages in the rewarding process of learning law, or studies blindly, lost in a perpetual, directionless cycle of uninspired work. The goal of this chapter is to introduce you to the basic elements of the law school experience so you can engage with confidence. By the end of this chapter, you will understand why reading law well is so important.

A. The Structure of Law School

Though different in many ways from other academic experiences, the study of law occurs in a coherent ecosystem that sustains itself. There is a predictable rhythm, a symmetry, to the development of the knowledge and skills shared by trained lawyers—and much of that rhythm is born out of the interactive processes of reading, thinking, talking, and writing about law that occurs in the law school classroom, in the preparation for those classes, and in the tests that are administered at the end of the semester.

The courses students take in the first year are expressly designed to create a laboratory experience where students read legal cases, discern patterns of law in those cases, discuss that law and confirm or alter their perceptions of those patterns, and—ultimately—are tested on their ability to apply the developed patterns they've observed to new fact situations. None of this knowledge—not the concrete rules that begin to emerge nor the inchoate factors that influence the development of those rules—is handed to students on a silver platter. The knowledge and skills acquired gradually in law school are the result of the interactive, fluid process of reading, thinking, talking, listening, re-reading, applying, guessing, writing, correcting, and trying again that marks the day in and day out intellectual activities of law students.

B. The Traditional Law School Casebook

In the first year of law school, much of the focus of law study is on courses arising from common law rules, from a combination of common law rules and statutes, from procedural rules of court, and from constitutional law. Rather than using traditional textbooks that talk *about* the law, these courses expose students directly *to the law* itself through reading assigned in casebooks.[1]

---

1. *See* Lisa Eichhorn, Hard Cases: Reading in the First Year of Law School (1998) (unpublished manuscript, on file with the author at the University of South Carolina School of Law). Professor Eichhorn notes that beginning students can easily (and

A traditional casebook focuses on only one area of law (for example, Torts or Criminal Law) and is divided into sub-topics that together cover the issues germane to that area of law.[2] Sub-topics in a torts book would include, for example, the intentional torts such as battery as well as issues surrounding negligence such as duty or standard of care. Within each sub-topic of an area of law, the casebook contains clusters of edited cases—actual opinions written and published by judges in various jurisdictions.

The cases have been carefully selected and carefully edited by the casebook author *based on what the author wants you to learn,* not based on the fact that the cases are necessarily earth-shattering, landmark cases (although some might be). Some of these cases may contradict one another (they are collected from different jurisdictions that may apply different common law rules), some show evolution in the law (juxtaposing an old case against a newer decision handling similar facts in a more modern context), some show exceptions to a dominant rule (situations where the general rule shouldn't be applied), and some are just poorly decided (included to make you think about what does and doesn't make sense).

In addition to the opinions themselves, casebooks often include some written material that is similar to analytical material you may have read in traditional textbooks in other disciplines. Sometimes the casebook author will reprint an article written by a recognized expert in this area of law, or the casebook author will summarize background information to help put the cases you will read into a useful context. In today's more modern casebooks, you will even see sidebar comments designed to add interesting contextual information.

---

wrongly) assume that law school casebooks are based on the kind of secondary material commonly found in undergraduate textbooks when, in fact, law school casebooks largely present *primary* material—the cases themselves. Such a misunderstanding, according to Professor Eichhorn, leads even good readers to make wrong assumptions about their reading purpose.

2. Increasingly, electronic casebooks are finding their way into the law school classroom. Chapter 15 explores ways to use electronic casebooks to your best advantage.

Following a cluster of cases or at the conclusion of a sub-topic, casebook authors often include a series of questions or comments to give you more to think about (or to give you hints about things that you could have been thinking about as you read the cases themselves). Often there are no right or wrong answers to these questions or concrete responses to the comments—the casebook authors are just providing you with food for thought. Even without right or wrong answers, however, these questions can help you identify right and wrong factors to be considered as you learn to process legal issues in the way that is common to lawyers. In short, they can give you an inside look at what lawyers think about when they read a case or compare related cases.

C. Really, How *Do* Lawyers Think?

As you read the assigned cases in your casebook, you will be exposed to the things that one judge thought about as he or she decided the legal question put before him or her. Most of the time, you will not be reading cases that were written at the trial level.[3] Rather, you will be reading cases decided by a court of appeals—a court given the task of deciding a case brought up on appeal because one or more of the parties involved thought an error of law (or, generally, more than one error of law) occurred at the trial or pre-trial level.

The court of appeals (sometimes an intermediate appellate court, sometimes the highest court in that jurisdiction) deciding the case does *not* retry or redetermine the facts of the conflict. The appellate court, for example, does not hear witnesses or re-think whether the light was red or green at the site of an accident. Rather, the appellate court looks at the legal question raised by the parties (presented in the form of written briefs submitted to

---

3. The majority of published opinions are written by appellate courts, not trial courts. Nonetheless, some trial courts—especially federal district courts and courts from larger states—do file written opinions explaining the legal conclusions they reach in the course of a hearing or trial.

the appellate court, sometimes followed by oral argument presented to the judges in court)[4] and decides if the court below did or did not commit reversible error.

In the process of reaching its decision, the court thinks about many things (including the existing controlling law as presented by the parties, the facts as presented by the court below, and sometimes the public policy issues involved). When its decision is reached, the court may decide to have one or more judges write an opinion expressing the reasons the court reached its result, or may decide to simply announce its result in summary form, without explanation. If a judge writes an opinion for the majority, other judges may write concurring opinions (opinions that support the result but express different reasoning) or dissenting opinions (opinions that express disagreement with the result of the case). The court may decide to publish the opinions in books called reporters[5] that are maintained by that court so that attorneys and/or the public can read the opinions in the future. Alternatively, the court may decide not to officially publish the opinions.[6]

---

4. If you are curious to see what an appellate brief looks like or to hear a real oral argument, you can find examples online from cases heard at the United States Supreme Court: https://www.justice.gov/osg/supreme-court-briefs. The U.S. Solicitor General files all briefs online here: https://www.justice.gov/osg/supreme-court-briefs. To hear audio excerpts of select oral arguments made in the Court, visit the United States Supreme Court website here: https://www.supremecourt.gov/oral_arguments. Many law school libraries also house appellate briefs from cases heard in state appellate courts and many state court websites make electronically filed briefs and recorded oral arguments available online. You can also check to see if your state's appellate courts allow the public to attend oral arguments, some of which can be heard online and some of which can be heard in person.

5. A reporter contains the published opinions for a particular court of law. These opinions are generally printed in consecutive chronological order by the date the court released the opinion. You will learn more about reporters in Chapter 14.

6. For a variety of reasons, including the cost of publishing opinions and the pressure not to publish opinions that do not have precedent-setting weight, a court might decide not to officially publish an opinion, issuing its opinion only to the attorneys for the parties to the case. Such unpublished opinions are often available through other sources,

What first year law students read most of the time, then, are opinions from an appellate court and occasionally from a trial court. These opinions (mostly published) were selected by their casebook authors because the written words of the court that decided the case express ideas and explore issues that the casebook author believes—if taken in conjunction with the background material and questions also included in the same section—will forward the students' understanding of the sub-topic covered in that part of the casebook.

D. Law Study as an Immersion Experience in the World of Law

In the beginning, it is a challenge for law students to try to figure out what is going on logistically in a given case. It can take forever to read even the shortest case. Cases are written in a whole new language based on understandings about the world of legal reasoning that judges and lawyers take for granted (although it's encouraging to remember that the language and conventions of law were new to all lawyers and judges at one time).

Because the language and assumptions about the legal process are familiar to judges and lawyers, the judges often write in a way that is clear to other experts in the field, but which is overwhelmingly confusing to a beginner. I have heard law students describe their first case reading and class experiences as being similar to a foreign language immersion course held in the foreign country and conducted completely in the new language. Learning about a foreign culture in an immersion course is not always comfortable, but eventually it works.

The secret to success in such an immersion course is to stay alert and pay attention to what you know and what you don't know. Learn as many new things as you can each day, while trying to let go of unimportant things so

---

but carry a different weight as authority for subsequent cases than do published opinions. The rules of court for any given jurisdiction determine how an attorney can use an unpublished opinion.

your brain is free to grab hold of what matters. Follow the language in your reading and in your classroom, but not blindly. Instead, draw inferences when you can, keep a dictionary close to your side, write your questions down, and get answers to those that leave you puzzled.

Do not let yourself "check out" mentally, hoping that somehow—perhaps by osmosis—things will all come clear. Instead, think all the time you are reading and all the time you are in class, writing down what you don't know and getting answers, and writing down what you sort of know but need to review. The more often you hear a new term and recognize it because you paid attention before, the more quickly that term (and the concept it represents) will move from your short term memory into long-term memory for retrieval later. Studying law with anything less than total intellectual engagement and insatiable curiosity about the new language and customs of law would be as ineffective as enrolling in a foreign language immersion course only to sleep all day, keep to yourself, and eat the food you packed before you left home.

The acculturation process that characterizes law study begins with your reading, but does not end there. Once you've read your assignments, you go to class where your professor initiates a dialogue about the cases you've read.[7] The professor often starts by bringing up a fact scenario different from those in the cases you've read, but then asks what a judge should do based on what was decided by the judges in your casebook. To participate successfully, you need to come to class armed with the ideas you have taken from your reading and build on those fledgling ideas through the class

7. Although law students are occasionally surprised by a class that is largely lecture in format, most law school classes are dominated by the "Socratic" method introduced by Charles Langdell at the end of the 19th century. The traditional Socratic class, and variations of it, remains the dominant form of classroom learning in law school. In a typical Socratic class, ideas are generated through questioning directed by the professor with the end goal being that students create new understandings about the topic at hand as new questions and responses (often in the form of "hypothetical" fact situations applied to emerging rules) challenge deeper, richer, and more concrete understanding of the area being studied.

discussion that grows from the reading. Your ideas take root as you listen to the ideas your professor expresses about the reading and to the ideas that your peers generate—paying particular attention to which ideas spark a warm reception from your professor.

As you participate in the class (largely by listening intently and by thinking as you listen), your original ideas will change, taking on new life and new meaning. In addition to listening for ideas about the particular case that is being discussed, you also want to be listening and watching *how* your professor thinks. What is important to your professor about this case? Why? Aside from the case itself, is your teacher exposing you to basic information about the practice of law (the kind of thing the judges who authored the opinion assume their readers know) that you should be holding on to and storing in your long-term memory?

E. What Happens Before and After Class?

After class, the learning process continues. The luxury of learning concrete pieces of information through lecture in class—or putting off fully understanding the issue discussed in a class until "later"—are luxuries that belong in your past. Time is critical in law school, where the next wave of new thoughts follows quickly on the wake of the last.

Instead of waiting to integrate information until the end of the semester or until the weekend, wise students learn to think about each class as it occurs. Similarly, rather than waiting to develop ideas until *after* hearing the professor's thoughts, wise students have learned to bring their own ideas *to* class, expecting to modify them there.

Law classes include a great deal of discussion and generate an endless stream of ideas as the students and professor struggle with cases together to find coherent patterns in the sub-topic covered in that class. Students who try to hold on to each contribution that comes up in class, hoping to process them all later, will quickly become overwhelmed. Experienced law students learn that most of the contributions made in class are part of a thinking *process* that is occurring spontaneously, right before their eyes. This process leads, ultimately, to the emergence of significant principles and illustrations of those principles in the area of law being discussed that day or in the series of days that the topic is on the table.

Once the process is complete and the principles and useful examples have emerged, many of the ideas that were explored along the way can be discarded. A carpenter who builds a fine piece of furniture can (and eventually should) discard the wood chips and sawdust whittled away from the final product. Similarly, a law student who has come to class with a framework of ideas about the specific topic at hand and listens and thinks in class while developing those ideas can (and should) discard much of the discussion and many of the contributing ideas once the final picture has emerged. The sooner the decision is made about what to keep and what to discard, the more mental room there is for new thoughts and new patterns to emerge.

F. Thinking Differently About Words

The ability to distill the details discussed in cases into the dominant, over-arching principles that manage each sub-topic covered in your course (or raised by a client in practice) is the most valuable skill a law student (or lawyer) can develop. The astute law student and the astute lawyer have to see the patterns that emerge over time as courts decide case after case, conflict after conflict.

Simply generating these principles and rules, however, isn't enough. Law in a common law country is not rooted in static, black and white rules because words are fluid, subject to multiple inferences and interpretations, and because times (and, therefore, perceptions of just results) change. Words that express rules gain shape as they are applied to new realities.

Law emerges in a never-ending process of word clarification as individual conflicts arise and are resolved and the facts of each new conflict add a rich new understanding to the rules relied on to resolve them. Here's a good example: if a teacher tells high school students to "behave" on a trip or risk suspension, what the teacher means and what the students understand may be two different things. If the students have known this teacher long enough to have been exposed to specific illustrations of what she considers misbehavior, or if the teacher gives concrete illustrations of what students have done in the past to get suspended on previous trips, the gap in understanding narrows.

Because the real meaning of rules rests in how they are applied to facts, the most astute law students and lawyers similarly train themselves to remember critical facts from illustrative cases so that they can use those examples to teach others (often, a judge in the future or a client needing counseling) the tangible meaning of the principles and rules that have emerged in any given area of law.

G. What's Up with Law School Exams?

Having the ability to move from the trees (specific, illustrative case conflicts) to the forest (over-arching principles emerging from patterns of cases) and then back again to the trees (to illustrate the validity of the principles or to compare new facts to them to see if the same principles should apply) is the essence of being an exceptional lawyer. This skill—the ability to move from the trees to the forest and back again—is what is tested on exams.

Although a traditional law school classroom provides little direct feedback from your professor on an individual basis until exam time, the opportunities to practice this skill (applying new facts to recognized legal principles) are plentiful, even before exam day. In law school, you practice discerning the rules and applying them to new situations (testing the boundaries of the rules, the soundness of a court's rationale) in your head while you listen in class. A good habit to develop is to reinforce yourself when you think you were on the right track and to correct yourself (without judgment) when it appears that your initial train of thought was wrong.

You also practice these skills by paying close attention to the ideas your peers and professors are expressing and by asking yourself which ideas and which illustrations make sense to you. If a significant emerging principle discussed in class does not make sense to you, you need to pursue it until it does. Listen to the discussion, honor the questions that are in your head (and write them down to think about later), ask a peer who does understand, or ask your professor after class. As the semester goes on, the enormous comfort that comes when you understand what is going on around you may be the most concrete positive feedback you'll get.

The life cycle that characterizes a typical semester of law study eventually comes full circle. Exams themselves, one of the great mysteries of legal education for beginning law students, are tied inexorably and rationally to the cases you've read and discussed throughout the year—but perhaps not in the way that many students anticipate. Exams are not tied directly to the specific facts in a case or to the specific statements a judge made in this case or that case. Rather, exams offer an opportunity for students to apply the principles that emerged from their reading and from the ensuing class discussion to facts that are similar to the kinds of facts that initiated the courts' initial discussions within the opinions in the first place. It is a lot like the school children discussed earlier whose teacher wanted them to "behave." Through experience and illustrations, the children would eventually see a pattern emerging in their teacher's expectations and could make rational decisions about what kinds of behaviors would result in suspension in the future.

Law school exams in the first year are most traditionally essay exams, but increasingly professors are also asking short-answer questions. On a traditional law school essay exam, you will have the opportunity to put pen to paper to test your developing ability to identify and remember important patterns in each area of law you've studied and to apply these patterns to concrete fact situations as you try to anticipate how a court might resolve the fact scenarios suggested by your professors on exams. On a typical short-answer exam, you will have similar opportunities to test your ability to remember patterns and distinctions among patterns, or to resolve hypothetical conflicts based on illustrations proposed in multiple choice scenarios or other objective questions.

It would be unusual in any law school exam to be asked only to regurgitate concrete facts from cases or hard and fast rules (often called "black-letter law"[8]). Most professors assume by exam time that you will know the rules and any facts from significant cases that have helped you understand the meaning of those words. What they want to test is whether you know how to use these rules (as developed richly in actual case applications) to anticipate the things a court would consider if it had to reach a result under a new set of facts made up for the exam (or, someday, brought in by a client when you are actually practicing law).

Reading, thinking, then writing about the law—all these experiences cause a subtle, gradual, successful shift to a new vocabulary and a new awareness of the intellectual world inhabited by lawyers. There is much hard work involved in uncovering, organizing, and then memorizing the principles that emerge from the many cases you'll read, and much hard work involved in learning how to clearly and logically apply those principles to an infinite number of potential fact scenarios on exams and in the practice of law.

Much of your success will depend on cognitive work that occurs at a level of which you may not be consciously aware. Developing steady, confident study habits that integrate your reading, your thinking, your listening, and your written notes—all while keeping your brain engaged—will lead to your eventual adoption of the new language and new culture that characterize the study and practice of law.

---

8. Bryan A. Garner, Dictionary of Modern Legal Usage 112 (3rd ed. 2011) (describing "blackletter law" as "legal principles that are fundamental and well settled"). Garner notes that the term "blackletter law" derives from the term "black-letter type," a "heavy Gothic" typeface used to print the "medieval Year Book" that contained summaries of legal rules and decisions. The term is commonly used today to denote hardline rules of law as opposed to more nuanced rules and related policy issues.

PRACTICE EXERCISES

Remember that you can visit caplaw.com/rll to see some of the responses I had in mind as I wrote the Practice Exercises at the end of each chapter.

1. Scholars of rhetoric (effective communication) would call the unique world inhabited by lawyers a "discourse community." A discourse community is a group of individuals who share a common language, common knowledge base, common thinking habits, and common intellectual assumptions. There is, for example, a medical discourse community. People with experience in the field of medicine share common assumptions, experiences, and means of expression that are not shared by people with no experience in medicine. Within the medical discourse community, there are numerous sub-discourse communities comprised, for example, of nurses or anesthesiologists or lab technicians. While these sub-discourse community members all share things in common with each other (because they're all members of the medical discourse community) they also have unique attributes and means of expression not shared by individuals outside their own sub-community. We are all members of numerous "discourse" communities and sub-communities.

   Name one discourse community that you are a member of:

   Is this discourse community a sub-community of a larger discourse community?

   Are there sub-communities within your immediate discourse community?

2. Name three vocabulary words that might have a special meaning within your discourse community, but a different meaning outside of your discourse community:

3. How did you become a member of this discourse community?

4. How would you help bring a novice into this discourse community? In other words, how could you teach someone what people who share this profession, this hobby, or this social network know, how they think, and how they express themselves?

5. How is the process you described in (4) above similar to the process followed in law schools as educators try to bring beginning law students into the legal discourse community? How is it different?

6. Why does the ability to read well (in an active, engaged, and effective manner) have such an important role in introducing newcomers to the legal discourse community?

CHAPTER 2

Basic Briefing

Developing an Initial Strategy for Managing Cases

A. Why You Need a "Schema" for Managing Cases

Educational psychologists talk about the importance of having a "schema," or framework, that allows us to think logically and efficiently about a situation we may see repeatedly. A schema is a cluster of information that we hold in our mind about a subject. Having a schema keeps us from having to approach a familiar situation from scratch each time. Schemata inform our perceptions, our assumptions, and our processing of information.

For example, because I can drive a car, I have developed a "schema" about driving. If I decide to drive my car to school, I know I will need keys and the car will need gas. I also know I should carry a driver's license and that my car has to have passed inspection. Eventually, I'll have to park the car someplace—I know I can't take it into class with me. If a friend says, "Would you mind using my car to give me a ride to work?" my "car driving" schema will be activated and I will want to know whether I have my driver's license on me and who has the keys to my friend's car. I may wonder if my friend's car is enough like mine that it will be easy for me to drive, and I might want to check to make sure there's enough gas for the trip.

Without experience, I can have no schema and the processing of information about a topic is inefficient and sometimes overwhelming. For example, if someone asked me to drive a tractor-trailer truck, the request might trigger my "car driving schema," but I'd have enough sense to know that this schema wouldn't get me very far. I would know I'd need fuel, and could guess I'd need a key. I imagine (but am not sure) that there are more than five gears and more than one clutch involved—but I don't know how to drive a vehicle with more than one clutch. I don't even know what type of fuel to put in a tractor-trailer—or where to fill it up, much less how to handle multiple gears. Someone with experience in driving large trucks would be able to call on a wealth of information (a schema) unavailable to me and would be in a much better position to drive the truck than I would.

Students who first enter law school know quite a bit about academics and quite a bit about law. They know what a traditional classroom looks like, and they can anticipate that learning in a professional school will involve homework, a teacher, and some form of evaluation. If they've grown up with access to mainstream T.V. and movies, they've seen pictures of courtrooms, reenactments of trials, and solved mysteries that turned on a fine point of law. They've probably seen movies or read books about law school itself. A day hardly passes that law of one kind or another isn't covered in the front pages of most newspapers. Some students who have taken undergraduate or professional courses involving law (for example, law and literature or the history of the Constitution) may even have read court opinions. Others may have read court records, helped attorneys prepare for trial, or served as witnesses in a trial.

As a result of these experiences, all students begin law school with some schemata (associations, expectations, plans) that will help put the study of law in a rational context. Like my "car schema," however, these prior frameworks may have limited usefulness as students open their casebooks and begin the process of decoding the opinions they will read—not because there's anything wrong with the reading schemata they come in with, but because the unique characteristics of law school may limit the applicability of their existing schemata in the same way that my prior experiences driving a car would not translate literally to the challenge of driving a truck.

Without a proper schema, students can't process information correctly or efficiently. Thus, the first step for a law student approaching the challenge of reading cases in a casebook is to develop a schema (plan) that will help the student organize the information contained in cases into predictable, manageable clusters of information. In short, beginning students need to know what to look for in cases and what to expect to learn from cases.

Over the years, the practice of "briefing" cases has evolved as a tool that law students, law professors, and lawyers can use to help organize the information presented in legal opinions in a way that makes that information manageable and easy to retrieve. This chapter is designed to introduce (or reintroduce) you to case briefing as a valuable schema (framework) that can help you organize your thoughts—quickly and efficiently—about any opinion you are reading.

B. What Will You See in Most Court Cases?

Unedited court decisions, published just as the court disseminated them, are found in books called "reporters."[1] Collectively, a court's bound reporters contain all the published cases ("decisions") in any given jurisdiction for a specific court from its earliest decisions to its current published cases.[2]

---

1. Although there is rarely any reason to reach beyond the edited version of a case contained in your casebook, if you are overwhelmed with curiosity, all the cases in your casebook can be found in their entirety in a reporter or, depending on the year of decision, online. Law students learn how to find cases in their first-year legal research classes. If you are not in law school, you can find the full, unedited version of a case by asking a reference librarian at a law school library, or, increasingly, by googling.
2. The majority of this book focuses on strategies for reading effectively and efficiently in a traditional law school casebook. In Section III of the book, however, the focus shifts to reading law in the real world. Chapter 14 expressly addresses strategies for reading *un*edited cases published in reporters.

If you've ever seen a portrait of a lawyer or judge with rows of matching books in the background, those books are probably reporters.

You will rarely see an unedited case, straight out of a reporter, in a traditional law school casebook. Rather, as you learned in Chapter 1, edited cases (cases that may have been shortened or paraphrased in part by a casebook author) comprise the bulk of the content in casebooks assigned to law students as their textbooks.

You can tell when a case has been edited because ellipses (...) or bracketed information ([ ]) will appear. Ellipses indicate that part of the case has been taken out. Brackets indicate that the information contained in the bracket, often paraphrased material, has been added by the casebook author for clarification. If a case has been edited by your casebook author, there is rarely (if ever) any reason to go back and find the original opinion. The edited parts have been excerpted or changed for a reason. Trust the author's judgment and read the case as it is presented in your casebook.

The caption for a case stands at the beginning of the case, and tells you three things: (1) the names of the parties in the original lawsuit or conflict (almost always the last name, and almost always only the name of one party for each side even if there were multiple parties); (2) the official reporter in which the case can be found, from which you can almost always infer the name of the court that decided the case and often the place of decision; and (3) the date the opinion was published (which can be several years away from when the original conflict arose, but it will give you an idea of the historical context of the case).

The name of the deciding judge or justice appears (sometimes in parentheses) on the first line of the edited case. Often, the judge's name is irrelevant. Occasionally, though, you'll recognize the name of the deciding judge and may know something about that judge's political persuasions or historical stature, which may influence what you expect to learn as you read the case. Cases by well-respected, widely known judges such as Justice Benjamin Cardozo or Justice Thurgood Marshall are often written in a particularly compelling style or carry particularly significant historical weight.

The remainder of the text is the opinion itself. There are no hard and fast rules for authoring an opinion, and judges' purposes in authoring opinions vary markedly.[3] Although there are no set opinion-writing guidelines anywhere, there are certain conventions that have evolved over time that can help you get oriented when you read a case. The following list describes six distinct pieces of information that are included in most court opinions:

(1) What led up to this opinion? Most opinions contain a statement of what happened to the case before it came in front of the present court. This part of the opinion is loosely referred to as the "procedural history" of the case. A full understanding of procedural history comes with experience and is dependent on how much you know about the development of lawsuits and the rules (and language) of civil procedure. In the beginning, you will be using your ability to infer and your ability to use a legal dictionary to understand the procedural history of the cases you read. You can pick up a lot about procedural history in the early weeks of class by listening carefully to your professors' and fellow students' explanations of what happened "below."[4]

(2) What's the conflict about? At some point, the court will tell the "story" of the parties—what was the conflict about in the first place? In the

---

3. Nancy Wanderer, *Writing Better Opinions: Communicating with Candor, Clarity, and Style*, 54 ME. L. REV. 47, 53 (2002) (noting that there are a number of intended audiences for judicial opinions, and that the purposes for writing such opinions in the American judicial system are wide and varied); *see also* Gerald Lebovits, Alifya V. Curtin & Lisa Solomon, *Ethical Judicial Opinion Writing*, 21 GEO. J. LEGAL ETHICS 237 (2008); Patricia M. Wald, *The Rhetoric of Results and the Results of Rhetoric: Judicial Writings*, 62 U. CHI. L. REV. 1371 (1995); Michael Well, *French and American Judicial Opinions*, 19 YALE J. INT'L L. 81 (1994).

4. When you read a case, it is important to understand the history of how the case wound its way through the courts to get to the present court. Lawyers refer to anything that happened in a case before it got to the present court as having occurred "below." You will learn more about the necessity of accurately understanding the procedural history of a case in Chapter 9.

American legal system, courts almost always reach opinions only in actual cases in controversy.[5] To a trained lawyer, discussing law without relating the law to the particular facts of the controversy that spawned the case makes little sense. Lawyers understand that you can't read a case without understanding the real-life facts as they happened to the parties because the legal words of an opinion taken out of the context of the underlying controversy have little inherent meaning. As you read more cases, you will develop a knack for visualizing the facts and figuring out which facts were "significant" (influenced the court) and which facts, although reported in the opinion, really didn't matter to the court when it reached its decision.

(3) What's the question the court is considering? Someplace in the opinion, the court must identify the legal question (or questions) it is answering. What is the court charged with resolving? In some opinions, the court makes it easy to find the legal questions by stating them in clear, express terms. Often, however, the question or questions are more challenging to find and require you to infer from the court's language and action exactly what the legal point in controversy was. Legal questions can be broad (for example, "does a plaintiff have to show actual physical harm to sustain a cause of action for intentional infliction of emotional distress?") or narrow (for example, "does occasional insomnia constitute sufficient evidence of physical harm to sustain a cause of action for intentional infliction of emotional distress?"). Neither of these versions of the question (the broad version or the narrow version) is itself "wrong" in the sense of being inaccurate. As will be discussed further in the next chapter, each represents a different way of framing the same issue. Astute students recognize the elastic nature of legal questions and pay attention to how their individual professors tend to conceptualize the issues in class.

---

5. On rare occasions, some courts will issue "advisory opinions"—opinions that answer questions that are important to the public before an actual controversy arises.

(4) **What's the answer?** The "holding" of a case is the court's actual decision concerning these parties. It is the answer to the question presented. Like the legal question, a holding can be stated by the court and by a student in broad terms or in narrow terms. Stated broadly, for example, the holding to a case might be that "evidence of actual, sustained, long-lasting physical harm is a critical element of a claim for intentional infliction of emotional distress." A more narrow statement of the same holding might be, "this plaintiff's claim was dismissed because she presented only evidence of occasional insomnia, which is not sufficient to support the damages element of a claim for intentional infliction of emotional distress."

(5) **What was the court thinking (its "reasoning")?** Many judges include a discussion of the court's reasoning in an opinion, and almost all opinions that are selected for casebook study include such a discussion. The reasoning articulated in the opinion is the students' clue to the kinds of factors judges consider when resolving issues in this area of the law. Reasoning can include policy rationales or moral justifications or can be a logical application of the dominant rule to the facts at hand.

The following statement is an example of what a judge might write to express a court's reasoning (reasoning that you may or may not agree with): "Because claims for intentional infliction of emotional distress often rest on intangible actions and require juries to infer a harmful intent, it would be unwise to allow such a claim without evidence of sustained, long-lasting physical injury to the plaintiff. To allow anything less would invite a floodgate of frivolous suits. Occasional insomnia is neither 'sustained' nor 'long-lasting' and therefore cannot support plaintiff's claim for intentional infliction of emotional distress."

(6) **What's the final word?** Finally, the disposition of the case will often (but not always) appear at the very end of the case and is frequently expressed in legal jargon understood by professionals at the time the case was written. Thus, a simple verb like "Reversed" or "Affirmed" or "Remanded" (sent back for further action) is often the "last word" in a case and gives you the actual judgment of the court.

C. Taking Notes ("Briefing" a Case)

Now that you know the primary components of most cases, you have the tools you need to enter the discourse of law. Knowing what to anticipate gives you a schema (a mental framework) for reading cases that helps you organize your thoughts before you begin a new case. Without that schema, you would have to reinvent the wheel each time you opened your casebook, starting from scratch to understand what you're reading. Starting your reading in an organized state of mind will make your reading more efficient and effective.

Taking systematic notes on what you're reading is the next critical step—especially in the beginning—to further develop your ability to read cases well. These notes reinforce your schema and free up your short term memory so you have more working memory available to actually think about the consequences/import of this case.

The importance of taking coherent notes is so significant in the study and practice of law that the notion of writing a "brief" of a case is universally recognized by law students and practicing attorneys alike. As law students become more experienced, their briefs often become "briefer," but the component parts remain the same. These component parts reflect the content of most opinions that you just learned about in the last section of this chapter. A typical beginner's brief for law school would be a hand-written or typed sheet of paper that would include the following components in the following order:[6]

6. I am grateful to my research assistant, Avery Auld, for suggesting that a good habit is to write briefs along the right hand two-thirds of your paper, leaving a substantial margin in which to add class notes to the left.

Case Heading (case name, date, place & court of decision, page in your casebook)

Parties' Names (which requires some reading in the case beyond just the case heading because the names on the heading may be only partially representative of the parties actually named in the suit; also reading further in the case helps you "visualize" who the parties are and develop a shorthand descriptor of their role to include in your brief)

Procedural History (in very truncated form, who filed what, what action did any court take below, and, finally—what action did this court take here [the disposition])

Facts (a quick reminder for yourself of the "story" of the conflict, making sure you have some way to remember the significant facts—facts that influenced the court's decision. It is not always easy to tell which facts influenced a court by reading only one case in your casebook; often reading related cases and "Notes and Problems" at the end of the casebook section clarifies what matters and what doesn't matter in this area of the law.)

Issue or Question Presented (paying attention to the case's context within the framework of the casebook, what is the legal question raised to THIS court that is resolved here. Remember to stay alert to whether your professor prefers you to focus on broad or narrow issues, and be prepared to state the questions presented both ways)

Holding (matching the Question Presented, what did the court decide? A broad question lends itself to a broadly stated holding/result; a narrow question should be matched by a narrow holding/result)

Reasoning/Rationale (stated succinctly, what do you think the court was thinking when it reached this result?)

Your Thoughts (it is a good habit to include any thoughts you may have had as you read the case so that you encourage your creativity and investment in the learning process. As you will learn in Part II of this book, reading cases is not about passively receiving information contained in the opinion. It's about making meaning by bringing your thoughts to the case, interacting with the author of the opinion, and learning from discussions in class that follow. If you don't write your thoughts down as they occur, you won't remember them and they won't be available to stir your thinking later.)

As they read law, lawyers make a distinction between language that speaks to the holding of a case and language that is often called "mere dicta." The holding of a case is what actually happened to these parties when this case in controversy was decided. The term "holding" can also be used more broadly to mean the rule that the court fashioned or relied on to reach the result in the case.

In reaching a holding, courts often discuss many other things as well. For example, a court might discuss the hypothetical resolution of a question not actually raised, or might speculate about arguments that could have been made but weren't, or might discuss the wisdom behind a particular line of precedent or a legislative act. These kinds of discussions are dicta—thoughts of the court. They do not have the weight of binding precedent (decisions that must be followed). However, dicta goes a long way towards helping an engaged reader see inside the mind of the court and draw rational inferences about where the court might go—or might be persuaded to go—in a future case. Hence, statements made as dicta are important, but must be separated in your mind (and in your notes) from language that leads to an actual holding.

The format of a traditional brief will give you the bare bones to join a class discussion of virtually any case you've read. It is a starting point, not a finishing point, but it will get you in the door. Learning to read carefully enough to write useful briefs, although only a beginning, can take weeks of hard work. There will be many times when you will miss the point of a case entirely, or misunderstand the facts, or assume the court was thinking one thing but (in retrospect) realize you were projecting your own thoughts on to the court. That's okay, and it's part of the learning process. The more you learn from these errors that arise naturally from inexperience, the less often you will make them. You will then make new (more sophisticated) errors based on new things you'll notice that you weren't even aware of before. You can begin to think of mistakes as your friends—without them, you'd get nowhere.

The more you learn about the world of law, the better your reading of cases becomes. The better your reading of cases becomes, the more you will understand from class discussion. The more you understand about what's being discussed at multiple levels in class, the better your reading of future cases will become. Eventually, through this cyclical process, you will find that you have become immersed in the language and culture of the law and this once-foreign land will start to feel like home.

PRACTICE EXERCISES

The practice exercises for Chapter 2 offer a chance to try your hand at reading a court opinion taken from a law school casebook.[7] Remember that you can visit caplaw.com/rll to see some of the responses I thought about as I wrote these practice exercise questions.

A. Read the following case and answer the questions that follow:

Leichtman v. WLW Jacor Communications, Inc.

Court of Appeals of Ohio, 1994

92 Ohio App. 3d 232, 634 N.E.2d 697

...Leichtman claims to be "a nationally known" antismoking advocate. Leichtman alleges that, on the date of the Great American Smokeout, he was invited to appear on the WLW Bill Cunningham radio talk show to discuss the harmful effects of smoking and breathing secondary smoke. He also alleges that, while he was in the studio, Furman, another WLW talk-show host, lit a cigar and repeatedly blew smoke in Leichtman's face "for the purpose of causing physical discomfort, humiliation and distress."...

Leichtman contends that Furman's intentional act constituted a battery....

In determining if a person is liable for a battery, the Supreme Court has adopted the rule that "[c]ontact which is offensive to a reason-

7. This case is reprinted with permission of Thomson West from Dan B. Dobbs & Paul T. Hayden, Torts and Compensation 42–43 (4th ed. 2001). It includes the original edits from that casebook.

able sense of personal dignity is offensive contact." It has defined "offensive" to mean "disagreeable or nauseating or painful because of outrage to taste and sensibilities or affronting insultingness." Furthermore, tobacco smoke, as "particulate matter," has the physical properties capable of making contact.

As alleged in Leichtman's complaint, when Furman intentionally blew cigar smoke in Leichtman's face, under Ohio common law, he committed a battery. No matter how trivial the incident, a battery is actionable, even if damages are only one dollar. The rationale is explained by Roscoe Pound in his essay "Liability": "[I]n civilized society men must be able to assume that others will do them no intentional injury—that others will commit no intentioned aggressions upon them." Pound, An Introduction to the Philosophy of Law (1922) 169....

We do not... adopt or lend credence to the theory of a "smoker's battery," which imposes liability if there is substantial certainty that exhaled smoke will predictably contact a nonsmoker....

...Concerning Cunningham, at common law, one who is present and encourages or incites commission of a battery by words can be equally liable as a principal....

With regard to WLW, an employer is not legally responsible for the intentional torts of its employees that do not facilitate or promote its business....

Arguably, trivial cases are responsible for an avalanche of lawsuits in the courts. They delay cases that are important to individuals and corporations and that involve important social issues. The result is justice denied to litigants and their counsel who must wait for their day in court. However, absent circumstances that warrant sanctions for frivolous appeals... we refuse to limit one's right to sue. Section 16, Article I, Ohio Constitution states, "All courts shall be open, and every person, for an injury done him in his land, goods, person, or reputation, shall have remedy by due course of law, and shall have justice administered without denial or delay."

...[W]e reverse that portion of the trial court's order that dismissed the battery claim in the second count of the complaint. This cause is remanded for further proceedings consistent with law on that claim only.

1. Is this an edited or unedited case? How do you know?

2. In what geographic region was this case decided? How do you know?

3. What was the general view of smoking as a health issue at the time this opinion was written? How do you know?

4. On a separate sheet of paper write a brief for this case.

5. What was the most difficult part of writing that brief for you? What made writing that part of the brief difficult?

B. Read the sample brief (below) that I wrote for this case. How does this brief compare to yours? How are they different? Are the differences meaningful or superficial? Are there things you would do differently if you had the opportunity to do your brief again?

TORTS—Battery (p. 42)[8]

Leichtman v. WLW Jacor Communications, Inc.
Ct. of Appeals of Ohio (1994)

Π: Leichtman (antismoking advocate)

Δ: WLW Jacor Comm. (radio co.) (& Furman? & Cunningham?)

PH: (1) Π filed complaint based in battery;

(2) Δ filed motion to dismiss that trial court granted;

(3) This court (ct. of app.) reversed dismissal on the battery claim.

F: Π, an antismoking advocate, appeared on Δ's radio talk show to discuss smoking and one of the company's other talk show hosts blew cigar smoke repeatedly in his face.

Q: Does the Π have a claim for battery based on these facts? In other words, can being "hit" with smoke ever constitute a battery?

H: Yes. Smoke is tangible enough to constitute an offensive contact.

8. To save time, it's easiest to use abbreviations to designate the various subsections of a brief. The Greek Pi sign (Π) and the Delta sign (Δ) are often used to designate Plaintiff and Defendant. In my brief, "PH" stands for Procedural History (legal facts—how the case got to this court); "F" for Facts (conflict facts between the parties); "Q" for issue or question (what the court looked at that's relevant to this course); "H" for holding (what the court decided about that question); and "R" for rationale. You can make up your own abbreviations—use whatever works for you.

Rule: Contact which is "offensive" to a "reasonable sense of personal dignity" is offensive contact.

R: Smoke (as "particulate matter") can make contact and, here, blowing smoke in Π's face could be sufficiently offensive to be a battery. The amount of damages can be negligible (even $1) and still be a battery.

My thoughts: Note that the company itself would not be liable for an employee's intentional tort (outside the scope of employment), but the other host might be if he encouraged or incited the act. Note also that this court didn't reach the question of whether smoking around someone would always constitute a battery.

CHAPTER 3

Advanced Thinking Leads to Advanced Reading

A. There Is Fun—and Power—in Reading Law Well

As I wrote this book, I gained a renewed appreciation of how hard it is to read. It is even harder to read in a new discipline, and in new formats, than it is to read in a discipline, and in formats, with which you are already familiar. By the same token, I've always thought of reading as fun. It can open your mind, take you places you would otherwise not go, and sometimes even introduce you to people and places that never actually existed or don't exist anymore.

Reading law is perhaps the most fun of all—it not only takes you to places and eras long gone as well as to places and eras that are the makings of today's headlines, it allows you to get a glimpse of the inner workings of this country's most powerful institutions and into the minds of some of our most profound thinkers and greatest leaders. Ultimately, as you become an expert yourself, reading law well will allow you to enter this discourse community as a peer, making the arguments and telling the stories that will influence the lives of people you've yet to meet—and may well result in decisions that will be included in the casebooks of the next century.

Reading law is second cousin to thinking about law. As one scholar has put it, "'[S]tudents must know the "meaning" of what they read in order to develop the reading "skills" they need to interpret . . . what they read.'"[1] In other words, a reader's ability to make sense of a new text depends not only on the knowledge presented in the text but also on a reader's prior knowledge and the "'level of inference that can be reasonably expected of her.'"[2]

There is a circular aspect to learning to read law like an expert: the better you read, the more you learn; the more you learn, the better your reading becomes. Words both capture ideas and create ideas. Without the right framework to capture the ideas represented by the words in cases, much of what is contained in the cases we read is lost to us.

This chapter will challenge you to think harder than basic briefing requires. In this chapter, you will learn to consider what lawyers and courts are actually doing when they resolve cases, draft and read statutes, advise clients, make arguments, and write opinions. By thinking hard about these issues, you will improve your understanding of what you read. Improving your understanding of what you read will, in turn, improve how you think about the law and your ability to make things happen in the field of law.

---

1. Elizabeth Fajans & Mary R. Falk, *Against the Tyranny of Paraphrase: Talking Back to Texts*, 78 CORNELL L. REV. 163, 171 (1993) (quoting Michael L. Johnson, *Hell is the Place We Don't Know We're In: The Control-dictions of Cultural Literacy, Strong Reading, and Poetry*, 50 C. ENG. 309, 312 (1988)).

2. *Id.* (quoting Marilyn S. Sternglass, *Writing Based on Reading, in* CONVERGENCES: TRANSACTIONS IN READING AND WRITING 151, 151 (Bruce T. Petersen ed., 1986)). *See generally* JEFFREY D. WILHELM, IMPROVING COMPREHENSION WITH THINK-ALOUD STRATEGIES (2001) (developing the recurring theme that readers cannot understand more than they can accurately visualize).

B. Logic: How Lawyers Think

It is widely understood and commonly repeated that the primary task of law school is to teach each student to "think like a lawyer." But, truth be known, lawyers don't think any differently than anyone else—not in the sense of how they reason. What is distinct about the thinking pattern of lawyers is the precision with which they think, the efficiency with which they view facts and measure facts against potential rules of law, and the willingness they exhibit to group facts and law in general or narrow terms, depending on which view best serves their end.

Lawyers, like everyone else, rely on three basic forms of logic to reach conclusions that seem consistent, fair, and rational. These basic forms of logic are: (1) deductive reasoning, (2) inductive reasoning, and (3) analogical reasoning.

(1) Deductive (syllogistic) reasoning is the heart and soul of clear legal thinking. In fact, the "modern" law school grew out of the belief commonly held in the 19th century that law was a "science," subject to verifiable application of truths reached through the rational application of scientifically sound deductive, syllogistic reasoning.[3]

---

3. Christopher Langdell, who served as Dean of Harvard Law School from 1870 to 1900, is among the most famous proponents of the nineteenth century "formalist" view of law as science. Langdell, who introduced the modern "case study" method still used in law schools today, believed that "[l]aw, considered as a science, consists of certain principles or doctrines. To have such a mastery of these as to be able to apply them with constant facility and certainty to the ever-tangled skein of human affairs, is what constitutes a true lawyer." Steve Sheppard, *An Introductory History of Law in the Lecture Hall*, 82 IOWA L. REV. 547 (1997), *reprinted in* THE HISTORY OF LEGAL EDUCATION IN THE UNITED STATES at 27 (Steve Sheppard ed. 1999) (quoting CHRISTOPHER C. LANGDELL, SELECTION OF CASES ON THE LAW OF CONTRACTS vi (Boston, Little Brown & Co. 1871)) (noting that Langdell viewed the law school classroom and the casebook as the functional equivalents of the scientist's laboratory). The formalists were shortly challenged by the "legal realists," including noted jurists such as Justice Oliver Wendell Holmes, Justice Benjamin Cardozo, and Professor Karl Lewellyn, who believed that law could not be reduced to inflexible, formal rules, but rather that flex-

Deductive reasoning is based on the development of a syllogism: a major premise (often thought of as a "rule"), a minor premise (often thought of as "facts"), and a conclusion that follows inevitably when the minor premise is applied to the major premise. For example:

> Major Premise (the rule): All responsible high school seniors may stay out one hour past curfew on prom night.
>
> Minor Premise (the facts): Your older sister, Mary, is a responsible high school senior.
>
> Conclusion (the result): Therefore, Mary may stay out one hour past curfew on prom night.

To be sound, an argument has to be based on a true major premise and a true minor premise, and the conclusion must flow from them. Where both the major premise and minor premise are accurate and the conclusion lines up with them, the conclusion must be true. However, if either the major premise or the minor premise are false, then the conclusion is not true, even if the two premises line up and sound rational.

If I want to call a conclusion into question, then, I simply have to discredit the major premise or the minor premise, or both. Here is an example of how I could discredit the sample syllogism above by disproving the minor premise:

> Major Premise (the rule): All responsible high school seniors may stay out one hour past curfew on prom night.
>
> Minor Premise (the facts): Mary is responsible, but she is not yet a high school senior.
>
> Conclusion (the result): Therefore, Mary may stay out one hour past curfew on prom night.

---

ibility and choice are inherent parts of the deductive and analogical reasoning that characterizes legal decision-making. For an interesting discussion of the important impact of Legal Realism on modern jurisprudence, see EVA H. HANKS ET AL., ELEMENTS OF LAW 509–537 (1994).

When you got to the conclusion (the result) of this second syllogism, you probably thought, "What? No, wait. That's not right!" There may be lots of reasons why Mary's parents might let her stay out late on prom night, but the rule as stated isn't one of them. That rule applies only to seniors. Therefore, the first syllogism was valid and sound (assuming Mary was a senior), and the conclusion was true. However, the second premise was not valid or sound (because it states that Mary was not yet a senior), and the conclusion was not true.

Much of the successful study and practice of law depends on the practitioner's ability to think in clear logic syllogisms, and to identify the syllogisms relied on by others in the field. The ability to think accurately in syllogistic form is important because the American legal system is based on an adversarial model, with each party represented by zealous counsel whose job it is to present the party's best argument to the decision-maker in the case. Each party wants the court to reach a different conclusion or the parties wouldn't be in front of the court.

To persuade the court that my conclusion is the correct one, I have to convince the court that my premises are true and that my conclusion follows from them. To persuade the court not to adopt the conclusion proposed by my opposition, I have to convince the court that at least one of their premises is false, or that their conclusion doesn't follow rationally from those premises.[4]

Thinking in deductive logic syllogisms on a routine basis takes practice, but eventually it will become second nature. One good way to practice this skill is to identify the various premises a court relies on in reaching a result (conclusion) when you read a case. Another is to identify (often by infer-

---

4. I am grateful to attorney Neal Ramee, an outstanding 2003 graduate of the University of North Carolina School of Law, for his many contributions to my understanding of legal logic. Mr. Ramee has contributed an interesting article on logic flaws to our writing program. If you are interested in learning more about common errors in logic, you are invited to read Neal Ramee, Logic and Legal Reasoning: A Guide for Law Students (2002) (available at caplaw.com/rll).

ence) the syllogisms the parties' attorneys put forward in their arguments to the court, and to identify what aspect of the losing party's syllogism was rejected by the court.

(2) **Inductive reasoning**, while not deductively verifiable,[5] is a type of thinking we're all familiar and comfortable with. It makes sense to us. Inductive reasoning is the process of reaching general conclusions about reality based on patterns that emerge from observing separate incidents and occurrences over time. Thus, if I see birds and no other kind of animal in the air, time after time, I may eventually conclude that birds can fly, but other animals can't. At some point, I may see a squirrel that appears to be flying. Then I will be confused and may need to rethink the conclusion I've reached about which animals can fly. Inductive reasoning is the basis of much of what lawyers do as they read case after case to try to discern patterns of rules and principles that can be articulated as a "major premise" in a logic syllogism reasoned deductively. The ability to find these patterns and accurately translate them into a rule that is, in fact, already being followed by the courts is a highly valued lawyering skill.

(3) **Analogical reasoning**, like inductive reasoning, is messier than syllogistic/deductive reasoning. We understand reasoning by analogy because we universally accept the basic assumption that things that are alike should be treated alike. Reasoning by analogy requires me to group things into like categories based on similarities they share, and to then draw conclusions about what will happen to one of those things based on what happened to its counterpart.

For example, let's return to the prom/curfew example used as an illustration of deductive reasoning above. If my parents allowed my older sister, Mary, to stay out late on prom night based on her status as a responsible senior, fundamental fairness would cause me to believe that I should be allowed to stay out late on prom night when I was a senior as well. Of course, the trick in analogical reasoning lies in the selection of the factors

---

5. *Id.*

that are deemed to be "similar." In the example above, I might be focusing on my status as a senior, which is actually only part of the rule. If my parents wanted to draw a distinction (refute the analogy I was trying to draw to my sister), they might focus on the word "responsible." They might argue that my situation is *not* analogous to that of my sister because I have not demonstrated sufficient "responsibility," whereas she had. My status as a senior might be irrelevant to them (although it is a trait I shared with my sister at the end of four years in high school) in light of what they consider to be lack of demonstrated responsibility.

C. Logic in Action: How Lawyers and Courts Use Logic Every Day

Lawyers use all three kinds of reasoning (deductive, inductive, and analogical) as they fashion arguments that they hope will persuade a court to rule in their favor, or as they predict what they think a court might do in an infinite variety of possible conflict scenarios. These tools work precisely because they are part of the discourse of law—it's how lawyers reason and how they communicate with one another. Lawyers understand intuitively or explicitly what Justice Oliver Wendell Holmes meant when he wrote, "What the courts will do, and nothing more, is what I mean by the law."[6]

Knowing "what the courts will do" is dependent not only on a lawyer's reasoning abilities, but also on the certainty that the actions and decisions of courts will be consistent. Governed by the doctrine of "stare decisis," courts within a given jurisdiction are bound to follow their own decisions of the past. Once a holding has been reached, that holding becomes "precedent" for all other cases that are substantially similar to it,[7] and the doctrine

---

6. Oliver Wendell Holmes, *Path of the Law*, 10 HARV. L. REV. 457 (1897).

7. You will sometimes hear lawyers, judges, and law professors use the term "on all fours" to indicate that one case is substantially similar to another. Cases are "on all fours" when their foundational properties square up: same (or rationally similar) parties; same (or rationally similar) facts; same (or rationally similar) legal question; same (or

of stare decisis dictates that the prior precedent will be followed in the subsequent case.

But decisions are not the result of neat cookie-cutter applications of a rule laid precisely on top of the next set of facts. Rather, there is ample wiggle room for rational legally trained minds to differ vehemently on the correct result in almost any given case. These differences of opinion arise by the very nature of the reasoning process itself. The selection of the major premise (rule) of any syllogism, and the characterization of the minor premise (facts) dictate the result that will follow. It's all in how the premises are framed.

Karl Llewellyn, author of a landmark collection of lectures presented to incoming law students at Columbia Law School in the late 1920s, explained the elastic nature of judicial decision-making by noting that the courts' adherence to precedent is "two-headed. It is Janus-faced....[8] [Precedent] is not one doctrine, nor one line of doctrine, but two, and two which, *applied at the same time to the same precedent, are contradictory of each other.*"[9]

Professor Llewellyn's point was that there are two ways to read a "rule." You can read it broadly or you can read it narrowly. If you read it broadly, you can take the actual words used by the court and more or less ignore the factual context of the decision, instead taking up the words themselves and allowing your audience to attach its own common-sense understanding of the words on their face. You would encourage this kind of broad reading of a court's rule if the rule as literally articulated in the case would carry your case to a favorable conclusion if adopted as your major premise.

---

rationally similar) policy/moral purposes. *See* BRYAN A. GARNER, DICTIONARY OF MODERN LEGAL USAGE 618 (2d ed. 1995) (indicating that the phrase "on all fours" is "useful legal jargon that refers to highly pertinent legal precedents" or to cases that are "squarely on point with regard to both facts and law").

8. Mr. Llewellyn's reference to "Janus" is to the Roman God, Janus, who is depicted with two faces, one on each side of his head.

9. K.N. LLEWELLYN, THE BRAMBLE BUSH 74 (3d ed. 1960).

On the other hand, a rule can be read narrowly. To read a rule narrowly, I would try to draw attention away from the words chosen by the court to express the rule, and instead focus my audience on the exact facts before the court when it made its ruling. By focusing the court on the exact facts that formed the minor premise in the prior decision, I can hope to convince the court that the conclusion the court reached was expressly tied to that specific minor premise, and cannot be viewed now apart from those facts.

As a strong advocate, I can also look past the words adopted by the court to the *principles or moral guideposts* behind the court's decision. If those principles would be undermined by application of the rule as stated to my new facts, I can free the court from the constraints of following the prior statement of the rule as precedent. Instead, I would attempt to persuade the court that the major premise in our new logic syllogism should be based on the underlying principles of the prior case, not on the superficial wording of the rule itself.

Another way to play with a rule or major premise is to use inductive reasoning to examine how the rule has actually been applied (not articulated, but actually applied) in many other cases. It might well be that a pattern is emerging in reality as courts apply a stated rule that belies the words of the rule itself. In that case, a gifted attorney can reframe or rephrase the rule to reflect the court's actions, persuading the court that the precedent to be followed is found rationally in the court's prior actions, not in the court's stated words.

For example, in the early part of the last century in North Carolina, there was a common law rule (not codified in statute) that allowed a teacher to corporally punish a child as long as the teacher did not act with "malice" and did not "permanently injure" the child.[10] Years later, a federal court sitting in North Carolina paraphrased the North Carolina rule as being one of "reasonableness" (as long as the teacher acted reasonably in punishing the child,

10. Drum v. Miller, 47 S.E. 421, 425 (N.C. 1904).

there would be no civil liability).[11] Within a decade of the federal decision, a North Carolina court agreed that North Carolina's rule was one of "reasonableness," but approved jury instructions in a corporal punishment case that directed the jury to find no liability unless the teacher had acted with "malice" or permanently injured the child, language taken straight from the old turn-of-the-century cases.[12] Is the North Carolina common law "rule" on corporal punishment one of "reasonableness" (as stated) or is it more specifically targeting only malicious behavior or behavior that causes permanent injury (as the jury was directed)? (Answer: if the jury is given specific instructions that do not allow jurors to apply a general rule of reasonableness, then the question of whether the teacher acted reasonably is not going to determine the teacher's liability. Instead, the jury will be allowed only to consider the more narrow questions of malice and permanent injury.)

What if, in carefully reading all of the corporal punishment cases in North Carolina, you could infer that the *principle* behind all the corporal punishment cases seemed to be to allow a teacher as much latitude as possible in managing a classroom? Could you use that information to help articulate a rule that would give the teacher maximum protection? (Answer: Yes. You could encourage the court to acknowledge that a teacher may corporally punish a child as long as the teacher doesn't act with malice or permanently injure the child because we have to trust a teacher's judgment about what is necessary for him or her to maintain order in a classroom.)

What if the underlying justification articulated in the older corporal punishment turned on an assumption that all school-aged children were used to being physically punished at home, and hence being corporally punished at school would be consistent with the discipline they were used to? Is that assumption (that all children are physically disciplined at home) still universally true? If not, does that factual inaccuracy call the old rule into question today? (Answer: Yes. An attorney who read the precedent-

---

11. Baker v. Owen, 395 F. Supp. 294, 300–301 (M.D.N.C. 1975), *aff'd* 423 U.S. 907 (1975).
12. Gasphersohn v. Harnett County Bd. of Educ., 330 S.E.2d 489, 493–94 (N.C. Ct. App. 1985).

setting cases carefully could call for a change in the *rule* by noting that the original rationale for the rule was no longer valid).

In addition to having wide latitude to go past the limiting words of a rule, judges (and attorneys making arguments or anticipating arguments to a judge) also have ample opportunity to group or cluster the information (facts) presented in minor premises in narrow or broad terms. For example, in a famous property case,[13] the court found that a fox belonged to the first person to "occupy" (gain control of) it, reasoning that a wild animal has no prior owner but would certainly not belong to the first person to see it or to try to pursue it. Is this rule limited only to wild animals? Would it also apply to abandoned animals? Would it apply to all property without a prior owner? Inductive and analogous reasoning can help a careful legal reader understand the breadth of a rule. For example, if a court in the same jurisdiction held that a meteorite that landed on the earth was "like a wild animal" and belonged to the first person to gain control of it, an astute reader could begin to see a pattern and might infer that the rule applied to any kind of property that did not have a prior owner (by asking himself or herself what the meteorite and the fox had in common that warranted application of the same rule).

Now imagine that you are practicing in that same jurisdiction and represent someone who has found a puppy all by itself on the side of the road. Your client would like to keep the puppy. Reasoning by analogy, what argument can you make that the puppy is up for grabs? Reasoning by analogy, what argument can you make that the puppy is NOT up for grabs? In other words, how is the puppy potentially similar to or different from the fox and the meteorite?

Successful lawyers are good at clustering facts in a fluid way, by finding broad commonalities or narrow distinctions. So, in our puppy case, an experienced lawyer could characterize this puppy as being the same as the meteorite and the fox by noting that all three are all things that appeared out

---

13. Pierson v. Post, 3 Cai R. 175, 2 Am. Dec. 264 (N.Y. Sup. Ct. 1805).

of nowhere and have no apparent first home. On the other hand, another competent lawyer could argue (say, on behalf of the owner of the mother dog) that the puppy is different from the fox and the meteorite, characterizing the puppy as a domesticated animal that had inadvertently wandered from its mother and care-taker, and the fox and meteorite (in contrast) as property with no home of origin.

These factual categorizations have an almost infinite elasticity to them, although they can be stretched beyond what a court is willing to accept. A teenager can be a minor child, a human, an artist, a threat, a runaway, an immigrant, a patriot, a family member, etc. Each categorization may be factually supported by evidence, but the art of good lawyering requires the lawyer to be flexible in how broadly or narrowly the facts that comprise the minor premise are presented. How broadly or narrowly the facts are drawn impacts heavily on the conclusion the court can reach deductively, on the patterns the court perceives inductively, and on the connections or distinctions a court is willing to make analogously.

D. What Might Laypeople Think of Lawyers' Logic?

A few years ago I was called up for jury duty in a criminal case. There were approximately fifty potential jurors in the jury room. The clerk of court called the names of the first twelve potential jurors at random from a glass jar, and each took his or her seat in the jury box. The attorney for the state asked the jurors a series of questions and excused those who gave answers troubling to the state's case. Next, the court-appointed attorney for the defendant asked the prospective jurors questions. Among the first questions she asked was "How do you feel about attorneys?" (Her strategy, I think, was to excuse anyone from jury duty who was hostile to her responsibility to present a strong defense.)

I was stunned when more than half of the seated jurors expressed significant concerns about how lawyers think. When the defense attorney asked for clarification from those jurors who said they had reservations about lawyers, the majority of them, all good-hearted people who wanted to do their civic duty, expressed concern that lawyers seemed to tamper with reality and were "slippery" (in the words of one juror) in their thinking.

I believe what I was witnessing was the difference in the discourse community of laypeople (to which I used to belong) and the discourse community of lawyers (to which I now belong). I interact with law students and lawyers almost every day, and have for nearly thirty years. I can't imagine thinking that lawyers "tamper with reality" or are "slippery" in their thinking. Where did this perception come from? I believe it is rooted, at least in part, in the "Janus-faced" nature of precedent that requires lawyers to develop a knack for being fluid in how they characterize a major premise and minor premise for argument.

Lawyers are not being disingenuous or slippery when they group facts into broad or narrow categories. Lawyers are applying important professional skills when they observe and articulate differences between the words used by a court and the actions it has actually taken, or when they abandon the bare words of a rule in favor of the underlying principles the rule is designed to protect, or when they recognize a rule of law as having broad or narrow implications.

This kind of rigorous thinking requires an enormous amount of moral and intellectual discipline resulting from years of practice that begins in the first weeks of law school. At the center of this thinking is reading—disciplined, focused, close, and critical reading. The ability to read carefully and critically is common to many professions, but is the hallmark of law and a skill shared universally by all great lawyers.

In the words of Abraham Lincoln, "If you wish to be a lawyer, attach no consequence to the *place* you are in, or the *person* you are with; but get the books, sit down anywhere, and go to reading for yourself. [Reading for yourself] will make a lawyer of you quicker than any other way."[14]

---

14. Letter from Abraham Lincoln to William H. Grigsby (Aug. 3, 1858), *in* ABRAHAM LINCOLN: SPEECHES AND WRITINGS 1832–1858, 484–85 (Don E. Fehrenbacher, ed., 1989) (emphasis in original).

PRACTICE EXERCISES

The exercises for this chapter are especially challenging. Enjoy the challenge and don't get discouraged if you struggle with these questions at first. Remember that you can visit caplaw.com/rll to see some of the responses I had in mind as I wrote the Practice Exercises at the end of each chapter. There are additional opportunities to practice logic as well as a very helpful article about logic by attorney Neal Ramee on the website.

1. It is widely recognized in tort law that the intentional tort of assault protects our interest in being free from the "fear of an unwanted touching." If someone alarms/scares us in a way that satisfies all of the requirements of a particular jurisdiction for a successful claim of assault, we are entitled to damages. In applying and developing this rule, courts have determined (among other things) that the person bringing a claim actually has to have been reasonably afraid *at the time the defendant acted*—it's not enough to find out about a scary situation later or to be threatened with a scary situation in the future and then to claim assault.

   Knowing that rule, write out in the space below a *deductively reasoned logic syllogism* that would allow a claim for a plaintiff who had attended a playoff game in the National Football League where the fans for the home team got progressively more verbally threatening about the visiting team, with some home-team fans even making physically threatening gestures in the direction of the visiting fans. The day after the game ended, the plaintiff read in the paper that numerous fights had broken out and at least one fan was hospitalized. (Hint: when you write out a logic syllogism, state your rule (the major premise) clearly and make sure that you state the facts (your minor premise) in language that parallels that of the rule.)

Can you write out a deductively reasoned logic syllogism that would NOT allow relief for that plaintiff?

2. Assume you are a first year law student reading a series of cases about assault in your casebook: (a) The first case concerns a situation similar to the one set out above but here the plaintiff attended a Division I college sporting event and sued a fan from the opposing team for assault where the over-zealous fan stood between the plaintiff and the plaintiff's car in the parking lot after the game. Assume in this first case that the court DID allow the plaintiff to bring a claim, reasoning that a reasonable person might have felt afraid of immediate harm from the over-zealous actions of the fan from the opposing team. (b) The second case concerns a situation where a group of friends go to the movies to see *Scream*. After seeing the movie, one of the friends tells another, "I'm going to hide someplace where you won't expect it and really scare you this week." The second student sues for assault. The court does NOT allow the plaintiff to bring a claim, reasoning that the fear has to be of a present action, and that vague verbal threats about the future won't support a claim. (c) The third case involves a claim for assault that arose after the plaintiff attended a Thanksgiving Day parade where a clown approached the crowd and appeared to prepare to spray water on the plaintiff, but sprayed only confetti instead. The court did not allow the parade-goer's claim for assault on the grounds that a reasonable person would have understood that the clown's action was in jest and was a normal part of parade activity.

You are now a judge. There is a case before you involving a claim for assault where the plaintiff was an all-state center on the local high school's basketball team. The player hit a winning three-pointer that won the Conference Championship for her team. Immediately after the game, a student fan who supported the losing team shoved a piece of paper in the player's hand as the player boarded the team bus. The paper said, "We'll see that you pay for that win. That's the last three-pointer you'll ever shoot." The star player is now concerned about her safety as the upcoming State Championship game approaches, and she wants to sue the fan for assault.

Reasoning *inductively* (forming a rule in your mind based on the statements about assault set out in Question 1 above and on the examples in the cases contained in this question), how would you state the rule for assault? Would you allow the star basketball player to bring a claim for assault against the student who gave her the note? Why or why not?

3. Assume that you are a lawyer practicing in a jurisdiction that decided the assault cases set out in the preceding two questions. You have a client whose fourteen-year-old daughter loudly yelled a threatening insult from ringside at a goalie during a professional ice hockey game. Reasoning by analogy, do you think a court in your jurisdiction would necessarily *have* to allow a claim for assault by the goalie to go forward? Why or why not? Reasoning by analogy, *could* a court in your jurisdiction allow a claim to go forward?

CHAPTER 4

Expert Reading

A New Take on a Familiar Skill

A. What Do Great Readers Have in Common?

Reading, something we learned to do in childhood, is not a single skill. Rather, it is a *skill set*—a collection of thinking tools we choose from as we interact with texts of many types.

Research on adult readers confirms that exceptional readers share certain reading behaviors in common with other exceptional readers.[1] Moreover, less proficient readers may not be doing some, or all, of the things that these experts do.[2] One reading scholar has noted that all great readers,

1. Michael Pressley & Peter Afflerbach, Verbal Protocols of Reading (1995); Jeffrey D. Wilhelm, Improving Comprehension with Think-Aloud Strategies (2001).

2. Pressley & Afflerbach, *supra* note 1; Wilhelm, *supra* note 1. Also, the following articles focusing specifically on reading in a legal context confirm that less proficient readers of law are doing things differently and net different results when they read law than do more proficient readers: Dorothy H. Deegan, *Exploring Individual Differences Among Novices Reading in a Specific Domain: The Case of Law*, 30 Reading Res. Q. 154 (1995); Peter Dewitz, *Reading Law: Three Suggestions for Legal Education*, 27 U. Tol. L. Rev. 657 (1996); Elizabeth Fajans & Mary R. Falk, *Against the Tyranny*

across disciplines, do most or all of the following.[3] As you read through this list, think about which of these behaviors describe reading habits you have already developed. Expert readers:

- "Personally connect" to the content of their reading;
- Accurately "decode text into words and meanings";
- Decide why they're reading before they start;
- "Make predictions (create hypotheses and continually adjust them in light of new information)";
- Visualize what's being described in the text;
- Ask questions in their minds as they read;
- Summarize in their minds as they read;
- Continually check to make sure their reading is making sense and use "fix-it strategies" when it doesn't;
- Are thoughtful about their reading—reflect and ponder;
- Think about ways to organize what they're learning and to apply what they're learning to new situations.

---

of Paraphrase: Talking Back to Texts, 78 Cornell L. Rev. 163 (1993); Christina L. Kunz, *Teaching First Year Contracts Students How to Read and Edit Contract Clauses*, 34 U. Tol. L. Rev. 705 (2003); Mary A. Lundeberg, *Metacognitive Aspects of Reading Comprehension: Studying Understanding in Legal Case Analysis*, 22 Reading Res. Q. 407 (1987); Laurel Currie Oates, *Beating the Odds: Reading Strategies of Law Students Admitted Through Alternative Admissions Programs*, 83 Iowa L. Rev. 139 (1997); James Stratman, *The Emergence of Legal Composition as a Field of Inquiry: Evaluating the Prospects*, 60 Rev. Educ. Q. 153–235 (1990).

3. Wilhelm, *supra* note 1, at 29.

B. Making Meaning As You Read

Current reading theorists recognize that reading is not a way to acquire static knowledge neatly packaged in a text, but rather is a way to *construct* knowledge—actually *make meaning*—as the reader's ideas interact dynamically with the ideas expressed by a text's author.[4] Thus, if I read a political commentary critically, questioning the statistics used and wondering about the political persuasion of the author, that commentary can become a springboard for deeper and richer thinking on my part about the topic covered. Similarly, if I read a travel book inquisitively, paying careful attention to the experiences and recommendations of the author, I may become full of new ideas for leisure travel—and may be well on my way to a fabulous summer vacation. If the reader brings little to the table, or fails to participate in the reading process fully, nothing much occurs. Some limited flat information may, indeed, be transmitted, but no new meaning can be created.

In the context of law, the importance of reading dynamically is critical. Just as storytelling is rooted in a rich oral history, and art is rooted in a rich visual history, law is rooted in a rich history of the *written word.* While argument can be presented and customs communicated in law orally, the development of law rests primarily on *written* precedent housed in centuries of court opinions and statute books. To be understood, law has to be read, and read well.

Merely adequate reading—reading for flat information—just won't do. Rather, the successful study and practice of law requires all students and all practitioners tow read with vigor and with accuracy, critically examining words in the context of action taken by the courts and legislatures, challenging assumptions, finding patterns, generating new ideas.

---

4. *See generally* sources cited *supra* note 2.

C. What Happens Next?

The remainder of this book will focus on how you can take your present reading skills—the skills you've developed your whole life—and apply them in the legal context. You may find that this transition is smooth and automatic, or it may require you to adjust your habitual reading style so that you can get the most out of reading law. Hands-on exercises are included in most chapters to give you an opportunity to apply the skills that you will be reading about.

In Part I, you learned a great deal about the legal discourse community. The chapters in the next section, Part II, will give you a chance to look at how to read cases in the context of casebooks assigned in law school. Most of these casebooks continue to be published in print form or as eBooks that provide purchasers with both a printed and an electronic version. The final section, Part III, will move outside of casebooks, exploring strategies that experienced law students and lawyers use when they read statutes and when they read unedited cases in practical skills courses or in the actual practice of law.

At the end of the book are several appendices: Appendix A gives you an opportunity to test your baseline reading speed (if you have had trouble reading in the past, you might want to start here); Appendix B presents a beginning reading checklist to help you develop the productive reading habits introduced in detail in Part II; Appendix C presents an advanced reading checklist to use when the habits discussed in Part II have become second nature and you want to speed up your reading; and Appendix D offers a list of additional resources on the topic of thinking and reading in the law.

Beginning with the next section (Part II), I have grouped the reading tools with the greatest pay-off for legal reading into seven skills. Out of necessity, I'll present each of these seven skills in its own chapter. However, it is not my intent for you to apply these skills in some set order. They are not a *sequence* of skills or activities as much as they are a *cluster* of reading behaviors available to you. There is overlap among the chapters and the concepts contained in them. The more of these strategies you consciously employ, the better the reading results you'll achieve.

I have adopted the acronym E.M.P.O.W.E.R. to help you remember these seven skills:

(1) Engage with Energy;

(2) Monitor your reading and read for the Main Idea;

(3) Always (always) read with a Purpose;

(4) Get Oriented (before you start) and "Own" your prior knowledge and experience;

(5) Identify the "Five Ws" (Who, What, When, Where, and Why);

(6) Evaluate what you've read; and

(7) Review, Rephrase, Record.

There are lots of things you can't control in law school. Many schools still grade on a "curve" (a grading system that compares your performance on exams to that of other students, rather than against a set standard) and base grades on one exam at the end of each semester; sometimes unplanned emergencies come up that interrupt even the best conceived study plan; sometimes you don't like or don't understand a particular professor's lecture style; and sometimes the workload alone is pretty overwhelming.

However, one thing you *can* control in law school is whether you're reading cases (and other assigned reading) as well as you are able to read them. Knowing that you're giving that important task your best shot can go a long way towards maintaining your confidence as you work hard to achieve academic and professional goals that are important to you.

PART II

Mastering Reading in a Law School Casebook

CHAPTER 5

Engage with Energy

A. The Consequences of Being a Novice

In the classic 1983 comedy, *Mr. Mom,* Michael Keaton plays the role of Jack Butler, an engineer who is laid off from his job in the automobile industry and switches roles with his wife, Carol, played by Teri Garr. Making a common mistake shared by many novices (newcomers to a task), Jack assumes that the tasks his wife has mastered as a full-time homemaker will be easy for him to take on as well. How hard can it be, he assumes, to manage a home while enjoying the company of his three small children? As anyone who has interacted much with young children already knows, the humor in the film lies in the error of this rash assumption.

As Jack quickly discovers, his wife's job only *seemed* easy because she had it successfully managed. She knew tricks to use to make the home run smoothly, had a support system in place to share the workload, and anticipated crises before they occurred. In short, she was an expert. He, on the other hand, was a novice.

On day #1, he was enthusiastic. Full of energy. Confident about the challenges that lay ahead. With only minor trepidation, he started the day with plans to drop his oldest son at school and to take the younger two to the grocery store. With a heavy rain falling and the children loaded into the station wagon, he approached the school and began to turn into the "entrance"—at least the entrance he had used to pick his son up in the past. The children called urgently from the back seat, "You're doing it wrong, you're doing it wrong!"

Ignoring their exclamations, he turned in anyway, sure that what had worked in the past would work again. Unexpectedly, his station wagon came nose to nose with a stream of cars driven by experienced stay-at-home parents who were trying to exit. With the rain streaming down, a volunteer crossing guard dressed in bright yellow rain gear knocked on his window. As he hesitantly rolled it down, she said, quietly, "Jack, you're doing it wrong."

The trick, of course, was that the experienced stay-at-home parents (and the children, who were also experienced) knew there was an unwritten but widely understood "rule" that switched the entry to the exit for drop-off, and vice versa for pick-up. The purpose of this rule was to allow children to get to the learning center in the morning without having to cross in front of cars. Being a newcomer, Jack followed the rule that had worked for him in the past—and failed to listen to the experts who were trying to tell him about a different rule.

Things went from bad to worse for Jack. The washing machine broke, the vacuum cleaner took on an aggressive life of its own, and, as he struggled to get things under control, lunch caught fire on the stove. Jack was exhausted and his initial enthusiasm for his new role waned. He quit shaving. He gained weight. He took up smoking. He stopped enforcing rules. He fell asleep on the sofa watching TV.

I've often thought of this movie as I've watched incoming law students face the challenges of their first weeks of heavy casebook reading—and as I remember my own early weeks in law school. Starting with confidence, energy, and palpable enthusiasm in the first days or even weeks of class, students quickly realize that they're "not in Kansas anymore." It is common for students to become overwhelmed and many, like Jack, begin to psychologically disengage and/or run out of physical energy.

B. Who Has More Energy: Experts or Novices?

In the last thirty years or so, cognitive psychologists have taken up the study of "expert/novice theory"—the understanding that individuals who are "experts" (the stars) in any field tend to do things differently than do "novices" (beginners or less proficient individuals). Studies show, for example, that expert taxi drivers have a different way of processing information about directions than do non-experts.[1] Similarly, expert chess players "see" the chessboard differently than do novices.[2] Experts are more efficient, plan better, remember more, and work at a deeper (more meaningful) level than novices.[3]

Not surprisingly, then, it actually takes *more* energy to try to carry out a complex task as a novice than it would as an expert. Thus, it is no surprise that Jack became discouraged by his lack of success before he learned the ropes, nor that he responded initially by disengaging, withdrawing, and becoming exhausted.

As Jack soon discovered, however, disengagement, withdrawal, and exhaustion constitute a prescription for disaster. Fortunately, as the movie progresses, Jack decides to face the challenge of managing a home and, ultimately, prevails. He prevails precisely because—and only because—he engages in the challenge and acquires the skills he needs to become an expert himself. It is a comedy with a happy ending.

---

1. Robert Glaser & Michelene T. H. Chi, *Overview*, *in* THE NATURE OF EXPERTISE xv–xvi (Michelene T. H. Chi et al. eds., 1988) (citing numerous studies of early research in artificial intelligence focusing on chess playing skills).

2. K. Anders Ericsson & Peter G. Polson, *A Cognitive Analysis of Exceptional Memory for Restaurant Orders*, *in* THE NATURE OF EXPERTISE 23 (Michelene T. H. Chi et al. eds., 1988).

3. *See generally* THE NATURE OF EXPERTISE (Michelene T. H. Chi et al. eds., 1988); MICHAEL PRESSLEY & PETER AFFLERBACH, VERBAL PROTOCOLS OF READING (1995) (exploring, in part, the nature of reading as a viable area of expertise).

Similarly, reading specialists are unanimous in their observation that skilled readers—readers who understand what they read at a more sophisticated level than their peers—engage with the text they are reading and read with enthusiasm. Moreover, not surprisingly, the more experience the reader has in the field covered by the reading being tested, the more enthusiasm the reader exhibits.

C. Becoming an Expert Legal Reader

This last fact (that expert readers are able to engage energetically and enthusiastically with text) illustrates why it is imperative that you learn as much about case reading and about the world inhabited by lawyers as you can, and that you learn these things as early in your legal education as you can. The more you know about law school reading assignments, the more quickly you will become an "expert" and the less likely you will be to lose confidence, experience confusion or perceive failure, and approach the reading task with self-defeating lethargy.

Effective reading requires action. It requires the reader to have the ability—both the physical and psychological energy—to connect with the text being read and to interact with it. Skilled reading is frequently described as a dialogue[4]—a conversation between the reader and the writer of the text. Such a conversation takes energy.

As we learned in Chapter 4, in addition to describing effective reading as the creation of a dialogue, reading experts describe reading as a way of building ("constructing") knowledge. To reading experts, reading is an activity that requires the reader to respond to the writer's message, construct-

---

4. I was first exposed to the concept of reading as a dialogue by Frank Kessler, instructor of reading at the Learning Center for the University of North Carolina at Chapel Hill, who has provided invaluable support to many law students over the years as they have struggled to learn new reading habits. *See generally* PRESSLEY & AFFLERBACH, *supra* note 3; JEFFREY D. WILHELM, IMPROVING COMPREHENSION WITH THINK-ALOUD STRATEGIES (2001).

ing new information from the exchange that occurs between the writer (who has a message to transmit) and the reader (who brings some knowledge to the interaction and leaves with new understandings).[5]

Less effective readers, however, mistake reading as a passive activity. They read methodically, moving from front to back of the assigned reading. They assume that the writer has information to transmit to them and they sit back, waiting to be taught. They are on the lazy river ride in the reading theme park.

Assuming that reading is a passive activity is an easy mistake to make. If you think about someone reading, you might visualize a retiree relaxing in a comfortable chair by a fire, a child sitting sleepily on a parents' lap, a teenager lolling on a blanket at the beach, or a student engrossed in a book in a wood-paneled library. Not one of these images conjures up a sense of action. To the contrary, you'd almost have to take the book out of the scene to begin to feel any energy or activity in the room.

Despite these images, however, it is a big mistake—a mistake of major magnitude—to assume that effective reading is a passive activity. It is not. Reading is intellectual weight-lifting. The more challenging the text, and the more intellectually demanding the purpose of the reading, the heavier the intellectual weight to be lifted. Law cases and casebooks present notoriously challenging reading.

Reading law effectively is about as far from an intellectually passive activity as you can get. As you will learn in the chapters that follow, the strategies

---

5. *See generally* Elizabeth Fajans & Mary R. Falk, *Against the Tyranny of Paraphrase: Talking Back to Texts*, 78 CORNELL L. REV. 163 (1993) (exploring the importance of developing constructively responsive reading skills in the law school setting); Laurel Currie Oates, *Beating the Odds: Reading Strategies of Law Students Admitted Through Alternative Admissions Programs*, 83 IOWA L. REV. 139 (1997) (discussing empirical evidence of the impact of active reading on academic performance in law school); Leah M. Christensen, *The Paradox of Legal Expertise: A Study of Experts and Novices Reading the Law*, 2008 B.Y.U EDUC. & L.J. 53 (2008); PRESSLEY & AFFLERBACH, *supra* note 3; WILHELM, *supra* note 4.

that lead to success in reading require active intellectual engagement. Skilled readers look over material before they begin, search their minds for what they may already know about the topic, develop a hypothesis about where the author may be going in the text, review and paraphrase frequently, evaluate the quality and content of the reading, and take notes to help remember significant parts of the reading.

D. Where Does the Requisite Energy Come From?

Because reading law requires active intellectual engagement, it requires a lot of energy. Sadly, however, the sheer volume of reading assigned—and the lack of knowledge about how to best approach the reading—leads many students down a disheartening path. Like the husband in *Mr. Mom*, some students are overwhelmed by the chaos that results from their lack of experience and they withdraw or engage in counter-productive behaviors. They lose their initial energy and enthusiasm, become discouraged and some even (metaphorically or actually) take up smoking, gain weight, and fall asleep watching TV. Ignoring all signs to the contrary, they persist in doing things exactly the way they've done them in the past—or they quit doing much at all. Like Jack, they end up "doing it wrong."

The first step to "doing it right" lies in accurately recognizing that effective case reading requires your full and unqualified attention. You must be engaged—i.e., be willing to intellectually *interact* with the case you're reading. In addition, you must be prepared to assess whether what you're doing is working and to be flexible if you find that it isn't. Anything short of enthusiastic engagement and flexible self-assessment does you a disservice—and wastes your time.

Total engagement in reading—just like total engagement in any other worthwhile activity—takes a lot of energy. Maintaining energy for reading the law won't happen by itself. You have to decide to "train" for this challenge, just as surely as you would train for a long distance race or rehearse for the lead role in a play. You have to commit to your goal.

Statistics documenting the connection between achievement and wellness are plentiful, and rest largely on the fact that wellness creates the energy necessary to achieve.[6] Few of us would question this connection—or the common sense of it—when the challenge faced is physical. Somehow, however, we have a tendency to throw common sense out the window when the challenge faced is intellectual. Statistics are equally plentiful, however, connecting intellectual and academic achievement with wellness—and for the same reason.[7] Intellectual achievement takes energy, too.

There are a few fundamental principles of wellness that we should all commit to, but law students who are serious about achieving in law school need to make a special effort to make these habits a priority.[8] Make sure

---

6. There are lots of disciplines studying the relationship of wellness to energy and achievement, ranging from exercise physiologists to recreational therapists to medical research scientists. For more information about this kind of research and wellness in general, you might enjoy exploring the following websites: http://wellness.com/; http://www.netwellness.org/; http://www.nationalwellness.org; http://www.healthypeople.gov; *see also* Sherry L. Leysen, *Brain Plasticity and the Impact of the Electronic Environment in Law and Learning*, 30 LEGAL REFERENCE RES. Q. 255 (2011).

7. *See, e.g.*, Mickey T. Trocket et al., *Health-Related Variables and Academic Performance Among First-Year College Students: Implications for Sleep and Other Behaviors*, J. AM. C. HEALTH, Nov. 2000, at 125. *See generally* internet sources cited *supra* note 6.

8. In addition to exploring the websites listed in note 6, *supra*, you can proactively commit to keeping life balanced. Some written resources that are helpful include: EDMUND BOURNE, THE ANXIETY AND PHOBIA WORKBOOK (6th ed. 2020); EDMUND BOURNE, BEYOND ANXIETY AND PHOBIA(2002); MARTHA DAVIS ET AL., THE RELAXATION AND STRESS WORKBOOK (4th ed. 1995); LARRY KRIEGER, ROASTING THE SEEDS OF LAW SCHOOL STRESS (available from the author at lkrieger@law.fsu.edu). Finally, Martha M. Peters, *Managing Law Student Stress*, FLA. LAW., Summer 1990, at 24–26, is still relevant today. You could also explore the many interactive wellness and relaxation resources available as free apps today. The website for the center for Counseling and Psychological Services (CAPS) at the University of North Carolina at Chapel Hill has a lot of interesting information, including this article on perfectionism (a trait shared by many law students): https://caps.unc.edu/self-help/stress-and-anxiety/perfectionism/. Above all, seek help at your school's counseling center or from your

that you have a plan in place that will allow you to have a healthy, balanced life:

- Throughout law school, keep contact with those you love. Help those who are important to you understand that your contact may not be as frequent or as lengthy as usual, but staying in touch with them is as important as ever to you.
- Make sure you get an optimum amount of sleep. Low-grade sleep deprivation over a prolonged period of time is as unhealthy as pulling the occasional all-nighter (which is also unhealthy and counterproductive).
- Eat well.
- Get regular exercise.
- Keep any anxiety in check.
- Take care of your personal values and spiritual needs.
- Seek whatever outside help you need to maintain these goals.

Our grandmothers often taught us that you can't get water from a stone. If your mind is wandering, take a break. Cognitive psychologists stress that the more prolonged your study time, the more frequently you will need to take breaks. The optimal time to try to concentrate on reading is about an hour, with short breaks (a minute or two to stretch) taken every fifteen minutes. If you are reading on a screen, give your eyes a needed break: take your eyes off the screen at least every twenty minutes and focus, instead, on something in the distance.[9] Do not read longer than an hour without taking a five minute break. Do not read longer than three hours, even with hourly breaks, without taking a big break (say, for lunch or a walk around campus).

Dean of Student Services if you find that you are chronically tired or anxious. Doing so will help you succeed.

9. Nick Bilton, *Do E-Readers Cause Eye Strain?*, Bits Blog of The New York Times (February 12, 2010), http://bits.blogs.nytimes.com/2010/02/12/do-e-readers-cause-eye-strain/.

Self-assessment is a good way to determine what your general state of health is at any given time. Before you start reading, and periodically as you continue reading assigned cases, check to see how you are feeling. Are you alert? Are you rested? Do you need to sleep? Do you need to eat? Are you thirsty? Do you need some exercise?

Health care workers often use a self-assessment scale during diagnosis that helps them understand how much pain a patient is presently experiencing. If you've been to the doctor for any kind of pain recently, you may have been shown a chart that asks you to rate your present pain level on a scale of 1 to 10. Each number on the scale is accompanied by a pencil sketch of an expressive face that illustrates levels of pain (with a number 1 face smiling calmly and a number 10 face showing much distress through deep wrinkles and a down-turned mouth).

You can use the following scale to assess your energy in the same way health care workers assess pain:

10. I'm full of energy and am ready to take on the world
9. My energy is high and I'm looking forward to the task at hand
8. I've got plenty of energy and am enjoying what I'm doing
7. I am enjoying what I'm doing but my mind is wandering some
6. I am able to focus but it is taking some energy to stay with the task
5. I am having trouble focusing and it is taking lots of energy to stay on task
4. My mind is wandering and I'm physically tired
3. I'm tired and can't focus
2. I'm very tired and don't want to try to focus
1. I am exhausted and am not getting anything done

Try using the scale now. Think about how you are feeling—right now, as you read this paragraph. Using the scale above, assign a number from 1 to 10 to your energy level. What is that number? Similarly, think about the last time you had a really positive experience. Think of an activity or event that really stands out in your mind. How would you have rated your energy level then? Now take a quick break. Stand up and stretch, do some shoulder rolls, breathe deeply and come back to reading this paragraph. Did your energy level go up?

As you approach a reading task in law, your energy level needs to be at least at a six on this energy scale for you to be able to engage actively with a text. If your energy level drops to five or below, you should stop reading. Instead, do something that will increase your energy, then go back to reading or engage in a less demanding study task.

Here's the bottom line: reading is often fun, but it is also hard work. When you are reading law, "Engage with Energy," or take a break until you can. If you can't engage with energy when you read, modify your expectations for your reading (see Chapter 7) or engage in a different study task until you get your energy back. If you are chronically short on energy and/or chronically have trouble getting invested in your law school reading, talk with someone who can help you turn that trend around.

PRACTICE EXERCISES

The practice exercises for this chapter give you a chance to think about yourself in relation to the task of reading law, day in and day out. Remember that you can visit caplaw.com/rll to see some of the responses I thought about as I wrote these practice exercise questions.

1. Name a time in your life when you felt your ability to learn was at a maximum:

2. What was characteristic of your life at that time (in other words, what stands out in your mind as you think about that period of your life)?

3. What is your greatest study skill? How can that skill be used in the study of law?

4. What is your greatest weakness in a learning environment? What can you do in the next week to minimize the impact of that weakness?

5. During what time of day do you have the most energy?

6. When your energy drops, what can you do to raise your energy that will not hurt your health in the long run?

7. What type of exercise program can you participate in at least twice a week throughout this semester? Are you willing to commit to that exercise program? Why or why not?

8. What teacher in your past contributed the most to your ability to think independently? What did that teacher do to encourage your independent thought?

9. Is reading an activity that you've enjoyed in the past? How might reading in law be different from other reading you've done?

10. What are your reasons for coming to law school? In what ways will earning a law degree be personally rewarding to you?

CHAPTER 6

Monitor Your Reading and Read for the Main Idea

In the preceding chapter, you learned about the importance of having enough energy to read actively when you are studying law. In addition to understanding the importance of reading with energy, skilled readers also pay attention to what they're doing. Rather than simply reading from the beginning of page one to the end of an assigned text, experienced readers think about what they're doing as they begin an assignment and as they move through a text. In short, they are in charge of their reading and monitor themselves as they read.

A. Nine Ways Experienced Law Students Monitor Their Casebook Reading

(1) Expert law students never (or hardly ever) read without being aware of time;

(2) Expert law students modify their reading strategies—often on the spot—to fit the task at hand;

(3) Expert law students develop a hypothesis about an area of reading and about a specific case *before* they actually read the cases;

(4) Expert law students happily modify a hypothesis if it becomes clear that they were initially wrong;

(5) Expert law students use common sense to check the validity of their hypotheses by making up questions and hypotheticals as they read—in effect, they "test" themselves as they move through text;

(6) Expert law students use the reading cues available to them to speed up their reading and the development of hypotheses about a case;

(7) Expert law students are aware of reading as a "social activity," and carefully choose whom to "engage with mentally";

(8) Expert law students read selectively;

(9) Expert law students pay attention to their feelings and don't read when they're too distracted to understand the material.

In this first section of this chapter, we'll explore each of these nine reading habits in detail.

(1) Time Is of the Essence

Scratch the surface of any law student, and you'll find a busy, busy person. Many law students (hopefully, MOST law students) enjoy learning and enjoy intellectual challenges. Despite the fact that learning is inherently interesting to them and that most have been conscientious students in the past, law students soon find that they cannot afford the luxury of immersing themselves in any given subject or in any given assignment to their heart's content. Rather, even students with the best time management skills are challenged to meet all of their academic and personal responsibilities.

It is typical for students to be assigned anywhere from twelve to twenty-five or more pages of casebook reading a night *in each class.* Not counting legal research and writing assignments, most first year law students meet with three classes on average per weekday. Thus, an average reading load could range from thirty-six to over seventy-five pages of reading on "school nights"—well over 2,000 pages of dense reading a semester.

Despite the high volume of reading assigned, reading cases is not the only thing that law students need to be doing to study successfully. In addition to managing all this reading, students need to attend each and every class with energy. Many students also find outside study groups to be useful[1] and the best students meet with their professors from time to time to clarify a question from class or from reading. As the semester wears on, students need to begin to synthesize information for exam review (often choosing to outline material) and they need to save time to practice writing exam answers (a whole skill set unto itself).

Thus, the speed with which students read cases—while still reading with accuracy—becomes a critical factor in their eventual success. Psychologists have known for years that a task will expand to fill the time allotted to it. Thus, if I have all day to clean the house, it will take me all day to do it. However, if I have only a morning to clean the house, I can still get a reasonable amount of house cleaning done—often with little or no sacrifice in the quality of the end result.

Law students can apply this principle to case reading by acknowledging that reading without a time limit is a luxury they can no longer afford. Instead, work within a rational time "budget" the way wise money managers work within a rational financial budget. Start with how much time you have to give the task, just as a wise money manager starts with how much money he or she has to spend, and get your reading done—as best you can—in the time allotted.

You can determine the time limit by dividing your available study time by the length of the assignment. Write down the starting time and the finish time for the assignment, and try your best to stick to your plan. Thus, if I have three cases to read and an hour and a half to read them in, I spend no more than thirty minutes reading and taking notes (including briefing) for

1. *See* Dorothy H. Evensen, *To Group or Not to Group: Students' Perceptions of Collaborative Learning Activities in Law School,* 28 S. Ill. U. L.J. 343 (2004); *see also* Christine P. Bartholomew, *Time: An Empirical Analysis of Law Student Time Management Deficiencies*, 81 U. Cin. L. Rev. (2013).

each case. If I get off my schedule by even ten minutes per case, I'm already thirty minutes behind. If I get thirty minutes behind in each of two or three more classes, I can easily end up being "short" over two hours of study time at the end of the day. Falling that far behind on a routine basis comes at the cost of being inadequately prepared for class, or at the cost of not maintaining the level of wellness you need in order to stay happy and healthy and to keep your energy at a productive level.

One way to increase the likelihood that you'll stay on task is to use well-established principles of behavior modification to monitor your time management as you read. Behavior modification principles teach us that behavior that is reinforced increases, and behavior that is punished decreases. The behavior I want to reinforce is studying in a focused, intense way that keeps me in healthy time limits. The behavior I want to "punish" (or at least not reinforce) is working past rational time limits, or working in a non-productive, unnecessarily time-consuming way.

Small things (like a candy lifesaver or a quick mental break) can be strongly reinforcing. Forcing yourself to move on when time is up (even if you didn't reach your goal) can be an effective "punisher" (and will speed you up unconsciously the next time). If you choose to read a case within a set time limit, train yourself to stick to that time limit and reward yourself when you do. Focus on having gotten as much out of the case as you could in the time allotted—and pick up more information about the case as the learning process continues in class. Don't lament the fact that you didn't completely master the case in the time available. Give yourself a pat on the back (or reward yourself with, literally, an M & M) for doing what the expert readers do—monitor your reading by sticking to the time limits you've chosen.[2]

---

2. Here's an important tip: As you choose time limits, assume that approximately two hours of preparation for every hour in class is what a strong student would shoot for on average. Note that only about 1.5 hours of that time could be devoted to reading for class because you have other important study tasks (such as reviewing and synthesizing class notes) to attend to as well. There are occasional days when you might need to go over this time limit (and days where you might be able to complete your

(2) Be Strategic and Flexible

Expert readers never wander willy-nilly into a reading project. Rather, they make deliberate decisions about how they will approach their reading. You'll learn more in the remaining chapters about some of the strategies that expert legal readers use when they approach assigned casebook reading. With experience, you'll develop additional strategies on your own. For now, it is important to know that you need to develop some strategies. After the first week or so of class, simply opening your casebook and beginning to read—no matter how earnest your effort—is just not going to be enough.

In addition to having reading strategies, expert readers monitor the effectiveness of the strategies they choose to apply as they move through a text. If they are not able to figure out the main idea of the reading, or meet any other purpose they may have for reading, they have enough conscious control of the process to stop what they're doing and try something different.

Similarly, skilled readers are honest with themselves about what they do and don't understand—and make wise decisions about resources they can use to save time to improve their understanding. A skilled reader who comes across a vocabulary word that is unfamiliar, for example, can quickly turn to a dictionary for clarification. Alternatively, the reader might use context cues to figure out the meaning of the word as it is used in the sentence. Similarly, a law student who comes across an unfamiliar term can make a strategic decision about the importance of looking up the word.[3] If it is a word that the student might see again and again, then looking it up

---

work in less time). On average, if you stick to this time limit you will end up doing heavily challenging intellectual work for about fifty hours per week (including the time you are preparing for class, the time you are engaged in class, and the time you study productively with others).

3. Finding the definition of a legal term often requires a specialized legal dictionary. *See, e.g.*, Black's Law Dictionary (11th ed. 2019); Bryan A. Garner, A Dictionary of Modern Legal Usage (3d ed. 2011).

makes all the sense in the world. Many students designate a place in their notebook or on their laptop to write down new words and their definitions.

Likewise, if the student is at high risk for being called on in class—or knows darned well that he or she WILL be called on in class—it might be a good idea to look up all unfamiliar words. Sometimes, however, a skilled reader (even in law school) might make an educated guess about the meaning of a word in context (being flexible about seeing if the guess makes sense as the reading goes on) or take a chance that the word is no longer in common usage and simply isn't important enough to spend time deciphering.

The point is, as you read in your casebook, you will need to develop new reading strategies and to exercise conscious control over the reading choices you make.

(3) Take a Guess About What You May Learn

Part of being an active reader is being willing to stick your neck out and take some intellectual risks. Before you begin any reading, you should develop a working hypothesis about the content of the reading. You might be wrong. You might be right. Either way, you'll be engaged.

Whether you realize it consciously or not, you probably already develop a hypothesis about the content of most things you read. As readers develop a hypothesis, they consciously or unconsciously take cues from the context of the reading—the title of the piece, the magazine or book it is in, things they may know about the author. If we're not speculating at all when we read, we're wasting a lot of time.

For example, if the title of an article handed out during law school orientation is "Writing Your Way on to the Law Review," I might speculate that the piece will contain useful tips about serious academic journal writing. If the title, on the other hand, is "Writing Your Way on to the Law Revue," (once I looked up "revue" and realized it was a synonym for a show comprised of humorous musical skits), I might speculate that the piece will contain useful tips for adapting karaoke lyrics to parodies of law school or writing scripts for skits or tag lines for funny photographs of professors.

I would certainly guess that I would laugh more reading the second piece than reading the first.

(4) Be Willing to Abandon Your Hypothesis If You're Wrong

Of course, once I started reading, I might find that my hypotheses (guesses) about these articles were wrong. It's certainly possible that the "Law Review" piece is one student's humorous parody of experiences with a journal competition or that the "Law Revue" piece is a serious explanation of the rules for joining the production staff of the end-of-the-year law school talent show.

Whether my initial hypothesis is right or wrong doesn't matter. I would be doing what an excellent reader should do just by having taken a guess in the first place—and then having enough sense to modify my hypothesis as my reading made it apparent that I was wrong.

This same principle applies to assigned casebook reading. Developing a hypothesis—which you're willing to modify as you read and then again when you go to class—will save you time and energy as you work through your assignments.

(5) Common Sense Can Help You Develop and Test a Reading Hypothesis

How would I know if my hypothesis is right or wrong? Approach your reading posing your hypothesis as a proposition and then test your proposition as you move through the text. "I'll bet . . ." is a good phrase to have in mind as you start reading a new section in a casebook or start reading a new case within a section.

As you move through the reading, ask yourself questions that will help you see if you are on the writer's wavelength. For example, let's say that I'm reading a cluster of cases about battery. The background reading prepared by the author just before the cases begin explains that battery is a tort that occurs when someone subjects someone else to a "harmful or offensive contact." Based on this background reading, I begin the first case by hypothesizing (speculating) that it will show me a situation in which a person bringing an action for battery was hurt or offended.

In the first paragraph of the case, however, I find that the action was disallowed because the court found there was no "harmful or offensive contact." I have enough sense to realize I need to change my initial hypothesis. Apparently this case is not going to show me a situation where a person was hurt or offended (or at least not in a way that the court would allow an action for battery), but perhaps the court is going to talk about what does and doesn't constitute harmful or offensive contact. I begin to think, "Maybe I will learn why this person's case did *not* constitute battery."

I now move forward assuming the case will be about a situation where someone was NOT subjected to a harmful or offensive contact, and hoping to learn more about the topic. As I read, I become confused about how a court decides when a contact is "offensive." I might develop a hypothesis that a contact is "offensive" if the plaintiff was *actually* offended by the contact, not just if he or she *might have been* offended. I would, then, pose some hypotheticals (imaginary situations) that I make up out of my head, like: "So, if I've gone to a lot of trouble to get my hair done and someone sprays me with water at the State Fair, then I'd really be offended by the contact and I could recover. BUT, if a teenager was at a party on a beach and got splashed with water and laughed, he would probably NOT be able to recover (because he wasn't really offended)—even if someone else might have been offended in the same situation."

As I read further in this case, however, I begin to wonder if this hypothesis (that a plaintiff can recover if he or she is personally offended by an unwanted contact) is accurate. I begin to lose confidence in my hypothesis because it is clear that THIS plaintiff in the case I'm reading was, in fact, personally offended when someone made a peace sign above her head just as a cameraman snapped a group picture at a class reunion. Nonetheless, even though she was offended, the judge did not allow recovery.

Hmmmmm . . . this result is perplexing. If I'm an "engaged" reader, I need to rise to the challenge and modify my hypothesis. I might ask myself a question at this point: "Well, darn. It doesn't look like someone can recover just because he or she is *personally* offended by an unwanted touching. But the casebook author says that 'offensive touching' is a battery. How can this be? I wonder if the key is that someone can recover if he or she was actually offended AND a *reasonable person*, in the same situation, would have been offended, too." Using the case in my hand, I could then test that hypothesis and see that it would cover the facts of that case—in the end, the court did NOT allow recovery even though this particular individual was offended because the court believed that a usual reunion-goer would have had a better sense of humor and would NOT have been offended.

(6) Context Cues Can Speed Up Your Reading and Help You Think About What to Anticipate

Casebooks are full (chock full) of all kinds of reading cues that help us formulate initial working hypotheses as well as questions to test our initial propositions. Using these cues will help you read faster and more effectively.

Every casebook has a Table of Contents that puts each case in the larger context of the subject being taught. There are usually running headers across the top of the page that repeat the Section Headings and Subheadings (from the Table of Contents) so you can stay oriented as you read. At the beginning of most new sections, many casebook authors include text that gives useful background information and/or summarizes the principles you will be reading about in detail in the accompanying cases.

In addition to the visual and textual cues provided in the casebook, the fact that cases are often clustered in related groups is helpful, too. When cases are grouped in clusters, one case can give lots of cues about the "main idea" of its companion cases. Finally, casebook authors mercifully include "Notes and Problems" or "Notes and Questions" at the end of each topic section. If you are having trouble figuring out what kinds of questions you should be asking yourself to test the meaning of a case, you can use the Notes, Problems, and Questions provided by the casebook author to jog your thinking and "get engaged" in your reading.

One of the things that sometimes confuses beginning legal readers about cases is that there are so many different "voices" included in a typical opinion.[4] Unlike a more traditional kind of writing where there is one author presenting one point of view, cases (although authored by a judge) often include multiple perspectives, multiple potential holdings, multiple lines of precedent, and multiple proposed rules of law before the court ultimately settles on the views it will adopt and the holdings it will reach. Wise readers can save time by paying attention to transitional phrases and other context cues to help them distinguish times when the court is introducing someone else's point of view (say, for example, that of the court below, or that of one of the parties, or that expressed in an older, precedent-setting case) from the times when the decision-making court is making statements that it has adopted as its own.

(7) Read Selectively

Not all parts of a case are equally important, and not all parts of a case require the same amount of attention to master. You'll read faster and more effectively if you choose what to focus on and what to skim. Often key transitional phrases can serve as "red flags" to warn you when to slow down. Words like "we hold; plaintiff argues; we fail to understand . . ." can foreshadow important reasoning points in a case. Other common transitional phrases ("the facts are . . ." or "we are asked to decide . . .") can point you to the sections of a case you may need to focus on to complete a brief for class.

(8) How You Feel About a Case Can Interfere with What You Can Learn From a Case (Unless You Handle Those Feelings Well)

No one comes to law school devoid of past life experiences. Memories of these experiences can be triggered by the facts of the cases we read, or

4. I am grateful to my colleague, Professor Bobbi Jo Boyd of Campbell University's School of Law and former Deputy Director of the Writing and Learning Resources Center at the University of North Carolina School of Law, for these observations about voice.

by the values discussed by a court, or by the law itself. These past memories can enhance your reading by adding richness to the text—making it personally meaningful to you. By the same token, if these past experiences and memories evoke strong emotional reactions, those feelings can create "interference" or "noise" that blocks your ability to read the case well.

You may be consciously aware of what you are feeling and associations you are making when you read a case, or those associations may occur only at an unconscious level. If you find you are resistant to a case or a concept, or that your energy level suddenly plummets when you read a case or every time you pick up a certain casebook, take time to consider whether something else may be going on. If you honor what you're feeling by attending to it consciously, you can move on and read the case more objectively—separating the past from the present.

(9) Reading Is a "Social Activity" with Strong Interpersonal Components

Although most of us would think of reading as a solitary activity, reading theorists have come to understand that reading has powerful social connotations. Reading research indicates that readers often think about other people as they read. For example, readers might think, "Have I read enough of this report to get through the upcoming Board meeting?" or "Can I explain these directions to my father?" or "Wow, my friend is sure going to think this is a funny email when I forward it to him."

In addition to imagining how they will interact with others in relation to whatever it is that they're reading, strong readers also engage in a semi-conscious social dialogue with the author of the text itself as they read: "I'm not sure this author knows as much about nuclear physics as I had hoped. I wonder how long she has worked in this field?" or [to the author of a history text] "You can't really mean that you think the Revolutionary War was caused by the French!?"; or [to a novelist] "Please don't give this story a sad ending;" or "What an incredible description—it makes me feel like I've been there myself."

This social component of reading has two important implications for law students. First, because the reading of cases is predictably followed by a lengthy class discussion—often in front of seventy-five or more classmates—students can easily get preoccupied with the potential opinions of other students or their professor, rather than focusing on making meaning of the case itself. If a reader is imagining the pressure of the spotlight, the temptation to think within safe boundaries looms large, and the importance of thinking creatively, deeply, and speculatively diminishes.

Second, because the authors of opinions speak with authority and conviction—often arising from actual authority and power—it is difficult to engage in even an imaginary dialogue with them. Years ago, a student brought me a bumper sticker that was popular at the time (representing a kind of anti-establishment message). The bumper sticker said, in bold, capital letters: "Question Authority." I kept that bumper sticker on my door for years to motivate students to engage in the kind of questioning dialogue that is required for effective case reading.

The importance of reading for the right purpose will be discussed in detail in the next chapter. For now, it is enough to recognize that you read with an awareness that you may eventually share the results of your reading with someone. Don't let the prospect of discussions in large classes loom larger than it should, and don't define the purpose of those discussions incorrectly. Class is there to help you develop and refine a hypothesis about the law—not to test your knowledge of a case. Your accurate reading of the details of a case (often those that are briefed) may be a prerequisite to a rich discussion of the case in class, but your reading purpose is not generally to "get" the case "right."

If you find your reading is dominated by a desire to avoid embarrassment in class, consider choosing other imaginary audiences (apart from your peers and the professor in class). For example, you can imagine talking about the case with a family member, a close friend, or the professor in the safety of a one-on-one setting, even if those conversations only rarely occur. Similarly, think about who wrote a case and what your image of that person means to you. Can you give yourself permission to "discuss" a case with the judge who authored it?

B. Most Importantly, Read for the *Main Idea*

Exceptional readers with experience in a particular field cut to the chase as they read. They look for large themes and important principles in their reading, actively pursuing "the main idea" of a text.[5] Inexperienced readers, or less proficient readers, instead march with determination through a text—methodically and carefully reading for detail that may be superfluous or unimportant in the end.

The challenge for beginning law students is that they don't have enough experience in the field of law (and law study) to know (at first) what may wind up being superfluous. It helps to know that, in all fields, development of "macropropositions" (the big picture) is dependent on the early development of "micropropositions" (the components of the big picture).[6] When readers first begin to read in a specialized field, such as law, they have to pay a lot of attention to mastering the "micropropositions" (the sub-parts of the big picture). As readers gain in experience, the macropropositions move appropriately into the foreground and the underlying micropropositions take the supporting role they deserve.

If you ever studied art, you may remember the impressionist era, represented by great artists such as Monet, Manet, Renoir, and Cezanne. During this era, the technique called "pointillism," most widely recognized in the work of Georges Seurat, became popular. You might have seen some of these pictures in museums or in books—one of the most famous shows an idyllic "Sunday Afternoon on the Island of la Grande Jaffe." The landscape is comprised of thousands of small points of paint (purples, blues, oranges)

---

5. *See* MICHAEL PRESSLEY & PETER AFFLERBACH, VERBAL PROTOCOLS OF READING 99 (1995).

6. *Id.*

that all blend (when you step back from the painting) to create the wonderful treatment of light and image that characterize that period of art. When you stand close to the painting, all you see are colorful dots. The dots make up a picture. They are not the picture itself.

Reading cases is the same kind of experience. The micropropositions (the dots of paint) are the details of a case that are emphasized in the early days of class. The macropropositions (the "big picture") are the themes, principles, and rules that emerge as we learn to read critically, searching for the main idea of the case in the context of its companion cases and accompanying notes and problems, considering each case as it relates to *this* course. For students searching for the main idea of their reading in a casebook, reading the case in the context of the course (asking, for example, why was *this* case chosen—what does it add to my understanding of this area of law?) is critical.

For students who are new to law study, the focus in the early weeks of class on the component parts of cases ("Ms. Garcia, can you tell us who brought the action in *Pennoyer v. Neff*?" or "Mr. Hunt, can you tell us the question before the court in *Gordon v. Steele*?") can lead them to believe that identification of these component parts *is* the "main idea" of their reading. It is not.

Being able to accurately identify the component parts of a case as described in Chapter 2 is a prerequisite step to being able to discuss the case at a deeper, more meaningful level. In the first days and even weeks of class, many professors will focus on the development of students' ability to read carefully enough to identify these foundational concepts. At this early point, it's entirely appropriate for students to focus on these details as they read—understanding these details is how the student will eventually have enough cards in hand to play the larger game of legal reasoning. Without them, the next step of reading (looking for the larger themes) can't be achieved.

Gradually, however, the discussion will shift. You'll begin to notice over a period of weeks that cases are no longer discussed in excruciating detail, but rather that hypothetical fact scenarios begin to dominate class discussions—shifting the focus to the outer boundaries of rules, to the commonalities and distinctions among related cases, and to the questions not expressly answered by the court in any of the cases studied.

Over the years, I have found another metaphor to the world of art helpful as this shift occurs. If you ever studied sculpture, or know someone who sculpts, you may know that people who truly appreciate sculpture are as intrigued by the "space in the sculpture" (the shapes created in the open area around the sculpture) as they are by the sculpture itself. Relating that image to law, you will find that, over time, your professors will take for granted that you can identify the "sculpture" of a case (the things you can touch and prove about a case—frequently the things we brief). What they really enjoy—and what expert legal reasoners consider to be the "main idea" of advanced casebook reading—is the "space" in the case (the things that are "indeterminate"[7] about the text, the questions not yet answered, the facts not dealt with adequately).

Making this shift from details (micropropositions) being the "main idea" of your reading to themes and patterns (macropropositions) becoming the "main idea" of your reading happens gradually. As long as you continue to read actively, and don't become complacent when you get good at understanding the tangible aspects of cases, you'll make the shift successfully.

---

7. Elizabeth Fajans & Mary R. Falk, *Against the Tyranny of Paraphrase: Talking Back to Texts*, 78 CORNELL L. REV. 163, 172 (1993).

PRACTICE EXERCISES

The practice exercises for this chapter will give you an opportunity to read an excerpted portion of a classic civil law case (*Compuserve, Inc. v. Cyber Promotions, Inc.*, 962 F. Supp. 1015 (S.D. Ohio 1997)). These exercises will allow you to focus on how you're monitoring your reading and how to read for the main idea. Remember that you can visit caplaw.com/rll to see some of the responses I thought about as I wrote these practice exercise questions.

1. You should set aside about 15 minutes to read this case. Write down your starting time and your anticipated finishing time here:

Assume this case is found in a Torts[8] casebook, in a section called (in the Table of Contents and the running header of the book) "Trespass to Chattels."[9] Read the excerpted portion that follows:

8. A tort is a civil action brought to compensate a party for a civil (not criminal) harm done to him or her. A law school Torts class (and its accompanying casebook) would explore the various causes of action (bases for a claim) upon which someone who has been harmed could seek a remedy under a tort theory. Negligence, for example, is a tort claim. Other tort claims include actions for slander, or for civil battery, or for intentional infliction of emotional distress.
9. "Chattel" is a term for personal property (as opposed to real property, like land).

CompuServe Incorporated vs. Cyber Promotions, Inc.

No. C2-96-1070

United States District Court, S.D. Ohio, Eastern Division

February 3, 1997

GRAHAM, District Judge.

This case presents novel issues regarding the commercial use of the Internet, specifically the right of an online computer service to prevent a commercial enterprise from sending unsolicited electronic mail advertising to its subscribers.

Plaintiff CompuServe Incorporated ("CompuServe") is one of the major national commercial online computer services. It operates a computer communication service through a proprietary nationwide computer network. In addition to allowing access to the extensive content available within its own proprietary network, CompuServe also provides its subscribers with a link to the much larger resources of the Internet. This allows its subscribers to send and receive electronic messages, known as "e-mail," by the Internet. Defendants Cyber Promotions, Inc. and its president Sanford Wallace are in the business of sending unsolicited e-mail advertisements on behalf of themselves and their clients to hundreds of thousands of Internet users, many of whom are CompuServe subscribers. CompuServe has notified defendants that they are prohibited from using its computer equipment to process and store the unsolicited e-mail and has requested that they terminate the practice. Instead, defendants have sent an increasing volume of e-mail solicitations to CompuServe subscribers. CompuServe has attempted to employ technological means to block the flow of defendants' e-mail transmission to its computer equipment, but to no avail.

This matter is before the Court on the application of CompuServe for a preliminary injunction which would extend the duration of the temporary restraining order issued by this Court on October 24, 1996 and which would in addition prevent defendants from sending unsolicited advertisements to CompuServe subscribers.

For the reasons which follow, this Court holds that where defendants engaged in a course of conduct of transmitting a substantial volume of electronic data in the form of unsolicited e-mail to plaintiff's proprietary computer equipment, where defendants continued such practice after repeated demands to cease and desist, and where defendants deliberately evaded plaintiff's affirmative efforts to protect its computer equipment from such use, plaintiff has a viable claim for trespass to personal property and is entitled to injunctive relief to protect its property.

I.

The Court will begin its analysis of the issues by acknowledging, for the purpose of providing a background, certain findings of fact recently made by another district court in a case involving the Internet:

> 1. The Internet is not a physical or tangible entity, but rather a giant network which interconnects innumerable smaller groups of linked computer networks. It is thus a network of networks. . . .
>
> 2. Some networks are "closed" networks, not linked to other computers or networks. Many networks, however, are connected to other networks, which are in turn connected to other networks in a manner which permits each computer in any network to communicate with computers on any other network in the system. This global Web of linked networks and computers is referred to as the Internet.
>
> 3. The nature of the Internet is such that it is very difficult, if not impossible, to determine its size at a given moment. It is indisputable, however, that the Internet has experienced extraordinary growth in recent years. . . . In all, reasonable estimates are that as many as 40 million people around the world can and do access

> the enormously flexible communication Internet medium. That figure is expected to grow to 200 million Internet users by the year 1999.
>
> 4. Some of the computers and computer networks that make up the network are owned by governmental and public institutions, some are owned by non-profit organizations, and some are privately owned. The resulting whole is a decentralized, global medium of communications—or "cyberspace"—that links people, institutions, corporations, and governments around the world. . . .
>
> . . . .
>
> 11. No single entity—academic, corporate, governmental, or non-profit—administers the Internet. It exists and functions as a result of the fact that hundreds of thousands of separate operators of computers and computer networks independently decided to use common data transfer protocols to exchange communications and information with other computers (which in turn exchange communications and information with still other computers). There is no centralized storage location, control point, or communications channel for the Internet, and it would not be technically feasible for a single entity to control all of the information conveyed on the Internet.

American Civil Liberties Union v. Reno, 929 F. Supp. 824, 830–832 (E.D. Pa. 1996). In 1994, one commentator noted that "advertisements on the current Internet computer network are not common because of that network's not-for-profit origins." Trotter Hardy, The Proper Legal Regime for "Cyberspace," 55 U. Pitt. L .Rev. 993, 1027 (1994). In 1997, that statement is no longer true.

Internet users often pay a fee for Internet access. However, there is no per-message charge to send electronic messages over the Internet and such messages usually reach their destination within minutes. Thus electronic mail provides an opportunity to reach a wide audience quickly and at almost no cost to the sender. It is not surprising therefore that some companies, like defendant Cyber Promotions, Inc., have begun using the Internet to distribute advertisements by sending the same unsolicited commercial message to hundreds of thousands of Internet users at once. Defendants refer to this as "bulk e-mail," while plaintiff refers to it as "junk e-mail." In the vernacular of the Internet, unsolicited e-mail advertising is sometimes referred to pejoratively as "spam."[1] CompuServe subscribers use CompuServe's domain name "CompuServe.com" together with their own unique alpha-numeric identifier to form a distinctive e-mail mailing address. That address may be used by the subscriber to exchange electronic mail with any one of tens of millions of other Internet users who have electronic mail capability. E-mail sent to CompuServe subscribers is processed and stored on CompuServe's proprietary computer equipment. Thereafter, it becomes accessible to CompuServe's subscribers, who can access CompuServe's equipment and electronically retrieve those messages.

Over the past several months, CompuServe has received many complaints from subscribers threatening to discontinue their subscription unless CompuServe prohibits electronic mass mailers from using its equipment to send unsolicited advertisements. CompuServe asserts that the volume of messages generated by such mass mailings places a significant burden on its equipment which has finite processing and storage capacity. CompuServe receives no payment from the mass mailers for processing their unsolicited advertising. However, CompuServe's subscribers pay for their access to CompuServe's services in increments of time and thus the process of accessing, reviewing and discarding unsolicited e-mail costs them money, which is one of the reasons for their complaints. CompuServe has notified defendants that

---

1. This term is derived from a skit performed on the British television show Monty Python's Flying Circus, in which the word "spam" is repeated to the point of absurdity in a restaurant menu.

they are prohibited from using its proprietary computer equipment to process and store unsolicited e-mail and has requested them to cease and desist from sending unsolicited e-mail to its subscribers. Nonetheless, defendants have sent an increasing volume of e-mail solicitations to CompuServe subscribers.

In an effort to shield its equipment from defendants' bulk e-mail, CompuServe has implemented software programs designed to screen out the messages and block their receipt. In response, defendants have modified their equipment and the messages they send in such a fashion as to circumvent CompuServe's screening software. Allegedly, defendants have been able to conceal the true origin of their messages by falsifying the point-of-origin information contained in the header of the electronic messages. Defendants have removed the "sender" information in the header of their messages and replaced it with another address. Also, defendants have developed the capability of configuring their computer servers to conceal their true domain name and appear on the Internet as another computer, further concealing the true origin of the messages. By manipulating this data, defendants have been able to continue sending messages to CompuServe's equipment in spite of CompuServe's protests and protective efforts.

Defendants assert that they possess the right to continue to send these communications to CompuServe subscribers. CompuServe contends that, in doing so, the defendants are trespassing upon its personal property.

II.

The grant or denial of a motion for preliminary injunction rests within the discretion of the trial court. *Deckert v. Independence Shares Corp.*, 311 U.S. 282, 61 S.Ct. 229, 85 L.Ed. 189 (1940). In determining whether a motion for preliminary injunction should be granted, a court must consider and balance four factors: (1) the likelihood that the party seeking the preliminary injunction will succeed on the merits of the claim; (2) whether the party seeking the injunction will suffer irreparable harm without the grant of the extraordinary relief; (3) the probability that granting the injunction will cause substantial harm to others; and (4) whether the public interest is advanced by the issuance of the injunction. *Washington v. Reno,* 35 F.3d 1093, 1099 (6th Cir.1994); *International Longshoremen's Assoc. v. Norfolk S. Corp.*, 927 F.2d 900, 903 (6th Cir.1991). None of these individual factors constitute prerequisites that must be met for the issuance of a preliminary injunction, they are instead factors that are to be balanced. *In re DeLorean Motor Co.*, 755 F.2d 1223, 1229 (6th Cir. 1985). A preliminary injunction is customarily granted on the basis of procedures that are less formal and evidence that is less complete than in a full trial on the merits. Indeed, "[a] party . . . is not required to prove his case in full at a preliminary injunction hearing." *University of Texas v. Camenisch,* 451 U.S. 390, 395, 101 S.Ct. 1830, 1834, 68 L.Ed.2d 175 (1981). . . .

2. In order to read efficiently, law students have to learn to read selectively. In the third paragraph of the case, the court wrote, "This matter is before the Court on the application of CompuServe for a preliminary injunction which would extend the duration of the temporary restraining order issued by this Court on October 24, 1996 and which would in addition prevent defendants from sending unsolicited advertisements to CompuServe subscribers." When you read this paragraph, was it clear to you what a "preliminary injunction" is? How about a "temporary restraining order"? If you have not been in a situation or a course where these terms were explained, there is no reason to expect yourself to know what they are. You could have googled those terms or looked them up in a legal dictionary (and found that both are orders issued by a court to prevent one party from taking an irreversible action until the court can resolve the situation at hand). Alternatively, you could have tried to guess from the context what those words

meant. What context cues are in the sentence, or appear later in the case, that could have helped you infer the meaning of the words?

3. If this case had been assigned in a Civil Procedure10 class, rather than in a Torts class, which portions of the case would have been the most important?

4. How much do you know about computers? Was there any information in the first paragraphs of Section I of the opinion that was "new" information to you? (The answer to that question would, of course, depend on how knowledgeable you are about computers). Why do you think the court felt compelled to include this information in such detail? (Hint: look at the date of the opinion. Do you think such detail is as necessary for today's reading audience?) If you are familiar with computers and the Internet, could you have skimmed these paragraphs?

5. Look at the footnote explaining the origins of the word "spam." Is this new information to you? Is it information that you need to hold on to in order to get the "main idea" of this case in the context of a Torts class?

6. Do you personally ever feel overwhelmed by "spam" in your own email account? Have you ever been involved with a company that was trying to earn a living by advertising on the Internet? How might these two experiences influence your reading of the case?

7. Who do you know (personally) who might find the facts of this case interesting?

8. Having read this much of the opinion, what is your best guess as to the reasoning the court will adopt in the remainder of the opinion (which was not included in your reading) to support its conclusion that "plaintiff has a viable claim for trespass to personal property and is entitled to injunctive relief to protect its property"? (Hint, go back to question 1 and look at what heading this case came under in our hypothetical casebook. If you're curious about the court's actual reasoning, and have time to read the whole opinion, ask a law librarian for help locating this opinion or check out our website at caplaw.com/rll.)

9. What time did you stop reading the case? Did you stay within your time limits? Did you finish more quickly than you anticipated, or did your reading take more time than you thought it would? In retrospect, are there things you could have done that would have saved you time when you first read this excerpted portion of the case?

10. Civil Procedure is a first-year course that explores the logistics of how cases are brought to a court and is generally based on the Federal Rules of Civil Procedure, which mandate procedures attorneys and courts must follow to bring a lawsuit based on any valid claim.

CHAPTER 7

Always (Always!) Read with a Clear Purpose

There are all kinds of good reasons to read. You can read for entertainment, you can read to expand your horizons, you can read to pass the time. You can also read for information, you can read for directions, or you can read so you have something to talk about at dinner.

Imagine, for example, that you are reading the classic novel, *To Kill a Mockingbird*, as part of an English class studying treatment of race relations in literature. Would you be looking for anything special as you read? What if you were reading the same book for a class on the Sociology of the South? What if, instead, you were a linguistics expert and you were doing research on how dialect is reflected in popular literature?

Each of these reading purposes would cause you to approach the novel from a different perspective, with different questions in your head. As you applied some of the strategies expert readers classically use (for example, reading selectively or reading for the main idea), you would make different decisions about what to focus on and what to skim, or what you considered the "main idea" to be, or which words were important to highlight or take note of. It is hugely inefficient—and often counterproductive—to read a text for one purpose when you ought to be reading it for another.

A. Intrinsic v. Extrinsic Reading Purposes

Choosing the right purpose of your casebook reading[1] is a critical threshold decision for all law students, and one that has a major impact on how effective your reading will be.

Here are some of the possible purposes (in no particular order) a student might have for reading in law school:

(1) to learn enough to impress someone (in or out of class);
(2) to be able to answer all the questions a professor might ask in class;
(3) to learn how courts function and how legal decisions are reached;
(4) to keep from being embarrassed if called on in class;
(5) to write a case brief;
(6) to be able to participate effectively in class;
(7) to learn principles/rules of law that are relevant in this section of the course;
(8) to get the assignment done;
(9) to try to improve legal reasoning abilities;
(10) to learn the right things to score high on exams;
(11) for fun.

You may be able to think of additional reasons why a law student might read material in a casebook and may already be reading for some other purpose yourself.

Some of these reading purposes, while commonly adopted by students in law school, are less beneficial to your educational progress than others. The

---

1. Chapters 13 and 14 of this book move beyond casebook reading to discuss how the "purpose" for your reading of a case (or statute) might change if you were reading in practice or as part of a skills-based class, rather than in the context of a casebook assigned as part of a more traditional law school class.

subject of law-student distress has been the object of scholarly investigation for years. In a recent article, the authors proposed that at least one source of law student distress (among many—including the subtle institutional pressure to work all the time) is the shift from *intrinsic* motivation to *extrinsic* motivation.[2] In that article, Professors Larry Krieger and Kennon Sheldon noted that healthy people thrive on pursuing activities that are intrinsically rewarding to them—that have some inherent internal value to that person. In contrast, people who pursue activities for external motivations (e.g., for status, or for money, or to avoid a painful consequence) are generally less happy (and less productive).

B. Strive to Read for a Purpose That Matters to You

These observations suggest that reading cases for intrinsically rewarding reasons would be better for you in the long run than reading them for extrinsically rewarding reasons. Not surprisingly, the reading purposes that are intrinsically rewarding are, for the most part, educationally more profitable as well.

Take another look at the list of reading purposes set out in the preceding section of this chapter. Which of those reasons are extrinsically motivated and which intrinsically motivated?

Reading to avoid being "wrong" in class is reading for extrinsic reasons. Similarly, reading to impress someone with your knowledge or reading solely to get high grades or to get the assignment done are all extrinsically motivated purposes.

In contrast, reading to learn something that you want to know for your professional growth, reading to improve your legal reasoning abilities (assuming *you want* to improve your thinking abilities), reading to learn

---

2. Kennon M. Sheldon & Lawrence S. Krieger, *Does Legal Education Have Undermining Effects on Law Students? Evaluating Changes in Motivation, Values, and Well-Being*, 22 BEHAV. SCI. & LAW 261 (2004).

principles that are central to your course of study (assuming you are committed to the course of study), and reading to learn more about how the legal discourse community operates (assuming that becoming a member of that discourse community is a personal goal with benefits personal to you) are all intrinsically motivated reasons to read. Interestingly, reading so you can participate intelligently if called on in class is the kind of "purpose" that can cut both ways—if you are interested in participating effectively because you want to learn and enjoy the dialogue, that's intrinsic motivation. If your vision of participating well is tied to impressing others or avoiding embarrassment, that's extrinsic motivation. Reading for fun (#11 on the list in the preceding section—which loosely translates into reading for the pure pleasure of it), sadly, is rarely your purpose for reading in law school because of the sheer volume of reading assigned. However, there's nothing to say that you can't enjoy some of the reading along the way, or can't—occasionally—decide to read a case for no reason other than to have fun with it.

C. Effective Purposes for Reading Law

After the first days and weeks of school, experienced law students who learn to excel eventually come around to understanding that they are reading cases in casebooks most of the time, in most classes, for one of the following three reasons (or a combination of these reasons). Each of these reasons will contribute to your development of the knowledge and skills you need to become comfortable in the legal discourse community:

(1) to read the assigned case well enough to get an accurate picture of what happened in the case [often synthesized in some form of a brief];

(2) to gather information about legal reasoning and the legal discourse community (how lawyers think, communicate, and take action); and

(3) to understand the "big picture" in this sub-topic of the course by reasoning inductively to see what this case adds in light of the information surrounding it in this section of the casebook.

In the first days and weeks of class, it will take most of your energy and skill to satisfy the first purpose set out above: getting an accurate picture of what happened in the case and briefing it. Over time, your ability to read cases accurately and to understand their content in terms of the clusters of thought represented in a typical brief will improve markedly. When that happens, you will be able to focus less consciously on that purpose. You will find you have the freedom to move forward and think consciously about how the court is reasoning in *this* case and how that type of reasoning might generalize to other cases you've read or will read in the future. You can start to tune into word usage, thought patterns, and values expressed by courts as they resolve a particular case in controversy. Eventually, a general understanding of how the legal discourse community functions will become integrated into the fabric of your own way of thinking and you will be more free to focus the bulk of your energy on the third purpose: understanding the big picture, looking for cues as to how this case enlightens your understanding of the sub-topic covered in this area of the casebook.

And, above all, you will be free to read closely, creatively, and critically when you remember that all reading is about speculation—about developing a hypothesis that you then test as you read, looping back and forward in the text to see if what you are thinking continues to make sense. In the study of law, this recursive process of looping back and forth in your reading is repeated again in class, where you bring your thoughts to the table knowing expressly that they will be revised, polished, discarded, and reborn before you fully understand a case—or a cluster of cases—and the issues it unveils.

PRACTICE EXERCISES

The following exercises will help you explore what it means to have a reading purpose. Remember that you can visit caplaw.com/rll to see some of the responses I thought about as I wrote these practice exercise questions.

1. Read the following passage for the specific purpose of identifying how many different rose cultivars (specific types, not classes) the author names. Assume that "time is of the essence" (in other words, assume that you need to read this passage quickly):

> Gardening with roses can be both a delight and a challenge. Roses are notoriously fussy about soil content and require frequent fertilizing, pruning, and treatment to prevent damage from insects. For those who enjoy a sensory experience in the garden, however, there is no single flower that can beat the rose for variety and range of color and scent. Roses are divided into various "classes," including climbing roses, shrub roses, hybrid tea roses, floribundas, and grandifloras, with numerous "cultivars" (individual rose species) within each class. Having a variety of rose classes and cultivars represented in your garden can enhance its overall beauty and visual impact. Among the climbing roses, "City of New York" is perhaps the most winter hardy and disease free, although "Joseph's Coat," with its bright blossoms, presents a more showy flower. Among the floribundas, "Apricot Nectar" stands out for its extreme hardiness in winter, and "Sonja" takes the prize for repeat blooms. If a gardener could plant only one rose, those with experience would recommend "Mister Lincoln," a perennial favorite, hands down. Hardy, disease resistant, and highly fragrant, this deep red rose will bloom repeatedly from May through October in many climates, making all the work that goes into growing roses worthwhile.

(a) How many specific roses were named?

(b) How did you keep track of them (monitor yourself) as you read?

(c) Did you figure out any reading "tricks" (visual cues) to help you locate the individually named species quickly? If not, look at the passage again and see if it would have helped to skim for capital letters and quotation marks.

2. Read the same passage above, but this time assume that you are considering planting a garden. You are a busy beginning law student and don't have much time or money for gardening. Nonetheless, you have decided to keep life balanced by finding a hobby that would distract you from reading law from time to time, and also allow you to share the fruits of your labor with those you care about.

(a) Would this article make you think twice about planting roses in your garden?

(b) If you had room for only one rose bush, which one would you choose? Why?

(c) Did it take you longer to read this passage for the purpose of deciding what to put in your garden than for the purpose of counting how many specific rose cultivars were named?

3. How does the notoriously large size of many law school classes influence students' choice of reading purposes?

4. Would your purpose for reading for class preparation shift if you knew there was a high probability that you would be called on in class the next day? Should it?

5. Why might you read and respond to the "Notes & Problems" at the end of a cluster of cases even if you knew you would not be called on in class or that your professor would not refer to those notes?

CHAPTER 8

Get Oriented and Own Your Prior Knowledge

A skilled reader would never (or hardly ever) jump into a text without testing the waters first. We have to know something about what we're going to read or the task would be completely overwhelming. Research shows that the more we know ahead of time, the more effective and efficient our reading will be.

For busy law students, then, it is critical to take the time to get oriented to a case before plowing into reading it. As you gain experience, you will be able to get oriented more quickly than you can as a beginner.

As we explored in Chapter 6, there are all kinds of external cues (cues outside of the case itself) that you can use to develop a hypothesis about what you're going to read. Similarly, there are all kinds of internal cues (prior knowledge) you've got inside your own head that you can use to quickly get situated and to enrich your reading.

These external and internal cues are so important that we are going to explore them in more depth in this chapter. Racing past these external and internal cues in an effort to save study time ends up costing you far more time than you save, and keeps your reading from ever reaching the kind of mature level it otherwise would.

A. Using Reading Cues to Get Oriented Quickly

(1) Reading Cues in the Casebook

(a) All casebooks have a Table of Contents that can help you get a grasp of what the whole course is about. By looking over the Table of Contents at the beginning of the school year, you can often develop a pretty good hypothesis about the content of this area of the law. Having a healthy overview, in turn, helps you take better educated guesses as to the meaning, in the larger scheme of things, of any particular case or group of cases you are reading. Always read the Table of Contents when you first begin a course, and review it often as you move into new sections. It's also a good idea to compare the Table of Contents with the course syllabus if your professor has provided one. No law course can teach you everything there is to know in any area of law. All you need to focus on are the components of this area of law that your professor considers to be sufficiently critical to include in the material covered by your class.

(b) A good casebook will divide a course into logical sub-parts, grouping related cases together. Pay attention to what the casebook authors call the subsection your case is contained in. Keep engaged. As you learn more about this subsection by reading background material and the cases contained in it, would you keep the title of the subsection that the author adopted, or would you edit it to something that makes more sense to you? If you can think of better wording, edit your copy of the book. Literally, cross out their section heading and write in your new one. Finding a sensible topic heading is a great way to develop your initial hypothesis about the main idea you should take from the cases included in that section of a casebook.

(c) Often casebook authors precede a cluster of cases with traditional text—a summary of this area of the law in the author's words (or a reprint of another authority's article on the topic). It is tempting to skip this kind of background information because it is rarely discussed in class—or, depending on your teacher, it is taught again in class lecture anyway. The significant advantage of reading such background material up front is that it can teach you more than you already know about a topic (thus increasing your background knowledge—see the following section of this chapter on "Internal Cues"). When you read such background material, keep your reading purpose in mind. In law school, you will rarely—if ever—be tested on such background material like you would have been in undergraduate school. Rather, it is a tool (one of several) you can use to speed up the process of developing a "working hypothesis" about the possible content of a case you will be reading before you actually begin to read. The kind of internal dialogue you might hear in your mind as you read background material in a subsection of your Torts book on "Intentional Torts" would be something like this: "Ah-hah! I get it. So *this* is what lawyers mean when they talk about 'intent.'" You don't actually have to have *intended* to hurt anybody. I'll bet the next case I read is going to play around with whether the defendant's actions were 'intentional' or not."

(d) Casebook authors make careful decisions before they cluster cases together. Hence, the content of the cases that surround a particular case can give you clues about the main idea of the case you're presently reading. In law school, you are always speculating, taking educated guesses, zeroing in on your target. Rarely are the lines around a rule of law so crystal-clear that they can be taught with absolute clarity. This is not simple math. Rather, this is complex math—an area of human thought dominated by gray areas, not bright lines. Thus, casebook authors will frequently present a case from a jurisdiction or an era when the bright-line rule was one thing. A beginning law student, when exposed to a bright-line case[1] like this, breathes a sigh of relief. "Thank goodness," the student thinks, "I have finally read a case that has taught me some law." Such relief, however, is frequently short-lived. Casebook authors will commonly follow such a case with another bright-line case (that makes just as much sense) from another jurisdiction or era that solved the same kind of conflict by applying a significantly different bright-line rule. Newcomers to the study of law then think, "How can this

1. I use the term "bright-line case" to describe the kind of case that states a clear, unequivocal rule and applies it in an equally clear way to facts that lead to what appears to be (at least at the time) a clear result.

be? Is the rule what I just read in the first case, or is the rule what I'm reading now? Heck, maybe I can't read at all. It makes no sense that the rule could be both these things." With experience, the student begins to understand that the cluster of cases being read will help him or her begin to identify the *tensions* in this area of law. It is the tensions, which you can identify only by reading many cases all wrestling with the same or similar topics, that help you learn the kinds of things the courts think about and the kinds of policy issues that influence them as they struggle to shape rules to solve disputes in this area of the law.

Thus, an internal dialogue I might have after reading a cluster of cases that all discuss the nature of "intent" within the meaning of the "intentional torts" could be something like this:

> [After reading the first case]: "So, this court dismissed the plaintiff's case for battery against the defendant because it felt the defendant was playing tug-of-war and never meant to hurt him. Maybe that means that you have to have meant to hurt somebody to have the "intent" required to be liable for an intentional tort like battery."
>
> [After reading the second case]: "Whoa. This court allowed a claim for the intentional tort of slander even though the harmful words that were sent over email to the listserv for the plaintiff's whole graduating class were sent by mistake. So, this court seems to think that the defendant is liable even though she never meant to hurt the defendant. I wonder if the difference has something to do with the fact that the plaintiff in the other case was also playing when he got hurt, but the plaintiff here got blind-sided by this email."

There isn't any way to "know" for sure what the "rule" or principles are at this point. This student, however, is *thinking* along the right lines and is asking himself or herself the right internal questions to "monitor" and test various educated guesses, important strategies introduced in Chapter 6.

(e) As you've learned, many casebook authors add one more reading aid (sometimes called "Notes" or "Notes & Questions") in most casebooks that is worth its weight in gold to an expert reader looking for cues to develop or test a hypothesis about a case or cluster of cases. Surprisingly, many students rarely use this tool. Ironically, the more confused many students are by apparent inconsistencies among the preceding cluster of cases, the *less* likely they are to explore these extra cues in depth. On the surface, it would seem that reading yet more hypotheticals or unanswerable questions would not be helpful—but, in fact, it really is.

The casebook authors include these notes expressly to help direct your thinking. They have designed these additional ideas to give you "free" hypotheticals and questions you can use to test the guesses that should have been developing in your brain as you read. So, the student described in (d) above who has begun to speculate about how to reconcile the two Tort cases on "intent" might continue his or her internal dialogue in the following manner:

> [After reading a Notes & Problems case presenting an entirely different perspective]: "Well, I'll be darned. I think I've got it. The point seems to be that a defendant has to have intentionally *acted* in order to be liable, but doesn't necessarily have to have intended a harmful *result* from the action. In the email case, the sender meant to send a private email to only the plaintiff, but sent the email to the whole class by mistake. Thus, even though the plaintiff meant no harm, she did mean to send an email. It was her act of hitting "send" that caused the harm, and thus she was liable for the harm the action caused. In the first case, though, the defendant meant to push the plaintiff in a game of tug-of-war, but since the plaintiff was involved in what he should have known was a contact sports event, the court felt there should be no liability even though the defendant intended to make the contact. It's a lot clearer now. Maybe the bottom line is that you're responsible for harm that results if you intend an action that is within your control and the other person hasn't consented to or invited your action. I'll see if what I learn in class is consistent with these ideas."

(2) Reading Cues in the Cases Themselves

There are external cues within the cases themselves that can help you develop educated guesses about the ultimate "main idea" of the case. **It is critical to take advantage of these external cues to speed up your reading and get more from a case.**

(a) Look at the place and date of decision (you'll be creating very different visual images and making different intellectual assumptions if you know a case was written in 1804, 1904, or 2004 and if it was decided in Burlington, Vt., Savannah, Ga., or Los Angeles, Ca.).

(b) Look ahead to the decision at the end of the case. Knowing who won lets you know where the court is going to eventually end up and makes it easier to follow its logic as it gets there.

(c) Take a quick skim of the whole case—how long is it, are the facts critical, does there seem to be a lot of dicta? Skimming gets you oriented quickly (especially in a long case) and allows you to monitor your reading more effectively.

(3) Reading Cues Available through Privately Published Resources

(a) *Privately Published Study Aids*: In addition to the rich array of external cues available through the casebook and cases themselves, there are privately published sources (study aids, hornbooks, and treatises) that can help, too. As a general rule, you don't need to use these privately published (and costly) study aids on a routine basis. You've got plenty of external cues *in the assigned reading itself* to get you oriented and help you develop a good working hypothesis about the cases you're reading. However, all of these study aids can be helpful from time to time if used wisely and as an aid to (not a substitute for) developing your own ideas.

Go to any law school bookstore and you'll be able to find a wide array of study aids ranging from books that present an entire course in outline form to books that summarize the content of a course in easy-to-read text.

Your law library or academic support office may have lots of these study aids available for free. Some study aids are written in a question and answer format (not a bad way to test the working hypotheses you're developing) and others use graphs and pictures to simplify complex ideas. Increasingly, online study aids are becoming available.

All of these study aids can be useful to varying degrees—but not one (not a single one) is a viable substitute for reading the cases in your casebook and attending class. Certainly not in the long run. As you learned in Chapter 7, you are reading cases in casebooks for three primary purposes: (i) to read the assigned case well enough to get an accurate picture of what happened in the case; (ii) to gather information about legal reasoning and the legal discourse community; and (iii) to understand the "big picture" in this sub-topic of the course by reasoning inductively to see what this case adds in light of the information surrounding it in the casebook.

If you use study aids heavily in lieu of reading cases on your own, you will sabotage your ability to learn to read cases without them. In addition, you will overload yourself with all kinds of information that the authors of the study aids included in an effort to be thorough—but that may well distract your attention from what *your* professor wants you to learn in this area of the law. It is your ability to discern your professor's understanding of the main ideas in the course—not the opinions of a study aid author or even your casebook author—that will determine your success as a student, and eventually, as a practicing attorney.

(b) *Treatises and Hornbooks*: A treatise or hornbook is also a useful external aid to help you develop and test your educated guesses about the rules/principles in an area of law. You can buy a treatise or hornbook (although they are really, really expensive) or you can almost always get them from the Reserve Desk at your law library.

Treatises and some hornbooks are recognized by authorities as the definitive word in a particular area of law. Many are used by your professors and by demanding appellate judges as a tool to help clarify muddy areas and difficult questions. Of course, a busy law student doesn't have time to learn everything there is to know about an area of law—he or she only has to learn what the professor has already determined is critical. Thus, a wise student would only turn to a treatise or hornbook to clarify an area of law where the gray areas have become unbearably foggy—or as a way to get enough high-level background information to fine-tune a developing hypothesis about a case or cluster of cases.

(c) *Using Study Aids in a Pinch*: There are two ways that study aids can be used successfully by a wise student in an emergency. First, if you find after the first weeks of class that you are an unbearably slow reader and are routinely taking more than two hours just to read and brief your cases for one class, consider finding a good study aid to use as an external reading cue (the same way you can use the background information provided by the author of your casebook at the beginning of some sections). Increasing your background knowledge about a case can help you form a hypothesis about your reading more quickly.

Similarly, there are some study aids that actually provide case briefs (summaries of the actual cases you're reading) for most casebooks. If you are sick or experiencing an unusual emergency and don't have time to read at all, you're better off reading the summarized version of a case than reading nothing at all. At least then you are able to go into class with a working hypothesis of this area of the law so that the discussion that follows in class can make some sense. If you're wise, though, you'll go back at some point to do a quick read of the actual case in your casebook to make sure you haven't missed anything important.

Also, if you are chronically moving at a snail's pace through cases or completely confused by them, a quick read of a summarized case brief can be a dynamite "external cue" for you. You can read a thumbnail version of what a private editor thought the case was about, use that author's ideas as a fledgling "hypothesis" as you begin to read the case and then modify the hypothesis as you interact with the real text yourself. Using these model briefs (which should *not* be assumed to be accurate) can improve your reading in the long term by giving you some direction if you are having trouble picking up the vocabulary and reasoning patterns common to law. Note that some commercial briefs, including some online commercial briefs, leave out important aspects of the case, such as the history of the case, the court's reasoning, or the parties' arguments. Those omissions make those briefs less valuable to you.

All of these emergency suggestions are good short-term fixes, but have to be limited to the short-term only. Relying on these sources habitually will keep you from learning how to read and think about cases independently. Learning how to read cases independently is critical to your eventual membership in the legal discourse community.

(4) Cues from Your Professor

Your professor is a great source of external cues that can speed up your development of a working hypothesis of the main idea of your reading. Pay attention to your syllabus if one is provided—be aware of where your present reading assignments fall in the overall context of the course design (as visualized by your professor). Listen to how your professor forecasts a case when it is assigned. Think about how a new section of cases you are beginning might fit into what you have learned in class in the past.

Staying alert to your professor's views on the course is also a good way to keep yourself from wandering too far away from the "main idea" of a case. As you experienced doing the Practice Exercise following Chapter 6, cases contain many compelling legal questions, any number of which could engage your attention for a prolonged period of time. Pay attention to your course syllabus and to your professor's directives about what topics and subtopics within the course are important. Learn those topics and subtopics, including their nuances as explored in the cases assigned, and let go of other aspects of the assigned cases that do not add directly to your understanding of those specified areas. I often think of this as "staying within the box" of the course as it has been laid out by your professor—the course designer.

(5) Cues from Your Peers

Don't forget your friends. Law students frequently talk about cases they have read or are planning to read. Keep your mind open and learn what you can from these kinds of conversations. As you listen to your peers, don't think of understanding cases as a competitive activity. It is not a question of who can brief a case first or who is the fastest reader or who has the most insight. Don't run a mental tape that says, "What's wrong with me—why didn't I see that point?" Instead, think of your peers as a resource—one more external cue—available to you as you explore the foggy, gray corners of the law.

B. Own What You Already Know

What we get from a text is strongly influenced by—and limited to—what we have experienced, what we know, and what we can understand. The more we know about the content of what we're reading, the more we will get out of it.

For example, if the author describes a warm sunny beach, I may be visualizing the Atlantic Ocean, you may be visualizing the Pacific Ocean, and someone else may be visualizing a quiet lake. As we all read on, we may come to find that the text we're reading is really about a sandy beach along the edge of the Mississippi River. If we're reading well, we'll modify the images we're visualizing accordingly (to get the author's message). There's no getting around the fact that, on the way to eventually visualizing the Mississippi River, we all brought our prior knowledge and experiences with us into the reading process. If I'm a reader who has never seen or heard of sand, then (without further description by the author), I'm hard-pressed to get a completely accurate image of the beach in the text.

On the other hand, if I'm a true lover of water and coastlines (an expert), I may have a hundred images of sand. I may be aware of different textures, different colors, and the kinds of shore birds and other animals that tend to live in certain kinds of water and soils. In such a situation, when I read about the beach on the Mississippi River set out above, there's a whole lot more going on in my head than in the head of the average reader. I am more likely to engage in a high-order "dialogue" with the author of the text.

I might question the author's description of a certain bird call, wondering what such a bird would be doing alongside a fresh water river. I might begin to speculate that the author must be describing the Delta area at the mouth of the Mississippi—otherwise, how would a saltwater shore bird have been there making the call in the first place?

The visual images I begin to create based on this prior knowledge are much richer than those of someone with less experience. My initial hypothesis is more likely to be accurate and I am also going to be more inclined to notice flaws in the author's descriptions or reasoning. Having such prior knowledge, then, can be a very good thing for a reader. Armed with prior knowledge, I will gain more from the text than I would have otherwise.

If I separate my prior knowledge and experience from the reading I'm going to do in law school, I handicap myself unnecessarily. Instead, I need to become deeply involved with the text of each case, "owning my prior knowledge." My prior knowledge of the historical or geographic context of a case, my prior knowledge of the legal issues raised, my understanding of the deciding judge's values, or my assumptions about vocabulary words can deeply enrich my ability to reach inside the case and extract meaning from it.

Let's say, for example, that a student in your class has played professional football and is now in law school. Your class has been assigned to read *Hackbart v. Cincinnati Bengals, Inc.*, 601 F.2d 516 (10th Cir. 1979), a case about tort liability for harm incurred by a player in a professional football game. When we see the running header at the top of the casebook ["Consent," within a Chapter on "Privileges"], we may all begin to guess that this case will deal with the limits on liability when participants in a dangerous sport are injured. Because of the former professional player's past experiences, however, he will be able to bring more to the case than the rest of us might. Those of us who played high school football, or who managed a team, or who love the sport might have other perspectives to add—and might anticipate different decisions and different outcomes in the case. Those with experience in football might think, "Cool. This is going to be a fun case to read. I think the sport is getting progressively more dangerous. I'll bet the court will allow recovery here to try to clean up the game." Others in the class, even engaged readers, who don't know a thing about football might be thinking something entirely different: "Uh-oh. I hope I'm going to understand what happened here. Who are the Bengals anyway?"

If I am reading cases well, words will trigger associations and associations will give birth to vivid images. My ability to speculate about what may be included in a case will depend on my ability to guess rationally at the meaning of the words the casebook author has chosen to headline this section of the casebook. I may encounter "old words with new meanings,"[2] but won't make the shift unless I am alert to the possibility that my earlier understandings may not be valid in this new context. Think about the word "competence," for example. As an educator, I think of competence in the sense of mastery of a subject. A lawyer practicing in the field of contract law would think of "competence" in the sense of "having sufficient mental capacity to be bound by a contract." A geriatric rehabilitation counselor, on the other hand, might think of "competence" in terms of functional life skills.

Using prior knowledge well as a useful context clue to help you get oriented to and engage in your reading requires a conscious awareness of the knowledge you're holding—and a willingness to question the applicability of what you knew before in the context of what you are now learning about law.

Thus, as we own our prior knowledge, it's also important to own what we *don't* know. Ironically, the more we know the less likely we are to accurately identify what we don't know (because we are likely to make assumptions

---

2. I am indebted to Professor Mary Beth Beazley, of The Ohio State University Michael E. Moritz College of Law, who first introduced this phrase at a session led by Professor Charles Calleros, of Arizona State University College of Law, at the 2004 summer conference for the Legal Writing Institute in Seattle, Washington.

based on our rich prior knowledge). One of the things we can't know unless we read a case carefully is how well a court handles information from a domain field that we may know something about. For example, if I'm a social worker and did my honors thesis on drug addiction among convicted felons, I may be confused if a court reaches a decision that does not include factual information that I know to be true.

Similarly, if I'm the professional football player discussed above, I run the risk of getting so distracted by what I know *for sure* about the realities of the sport that I do not ever fully understand the case *as the deciding court understood it.* One of the reading skills experienced lawyers develop is the ability to separate the reality they know to be externally verifiable from the "reality" adopted by a court in any given case. Having enough prior knowledge to make these kinds of distinctions (separating the "Minor Premise" [as discussed in Chapter 3] that the court actually used from the "Minor Premise" you think the court *should* have used) is one of the critical reading skills expert legal readers can develop.

Stay intellectually engaged with your reading by staying in touch with your thoughts as you read. Visualize and imagine. Then, as you learned in Chapter 6, monitor your assumptions and modify them as you move through the case. Is the court coming from the same political or moral base that you are? How does that political or moral base impact the assumptions you or the court are making? Is the court aware of the reality as you understand it, or has it adopted a different view of the facts?

Your prior intellectual knowledge and experiences combine to give you valuable internal cues that can get you started down the right path when you enter a new area of law or begin a new case. By integrating these internal cues with the external cues provided by your casebook author, your professor, and other resources, you can save yourself valuable time reading cases while netting meaningful, sophisticated results.

PRACTICE EXERCISES

The exercises in this chapter will give you an opportunity to use context and your prior knowledge to read a case in context. Remember that you can visit caplaw.com/rll to see some of the responses I thought about as I wrote these practice exercise questions.

1. Read the following excerpt from the "Summary of Contents" of *Property and Lawyering*,[3] a popular Property casebook. In the space provided here, take a guess as to why the casebook authors may be treating "Gifts of Personal Property" and "Gifts of Land" in separate sections in Chapter 3:

Summary of Contents

3. James L. Winokur, R. Wilson Freyermuth, & Jerome M. Organ, Property and Lawyering, at xv–xvi (2002), reprinted with permission of Thomson West.

2. Read the following excerpt from the beginning of Chapter 3 of the *Property and Lawyering* casebook:[4]

Chapter 3

TRANSFERRING PROPERTY BY GIFT

. . .

A. GIFTS OF PERSONAL PROPERTY

The most common type of gift (such as the typical Christmas, Hanukkah, birthday, or wedding gift) is an *inter vivos* gift (literally, a gift "between the living"). For such a gift to be legally effective to transfer ownership, there are three requirements—the donor must have *donative intent* (*i.e.*, the intent to make an immediately effective gift), the donor must *deliver* the object of the gift, and the donee must *accept* the object of the gift. Most gifts occur in personal and family relationships, and most take place without dispute. In some cases, however, a dispute arises regarding whether a donor made a valid gift. Often, these disputes arise after the donor's death, and they typically involve questions regarding whether the donor made an effective delivery of the object of the gift during the donor's life. Why does the law require delivery of the object of the gift? What purposes does the delivery requirement serve? What actions are (or should be) necessary to constitute an effective delivery?

---

4. James L. Winokur, R. Wilson Freyermuth, & Jerome M. Organ, Property and Lawyering, at 200 (2002), reprinted with permission of Thomson West.

In the space below, write out some tentative answers to the three questions the casebook authors raise at the end of that paragraph (remembering that there is NOTHING up to this point in the casebook that would have provided you with answers to these questions. The casebook authors are expecting you to hypothesize—take a guess—based on your life experience and common sense):

(a) "Why does the law require delivery of the object of the gift?"

(b) "What purposes does the delivery requirement serve?"

(c) "What actions are (or should be) necessary to constitute an effective delivery?"

3. Read *In Re Estate of Evans*, reprinted below, which is the first case in the *Property and Lawyering* casebook following the section you read immediately above about "Gifts of Personal Property."

Before you begin reading, venture a guess (in writing below) as to what you think the primary legal issue is that you're going to be reading about in this case in this part of this Property casebook. (Note: you may think that more than one issue will be covered—and you could be right!)

In Re Estate of Evans

Supreme Court of Pennsylvania 467 Pa. 336, 356 A.2d 778 (1976)[5]

NIX, JUSTICE. Appellant, Vivian Kellow, objected to the inventory, proposed schedule of distribution and final accounting of the executor of the estate of Arthur Evans. After appellant finished the presentation of her case, the lower court granted appellees' motion to dismiss appellant's objections. . . . The thrust of her appeal to this Court is that certain contents of a safe deposit box were the subject of an inter vivos gift to her from Arthur Evans, the deceased, and, consequently, should not have been included in his estate.

Appellant, the niece of Arthur Evans' deceased wife, began working for the Evans family when she was 16. For several years she took care of Mrs. Evans who for some years prior to death was an invalid. Appellant cooked meals for the Evanses, cleaned their house, did their laundry and generally cared for Mrs. Evans. She received adequate compensation for performing these needed services. When Mrs. Evans died, appellant continued to cook at least one hot meal a day for Mr. Evans, do his laundry and make sure his house was tidy. After

5. Reprinted from JAMES L. WINOKUR, R. WILSON FREYERMUTH, & JEROME M. ORGAN, PROPERTY AND LAWYERING, at 201 (2002) with permission of Thomson West.

appellant was married, she continued to perform these same services and visited Mr. Evans once a day. In May of 1971, following one of his four hospitalizations, the deceased moved into appellant's home.

Although at times Mr. Evans was confined to his bed because of water in his legs, he frequently took walks, had visits with his lawyers and made trips to his bank. On October 22, 1971, appellant's husband drove Mr. Evans and a friend of his, Mr. Turley, to town so that Mr. Evans might go to the bank. Turley testified that Mr. Evans spent about one hour going through the contents of his safe deposit box. Before leaving the bank, the deceased obtained both keys to the box.

Various witnesses presented by appellant testified to seeing the keys to the safe deposit box beneath appellant's mattress and to statements by Mr. Evans to the effect that the contents of the safe deposit box had been given to appellant. Mr. Evans entered the hospital for the last time on November 5, 1971. During this last hospital stay, Reverend Cunnings visited with him and was told that Mr. Evans was giving the Reverend's church $10,000.00 and that he had given the rest of his possessions and the keys to his safe deposit box to appellant. Mr. Evans expired on November 23, 1971.

Appellant relinquished the keys to the safe deposit box to a bank officer, but not without protesting that the contents of the box were hers. The box revealed a holographic will of Mr. Evans dated September 16, 1965, and approximately $800,000.00 in bonds, preferred and common stock and several miscellaneous items.

The lower court correctly noted that the requirements for a valid inter vivos gift were donative intent and delivery, actual or constructive. With respect to donative intent, the court found: "Turning to the facts of this case, certainly no one can reasonably argue that Arthur Evans lacked sufficient motive to make a gift to Vivian. The record clearly manifests, both by his conduct and his statements, donative intent, the first prerequisite."

Nevertheless, the court ruled that no delivery had been made. This result was predicated upon a finding that the deceased had not divested himself of complete dominion and control over the safe deposit box. After properly noting that constructive delivery is sufficient when manual delivery is impractical or inconvenient, the court reasoned:

> The record contains no evidence of circumstances which were such that it was impractical or inconvenient to deliver the contents of this box into the actual possession or control of Vivian. Arthur Evans, although suffering physical infirmities and apprehensive of death, was nonetheless ambulatory. On October 22, 1971, he appeared at the Nanticoke National Bank in the company of Harold Turley and Leroy Kellow and spent approximately one hour going over the contents of his safe deposit box in a cubicle provided in the bank for that purpose. He left the bank after redepositing the contents and took with him only the keys which independent testimony indicates he delivered to Vivian the next day. There was no manual delivery of the contents. The contents of the box remained undisturbed. The box, and its contents, were registered in the name of the decedent at the date of his death. The objects of the gift were not placed in the hands of Vivian, nor was there placed within her power the means of obtaining the contents.

Appellant now asserts . . . that the lower court erred in ruling there was insufficient delivery to sustain the inter vivos gift. . . . We find these arguments unpersuasive and, therefore, affirm the decision of the lower court. . . .

The law in this Commonwealth is well settled concerning the requirements of an inter vivos gift. In *Tomayko v. Carson*, 368 Pa. 379, 385, 83 A.2d 907, 908 (1951) we stated:

> A claim of a gift *inter vivos* against the estate of the dead must be supported by clear and convincing evidence. In order to effectuate

> an *inter vivos* gift there must be evidence of an intention to make a gift and a *delivery*, actual or constructive, of a nature sufficient not only to *divest* the donor of all dominion over the property but also *invest* the donee with complete control over the subject-matter of the gift. It is claimant's burden to prove by *clear and satisfactory evidence* that a gift in fact was made. [citations omitted]

In the instant case, the controversy focuses on whether there was an adequate delivery. In *Allshouse's Estate*, 304 Pa. 481, 487B488, 156 A. 69, 72 (1931), we elaborated on the requirement of delivery:

> As said in *Walsh's App.*, 122 Pa. 177, 187, 15 A. 470, 471, 1 L.R.A. 535, 9 Am.St.Rep. 83: "If there remains something for the donor to do before the title of the donee is complete, the donor may decline the further performance and resume his own," and again, at page 190 of 122 Pa., 15 A. 470, 472: "[i]t is not possible that a chancellor would compel an executor or administrator to complete a gift by the doing of any act which the alleged donor if living might have refused to do, and thereby revoked his purpose to give." In *In re Campbell's Est.*, 7 Pa. 100, 47 Am. Dec. 503, Chief Justice Gibson stated: "A gift is a contract executed; and, as the act of execution is delivery of possession, it is of the essence of the title. It is the consummation of the contract which, without it, would be no more than a contract to give, and without efficacy for the want of consideration." Again, as we stated in *Clapper v. Frederick*, 199 Pa. 609, 613, 49 A. 218, 219: "Without a complete delivery during the lifetime of the donor there can be no valid gift inter vivos. 'Though every other step be taken that is essential to the validity of the gift, if there is no delivery, the gift must fail. Intention cannot supply it; words cannot supply it; actions cannot supply it. It is an indispensable requisite, without which the gift fails, regardless of consequence': Thornt. Gifts, p. 105." The consequence is that

> no matter how often or how emphatically the desire or intention of the donor to make the gift has been expressed, upon his death before delivery has been completed, the promise or purpose to give is revoked. *Scott v. Lauman*, 104 Pa. 593; 28 Corpus Juris, page 651.

We have recognized that in some cases due to the form of the subject matter of the gift or due to the immobility of the donor actual, manual delivery may be dispensed with and constructive or symbolic delivery will suffice. In *Ream Estate*, 413 Pa. 489, 198 A.2d 556 (1964), for example, the Court found there had been a valid constructive delivery of an automobile where the donor gave the keys to the alleged donee and also gave him the title to the car after executing an assignment of it leaving the designation of the assignee blank. The assignment was executed in the presence of a justice of the peace and the evidence was overwhelming that the name of the donee was to be inserted upon the death of the decedent.

In *Elliott's Estate*, 312 Pa. 493, 167 A. 289 (1933), we held there was a valid constructive delivery of the contents of a safe deposit box where the donor turned over to the alleged donee the keys. There, however, just prior to the delivery of the keys a doctor had informed the non-ambulatory donor that death was imminent. Under those circumstances manual delivery was impossible.

Appellant relies heavily on *Leadenham's Estate*, 289 Pa. 216, 137 A. 247 (1927), and *Leitch v. Diamond National Bank*, 234 Pa. 557, 83 A. 416 (1912). These decisions, however, support the Court's finding that there was no delivery in the instant case. In *Leadenham's Estate, supra*, the donor had rented a separate safe deposit box in the name of the intended donee, put the contents of his box into the newly rented one and delivered the keys to it to the donee. On those facts we held that the constructive delivery of the keys was sufficient to sustain the inter vivos gift because the donor had divested himself of dominion and control and invested the donee with complete dominion and control.

In *Leitch v. Diamond National Bank*, *supra*, the donor and donee were husband and wife and had lived together harmoniously for many years. The husband had three safe deposit boxes registered in his name and the name of his wife and he designated one of them as his wife's. He gave her the keys to that box. The Court found that she had complete control over that box and that he only entered it with her permission. Since she had complete control over the access to the box the Court found there was a valid delivery of the contents of the box to her.

In both of these cases, the determinative factor was that the donee had complete dominion and control over the box and its contents. In that posture we ruled that giving the keys to the box to the donee was a valid constructive delivery. In the instant case, appellant did not have dominion and control over the box even though she was given the keys to it. The box remained registered in Mr. Evans' name and she could not have gained access to it even with the keys. Mr. Evans never terminated his control over the box, consequently he never made a delivery, constructive or otherwise.

Although appellant suggests that it was impractical and inconvenient for Mr. Evans to manually deliver the contents of his box to her because of his physical condition and the hazards of taking such a large sum of money out of the bank to her home, we need only note that the deceased was obviously a shrewd investor, familiar with banking practices, and could have made delivery in a number of simple, convenient ways. First, he was not on his deathbed. He was ambulatory and not only went to the bank on October 22, 1971, but took walks thereafter and did not enter the hospital until November 5, 1971. On the day he went to the bank he could have rented a second safe deposit box in appellant's name, delivered the contents of his box to it and then given the keys to appellant. He could have assigned the contents of his box to appellant. For that matter, he could have written a codicil to his will.

> The lower court noted that the deceased was an enigmatic figure. It is not for us to guess why people perform as they do. On the record before us it is clear that regardless of Mr. Evans' intention to make a gift to appellant, he never executed that intention and we will not do it for him. On these facts, we are constrained to hold that there was not an inter vivos gift to appellant and that the contents of the safe deposit box were properly included in the inventory of Mr. Evans' estate. . . .

4. Answer the following questions about your reading of this case:

   (a) Why do you think the court was careful to include the information about Mr. Evans' trip with Mr. Turley into town?

(b) In the sixth paragraph, the court states, "The lower court correctly noted that the requirements for a valid inter vivos gift were donative intent and delivery, actual or constructive."

i. Is this statement exactly the same as the one the author's made in the section of the casebook set out in Question 2 above? What does it add or take away? Do you think this court's statement is inconsistent with that made by the casebook authors, or is it just a different way of saying the same thing (or does it emphasize a different part of the casebook authors' statement, or expand upon it)?

ii. Look back at the guess you made concerning what topics this case might cover in answer to Question 3 above. Once you read this sixth paragraph, did you need to modify your guess? If so, how?

iii. In 1976, in the State of Pennsylvania, under what circumstances could the transfer of a gift be made "symbolically"?

iv. One good way to save time when you read is to figure out (as soon as you can) whether an author is introducing a new concept when a new word is introduced, or if the author is merely introducing a synonym for the same concept. In the middle of the opinion, this court discusses an older case called *Ream Estate* (the case about the transfer of the automobile). In discussing that case, does the court use the words "symbolic" and "constructive" interchangeably? Is use of "shifting terms" (use of more than one word to describe what is probably one concept) helpful or confusing to you as a reader?

5. One of the things this Chapter emphasizes is the importance of recognizing that our prior personal experiences can influence how we read a case. Have you had any experiences with situations similar to the facts described in this case? For example, have you cared for an elderly relative or friend? Do you have an aging parent, grandparent, or friend who may need help in the future? Have you been the recipient of an inheritance? Have you studied the concept of inheritance in another subject or discipline? Do you or your family have strong feelings about rights of inheritance? Do you or your family have strong feelings about honoring the wishes of elders? About paying back good deeds?

If so, did any of these experiences influence how you thought this case would turn out?

If you could choose one word to describe the emotional feelings that reading this case brought up in you, what would it be? Were any other feelings touched on as you read this case?

6. Go back now and reread the opening paragraph of this case and the facts as presented in the next four paragraphs. How much money was in the safety deposit box? ____________________. If Ms. Kellow had won this case, who would have gotten all of that money? ________________. What amount did she end up with instead? ________________________. The court here found, as a matter of law, that the trial court was correct in dismissing this case (not allowing her claim to be heard by a jury) because it found that Mr. Evans did not properly execute his intent to deliver the contents of the safety deposit box to Ms. Kellow.[6] As the judge who wrote this opinion made decisions about how to write it, why do you think the judge did not specifically name the amount of money involved in the opening paragraph of the opinion, but rather chose to include it inconspicuously several paragraphs later?

6. Note that the casebook authors did not include language that expressly confirmed this specific decision on the court's part, but you could read between the lines (especially reading the last paragraph of the opinion in the context of the first) to figure out that this is what happened. If you are new to legal reading, this would have been a challenging inference to reach and an example of how reading in law becomes easier with experience.

7. Go back up to Question 2 above and rethink your answers to the three questions raised by the casebook authors. Would you change any of your answers now that you've read the accompanying case? In your own words, in four or fewer sentences, write out what you think the "main idea" of this case is within the context of the casebook.

8. Do you feel intellectually and emotionally comfortable with the result the court reached? Would you have decided the case differently? If you're curious, and have time, you can go to caplaw.com/rll to read a strong dissenting opinion from a judge who would have allowed Ms. Kellow to have her day in court. If you choose to read this dissenting opinion, which is included in the casebook itself, consider how the thoughts it contains might have saved you time answering some of the other questions raised in this Exercise, relieved any emotional angst you felt when you finished the majority opinion, or helped you understand this area of law more thoroughly.

9. It's always a good idea to think about time when you are reading law. Before you began, did you estimate how long it might take you to read the opinion set out in Question 2 above? If you did estimate a time before beginning , did you write it down and stay within your limits? If you did not estimate a time, can you take a guess now about how long it took you to read that case?

CHAPTER 9

There's More to the Five Ws (Who, What, When, Where, and Why) Than Meets the Eye

As you learned in Chapter 7, the best reasons to read the cases assigned in your casebooks are:

(1) to read the case well enough to get an accurate picture of what happened in the case [often synthesized in some form of a brief];

(2) to increase your understanding of legal reasoning and the legal discourse community (how lawyers think, communicate, and take action); and

(3) to understand the "big picture" in this sub-topic of the course by reasoning inductively to see what this case adds to your understanding of the controlling principles/rules explored in this section of the casebook.

To accomplish each of these things, you have to first be able to identify two kinds of facts in any case you read:

(1) the *legal* facts (for example, facts about how this case came up through the courts, facts about how pre-trial papers were filed or

a trial was conducted, facts about the legal arguments the parties may have made to the lower courts before the case came up on appeal);

(2) the *conflict* facts (facts about the real-life events that happened between the parties that gave rise to the present disagreement).

With a good understanding of both of these kinds of facts (legal facts and conflict facts), you can engage in a sophisticated dialogue with the judge who wrote the opinion—and you have enough information to think deeply about the legal principles discussed by the court. You can do these things because you have an accurate understanding of the case as the court experienced it.

Judges include only select facts from the record when they write an opinion. Cases in casebooks are further edited by the casebook author, so those selected facts might be further excluded from the version of the opinion you are given to read. Because the original authoring judge, and then the casebook author, make decisions about which facts to include in an assigned opinion, your view of a case will always be somewhat limited. You weren't there, didn't hear the witnesses, and can't weigh all the evidence.[1] You will

---

1. A few opportunities to explore the "bigger picture" of what occurred in a legal conflict do exist. As an example, Professor Thomas B. Metzloff directed "The Distinctive Aspect of American Law Project" at Duke University School of Law a number of years ago. Through this project, Professor Metzloff developed a series of video documentaries recounting the history and stories behind leading United States Supreme Court cases, on the belief that students of the law can better understand what they are reading in cases if they can first "see" the reality of a case through the eyes (and in the voices) of those involved from the inception of a conflict through the filing of pleadings and the resolution of the case. Similarly, many law schools offer Law & Literature classes for upperclass students that explore, among other things, books depicting real-life cases. *See also* Elizabeth Fajans & Mary R. Falk, *Against the Tyranny of Paraphrase: Talking Back to Texts*, 78 CORNELL L. REV. 163, 195–99 (1993) (describing how a law professor could use the real-life context of a case, such as the testimony at trial, in comparison to the court's presentation of the facts, to challenge students to "hear" the many voices in the text of an opinion); *cf.* Patricia L. Bryan, *Stories in*

need to piece together the puzzle of what happened in the case from the facts in front of you. From those facts, a good reader can infer the "conflict facts" (the essence of the disagreement between the parties or of the crime committed), and the "legal facts" (what happened once the disagreement or crime became absorbed by the legal system).

Class discussions, especially at the beginning of the year, are often dominated by professors' questions about these conflict facts and the accompanying legal facts. This preoccupation with the "who, what, when, where, and why" that underlie cases occurs because professors recognize the importance of both of these kinds of facts. Because these facts are important, professors spend significant class time in the beginning to ensure that students are reading cases well enough to correctly visualize them.

When professors move away from devoting large amounts of class time to these matters, it is still necessary for you to discern these facts yourself when you read (or you risk misunderstanding the case). It becomes less necessary for the professor to spend class time teaching students how to accurately identify these things because, after the first several weeks, students will have learned how to do so on their own.

A. The Legal Facts

If we lived in an ideal world, judges and casebook authors would lay out the legal facts in every case in a crisp and linear way, using language that is easily accessible to lawyers and beginning law students alike.[2] They don't. It's not their job. Judges do not write cases so that law students can have an easy

---

Fiction and in Fact: Susan Glaspell's A Jury of Her Peers and the 1901 Murder Trial of Margaret Hossack, 49 STAN. L. REV. 1293 (1997) (juxtaposing the facts surrounding the murder trial of an abused spouse at the turn of the last century with the moving fictional account that grew from it). Foundation Press has released a series of books (e.g., CONSTITUTIONAL LAW STORIES; CIVIL PROCEDURE STORIES, etc.) that unveil the facts underlying select landmark cases memorialized in popular casebooks.

2. *See* Nancy A. Wanderer, *Writing Better Opinions: Communicating with Candor, Clarity, and Style*, 54 ME. L. REV. 47 (2002) (and articles cited therein).

time preparing for class discussions. Rather, they write opinions to explain their reasoning when they reach decisions in the cases that have been tried or appealed before them. They write these opinions for the particular parties in the case and their lawyers, and sometimes also with an eye towards the fact that some other lawyer in the future might use the case as a basis for an argument made in a new case.

If judges don't make a practice of writing the legal facts and procedural history of a case in some kind of crisp, accessible manner, what's a law student to do? The best way to get good at identifying the legal facts underlying a case is to keep your eyes and ears open. Work with a legal dictionary or dictionary of legal usage by your side. Stay alert to nuances in language and be willing to piece things together by inference. Adopt whatever learning tools are effective and efficient for you—draw flow charts, outline, rephrase—so that you can accurately learn how a case got up to its present level.

In addition to including the kind of "procedural" legal facts that help a reader understand the circuitous route a case may have taken on its way to the written opinion you are holding in your hand, cases also contain legal facts about evidentiary issues, how the trial was conducted, how pre-trial motions were filed, etc. As one example, it really matters (a lot) to lawyers whether the plaintiff in a case has the "burden" of persuading a judge or jury that he should win. It matters because I can be *just as* "right" as the other side, but if the burden is on me to be *more* than half-way right, I'll lose. If I don't have that "burden," then I can win even if I'm only 50% correct.

How much attention should you give to these kinds of procedural and underlying legal facts when you read a case? The answer depends on what your *purpose* is on the day you are reading. If you are functioning in your normal routine as a student striving for excellence, you should be trying to get as clear and accurate a picture of all of the underlying legal facts as time will reasonably allow. Accurately understanding the underlying legal facts leads you to excellence because: (1) it makes you a more proficient legal reader (because there's a finite number of legal facts that you tend to see over and over, so you're increasing your knowledge base every time you learn something new about how the legal world functions); and (2) you will have a better image of what happened in this case, and hence can draw better inferences about the court's reasoning and result. Accurately understanding the underlying legal facts, however, ONLY leads to excellence if you leave time to also get the main idea from the case (see Chapter 6) and also leave time to read this case and others with enough energy to stay engaged (see Chapter 5).

To read for underlying legal facts quickly and efficiently, develop the habit of using all the resources at your fingertips. Don't keep re-inventing the wheel, case after case. Instead, keep a section in your notebook or in your computer files to save new vocabulary and new understandings about how the legal world operates. When you get a new concept, write it down. When you see it again, go back and review what you wrote. It only takes a second, but pretty soon all these new things you're learning will become part of the general background knowledge you have when you approach any case in the future. The more you know, the more you'll be able to learn. Your understanding gets better and better, easier and easier.

Also, don't try to figure things out in a vacuum. Even trial lawyers with years of experience don't necessarily understand the procedural history or other legal facts in the kind of antiquated cases that often populate casebooks. The norms of practice and vocabulary used by courts to describe their actions may have changed dramatically over the years. Take your best guess, use a dictionary, ask a friend—then use your best judgment about moving on.

As you think about moving on, see if you can develop a rational hypothesis about the case without completely solving the mystery of the underlying legal facts. If the case is largely *about* the underlying legal fact (see, for example, Question 4 in the Practice Exercises following Chapter 6), then you will want to hang in there longer or use more external resources to clear up any confusion you have about that legal fact.

For example, if you're in a Civil Procedure class and you are studying summary judgment motions, then a case with some confusing legal facts about summary judgment would demand more attention because figuring it out might well BE the "main idea" of that case in the context of that course. In a Torts class, however, you might be wise to selectively read beyond a throw-away statement about the summary judgment motion made at trial, focusing instead on the "main [torts] idea" to which the Table of Contents and background information direct your attention.[3]

Exceptional readers, in all domains, know when an issue is central to understanding the main idea of a text and read selectively, searching for the critical information. In short, they are willing to let go of a thorny side issue in a text if they can still understand the main idea of the text. Exceptional legal readers are willing to read selectively, too, sometimes jotting down a question about a side issue or moving on if they can still get their mind around the main idea of the case in the context of the course.

B. The Conflict Facts

As a general rule, conflict facts occur before any legal facts come into play. In other words, most cases arise because of a conflict between parties or because a crime is alleged to have been committed, well before any legal action is taken.

For most of us, understanding the conflict facts in a case is a whole lot easier—especially at the beginning—than understanding the legal facts.

---

3. There would be exceptions to this general rule when your reading purpose is unusual. For example, if your professor has expressly told you that he or she will call on you tomorrow, then pretty much any question about the case is fair game. You might, in that situation, want to go the extra mile to make sure you know the case up one side and down the other—which, incidentally, can mean knowing it well enough to explain to the professor *why* you made certain inferences based on the text itself. It's okay to be wrong, and especially okay to be wrong if you have a rational basis for the conclusions you've drawn. As you learned in Chapter 5, the success of any law school classroom depends on the quality of the dialogue that emerges between the professor and a student concerning an assigned case. That dialogue can be of very high quality even when a student misses some of the details of the conflict and legal facts, as long as the student is willing to learn as the discussion unfolds.

This is because we all have more experience reading facts in other contexts than we do reading law in the context of a case. We have more prior knowledge and hence something to relate our reading to. If we run into the occasional vocabulary word we don't understand, we know how to use a regular dictionary or how to figure out the meaning of the word in context.

Also, especially for a novice, reading conflict facts is often inherently more interesting than reading about the procedural history of the case. Reading the conflict facts in a case is a lot like reading a short story—only all the people, places, and things involved are real. For people who like stories (and who doesn't?), cases often present dramatic, engaging scenarios with which many of us can identify.

Nonetheless, despite the comparison to our common prior experiences with reading stories, there are good ways and better ways to read the conflict facts in a case.

Details about facts matter a whole lot to courts. However, not all details matter equally. It is a waste of time and energy (and leads to the development of sloppy thinking habits) to treat all facts the same. Instead, once you get a sense of the "plot" of a conflict, you then need to work on developing a sixth sense for the "germane" or "legally relevant" facts. These are the facts that are worth your time and energy. A fact is legally relevant if its presence or absence would make a difference in the court's final result. For example, consider a rule that says residency is established by proof of the intent to stay someplace "indefinitely." If the facts indicate that a student moved all of her belongings to a new state, that fact would be relevant (because it would speak to the question of how long she intended to stay there). The fact that the person moved on a Saturday probably wouldn't matter.

As you learned in Chapter 3, lawyers often think of the facts in a case as representative of larger groupings of similar facts. For example, if the plaintiff in a particular case is a six-year-old boy from Alabama, an experienced lawyer wonders if the outcome of the case would apply only to all children, to all male children, to men in general, to Southerners, or to all people.

Similarly, if a defendant accused of larceny stole a wallet from an unoccupied model home in a new development, an experienced legal reader would play around in his or her mind with questions about whether it mattered that the building was a residence, whether it mattered that the residence was unoccupied, or whether it mattered that the building was a free-standing house. Thus, the way the reader conceptualizes any particular fact in a case directly influences the breadth of the application of the holding adopted in the case. Is the "rule" that arises from the case one that has broad applicability, or does the rule apply only under narrowly similar facts?

As with all reading, when you are reading for the conflict facts in a case, know your purpose and read strategically. When you first read a case, you can skim the facts to get an overview of the "story." Who are the people involved? What actually happened? When did things happen (in what sequence, over what period of time, in what historical context)? Where did the conflict or legal question arise (in what type of setting, in what political climate, in what geographical region)? Why did this conflict occur (What is at stake? Why wasn't some more peaceful solution reached? Who was harmed?)?.

The more accurately, vividly, and quickly you can visualize the reality of what happened to the parties involved in a case, the closer you will be to gaining a sophisticated, effective understanding of the main idea of the opinion you are reading. If the facts are complex, try these techniques: (a) draw a timeline summarizing events; (b) make a list of everyone involved in the conflict and their relationship to each other; (c) draw a quick picture of everyone involved as you visualize them and draw lines connecting them, as appropriate, to each other.

Exceptional reading calls for an exceptional imagination. Many outstanding students keep actively engaged in case reading (and remember more about the cases they read) by creating a film in their heads of the events in the case. If you are reading an 1888 case about two ranchers set in Arizona, you might cast John Wayne as one of them and Clint Eastwood as the other. See the tumbleweed. Feel the dust in the hot air. By associating these vivid visual images with the facts of the case, you help the case come to life and the legal issues raised in it will stick with you longer.

When the underlying conflict facts come to life, the underlying *legal* facts and the ultimate outcome become more engrossing than they otherwise would be. The future of these people—the actual result reached in the case—lies within the pages of the case you're reading. The more clearly you see what happened—in the courts below and to the parties involved—the greater the odds that you'll care about (and remember) the legal principles the case was chosen by your casebook author to illustrate.

PRACTICE EXERCISES

These practice exercises will give you an opportunity to explore ways to decipher challenging opinions so that both the legal facts and the conflict facts become clear to you. Remember that you can visit caplaw.com/rll to see some of the responses I thought about as I wrote these practice exercise questions.

1. In determining the meaning of a particularly difficult sentence or paragraph in an opinion, it is often helpful to simplify the court's words or sentence structure. One trick when rephrasing a complex sentence is to change the "voice" of the speaker, taking the words from the judge and putting them into the "voice" of whoever the judge is attributing the thought to. Another good reading trick is to break a long sentence into several shorter sentences and/or to add more punctuation to the existing sentence. Finally, it is often helpful to *add missing* words or thoughts to a sentence to clarify its meaning. Read, for example, the following unedited excerpt from *Parker v. Twentieth Century-Fox Film Corp.*, 3 Cal. 3d 176, 474 P.2d 689 (1970):[4]

> "As stated, defendant's sole defense to this action which resulted from its deliberate breach of contract is that in rejecting defendant's substitute offer of employment plaintiff unreasonably refused to mitigate damages."

---

4. The *Parker* case concerns an employment contract dispute between actress Shirley MacLaine and Twentieth Century Fox Film Corporation. The facts in the opinion show that she was initially signed to star in a musical to have been filmed in California but that the film never went into production. The film company offered her alternative employment in a Western that would have been shot in Australia. She turned down the role in the Western and sued the film company for breach of contract.

That sentence is hard to understand in only one reading. To make comprehension easier, the reader could have rewritten the sentence more simply. Here's an example:

> "The defendant, whose breach of [employment] contract caused this action, raises only one argument in defense. The defendant argues that the plaintiff unreasonably refused to mitigate damages when [she] rejected the defendant's offer of substitute employment."

Rewriting complex sentences to ease understanding is a good reading habit to develop in law. Such rewriting can be done in actuality, in the margin of the casebook, or merely in your head as you read. Try it with the following phrase, taken from the same case:

> "No expertise or judicial notice is required in order to hold that the deprivation or infringement of an employee's rights held under an original employment contract converts the available 'other employment' relied upon by the employer to mitigate damages, into inferior employment which the employee need not seek or accept."

One possible rewrite (or mental paraphrase) for this difficult passage could have been:

> "This court is free to hold that, when an alternative employment offer made by an employer infringes on an employee's rights under an original employment contract, the substitute employment is 'inferior.' An employee is not required to seek nor to accept 'inferior employment' in order to mitigate damages that may result from the employer's breach of the original employment contract."

How does this rewrite compare to yours? Does yours work, too?

In the space below, explain what is effective about each of the paraphrases (including your own) that was less effective in the original excerpt taken from the opinion itself:

2. The following is a challenging case to read. It was decided in 1853, when writing conventions were very different than they are today. Read the case first to see if you can understand what the legal conflict is about. It will help to know that a "conflagration" is a massive fire. It will also help to know that this case appears in *Torts and Compensation*, a Torts casebook by Dan B. Dobbs and Paul T. Hayden.[5] The case appears in "Chapter 4: Defenses to Intentional Torts—Privileges" in Subsection 3, labeled "Privileges Not Based on Plaintiff's Conduct."

After reading the case enough times to "see" the factual situation underlying the conflict between the parties, answer the four questions that follow the case.

Surocco v. Geary

Supreme Court of California, 1853 3 Cal. 69

MURRAY, CHIEF JUSTICE, delivered the opinion of the Court.

This was an action, commenced in the court below, to recover damages for blowing up and destroying the plaintiffs' house and property, during the fire of the 24th of December, 1849.

Geary, at that time Alcalde of San Francisco, justified, on the ground that he had the authority, by virtue of his office, to destroy said building, and also that it had been blown up by him to stop the progress of the conflagration then raging.

It was in proof, that the fire passed over and burned beyond the building of the plaintiffs', and that at the time said building was destroyed, they were engaged in removing their property, and could, had they not been prevented, have succeeded in removing more, if not all of their goods.

---

5. DAN B. DOBBS & PAUL T. HAYDEN, TORTS AND COMPENSATION 94–96 (4th ed. 2001), reprinted with permission of Thomson West.

The cause was tried by the court sitting as a jury, and a verdict rendered for the plaintiffs, from which the defendant prosecutes this appeal under the Practice Act of 1850.

The only question for our consideration is, whether the person who tears down or destroys the house of another, in good faith, and under apparent necessity, during the time of a conflagration, for the purpose of saving the buildings adjacent, and stopping its progress, can be held personally liable in an action by the owner of the property destroyed. . . .

The right to destroy property, to prevent the spread of a conflagration, has been traced to the highest law of necessity, and the natural rights of man, independent of society or civil government. "It is referred by moralists and jurists to the same great principle which justifies the exclusive appropriation of a plank in a shipwreck, though the life of another be sacrificed; with the throwing overboard goods in a tempest, for the safety of a vessel; with the trespassing upon the lands of another, to escape death by an enemy. It rests upon the maxim, Necessitas inducit privilegium quod jura privata."

The common law adopts the principles of the natural law, and places the justification of an act otherwise tortious precisely on the same ground of necessity.

This principle has been familiarly recognized by the books from the time of the saltpetre case, and the instances of tearing down houses to prevent a conflagration, or to raise bulwarks for the defense of a city, are made use of as illustrations, rather than as abstract cases, in which its exercise is permitted. At such times, the individual rights of property give way to the higher laws of impending necessity.

A house on fire, or those in its immediate vicinity, which serve to communicate the flames, becomes a nuisance, which it is lawful to abate, and the private rights of the individual yield to the considerations of general convenience, and the interests of society. Were it otherwise, one stubborn person might involve a whole city in ruin, by refusing to allow the destruction of a building which would cut off the flames and check the progress of the fire, and that, too, when it was perfectly evident that his building must be consumed. . . .

The counsel for the respondent has asked, who is to judge of the necessity of the destruction of property?

This must, in some instances, be a difficult matter to determine. The necessity of blowing up a house may not exist, or be as apparent to the owner, whose judgment is clouded by interests, and the hope of saving his property, as to others. In all such cases the conduct of the individual must be regulated by his own judgment as to the exigencies of the case. If a building should be torn down without apparent or actual necessity, the parties concerned would undoubtedly be liable in an action of trespass. But in every case the necessity must be clearly shown. It is true, many cases of hardship may grow out of this rule, and property may often in such cases be destroyed, without necessity, by irresponsible persons, but this difficulty would not be obviated by making the parties responsible in every case, whether the necessity existed or not.

The legislature of the State possess the power to regulate this subject by providing the manner in which buildings may be destroyed, and the mode in which compensation shall be made; and it is to be hoped that something will be done to obviate the difficulty, and prevent the happening of such events as those supposed by the respondent's counsel.

In the absence of any legislation on the subject, we are compelled to fall back upon the rules of the common law.

The evidence in this case clearly establishes the fact, that the blowing up of the house was necessary, as it would have been consumed had it been left standing. The plaintiffs cannot recover for the value of the goods which they might have saved; they were as much subject to the necessities of the occasion as the house in which they were situate; and if in such cases a party was held liable, it would too frequently happen, that the delay caused by the removal of the goods would render the destruction of the house useless.

The court below clearly erred as to the law applicable to the facts of this case. The testimony will not warrant a verdict against the defendant.

Judgment reversed.

(a) Even the opening sentence of this case is confusing. "This was an action, commenced in the court below, to recover damages for blowing up and destroying the plaintiffs' house and property, during the fire of the 24th of December, 1849."

   i. Who suffered damages? (Note that it's hard to figure out because the opinion does not say expressly who the "actor" in the sentence is.)

   ii. Who allegedly destroyed plaintiffs' house and property? (Note that one of the confusing things about this sentence is that it does not identify who caused the damage, but seems to assume the reader knows. You have to move to the second sentence to have enough information to infer who may have caused the damage.)

   iii. As you read this sentence, did you imagine that the words "house and property" were redundant or that there was a house and there was also separate property (perhaps contained in the house or outside, around the house)? As you read further in the case, did your initial "vision" become more clear?

iv. Did you notice that this fire occurred in San Francisco on Christmas Eve in 1849? What kind of fire prevention technology might have existed in that era?

(b) The second sentence of the opinion is: "Geary, at that time Alcalde of San Francisco, justified, on the ground that he had the authority, by virtue of his office, to destroy said building, and also that it had been blown up by him to stop the progress of the conflagration then raging."

i. Do you know for certain what an "Alcalde" is?

ii. What do you imagine an "Alcalde" is?

iii. What is the best reading cue in the sentence to help you figure out what an "Alcalde" might have been in 1849?

iv. What might the word "justified" mean, in more modern terms, in this sentence?

(c) The third sentence reads, "It was in proof, that the fire passed over and burned beyond the building of the plaintiffs', and that at the time said building was destroyed, they were engaged in removing their property, and could, had they not been prevented, have succeeded in removing more, if not all of their goods."

   i. Why does it matter that the fire burned past the plaintiffs' house and property?

   ii. Who is the "they" referred to in this sentence?

   iii. Who prevented the actors from removing their property from the burning building? Why were the actors prevented from removing more of their property?

(d) In your own words, write out a short description of what happened between the parties in this case (or, alternatively, draw a diagram with stick figures that illustrates the events of the underlying conflict):

3. Reread the case again, this time focusing on the "legal facts" of the case. When you are finished, please answer the questions below:

(a) Note that there is only one party named as the plaintiff in the heading of the case (Surocco), but the court refers consistently to the plaintiffs in the plural. Who do you imagine the plaintiffs are in this lawsuit? You don't have any way, given the facts as presented in the casebook, to confirm that understanding. Do you need to confirm that understanding to continue to read for the "main idea" of this case?

(b) Was there a jury in this case? If not, who decided the outcome of the case?

(c) What do you imagine (even if you have never studied the "Intentional Torts" referred to in the title of "Chapter 4" of this casebook) the plaintiffs think gives them a right to recover for the loss of their property? In other words, what is the legal theory upon which they based their original claim in the trial court?

(d) Looking only at the second paragraph of the case, what do you think the defendant's legal theories are for why he should not have to pay for the plaintiffs' property damage? In other words, why do you think the defendant thinks he should have won in the trial court? [As an aside, do you think I am right to assume that the defendant is a "he"? Are there any actual facts in the case, or words used by the court, that give me the gender of the defendant? Even without any reference to gender by the court, would I have any historical grounds for making the assumption that the defendant is male?]

(e) If the fire burned past the plaintiffs' house, then did it do any good for the Alcalde to blow up the house? Did the court care?

4. List at least four words or allusions that you did not understand when you read the case. Did you need to understand them to continue to read for the "main idea" of the case within the context of a Torts casebook?

(a)

(b)

(c)

(d)

5. If you were going to read this case in preparation for a class discussion in Torts tomorrow, what could you take as your "working hypothesis" of the "main idea" of the case?

6. As you have learned throughout this book, it is a good habit to keep track of time when you are reading law. How long did it take you to read this case? When did you start? When did you finish?

CHAPTER 10

Evaluate What You're Reading—Your Ideas Matter

Expert readers evaluate what they read. They don't assume the author is an authority whose written contributions are beyond their reach. Rather, to "make meaning" of text, expert readers make judgments about the content of what they're reading as they read, learning from the author but also forming opinions about the content, style, validity, and power of what they're reading. Interestingly (but predictably), the less a reader knows about the subject of a text, the less inclined the reader is to evaluate the text.[1] Also, if the reader assumes the text is merely transmitting objective information, the reader is less inclined to evaluate the text.[2] The more a reader knows about a subject and the more the reader expects to glean from the reading, the more meaningful his or her engagement with the text becomes.

Like all expert readers, expert law readers engage heavily in evaluating the law they are reading. The more experienced the law reader, the more

1. MICHAEL PRESSLEY & PETER AFFLERBACH, VERBAL PROTOCOLS OF READING: THE NATURE OF CONSTRUCTIVELY RESPONSIVE READING 75 (1995). Note also that one of the well-recognized challenges with online reading is being able to identify the source of information so you can rationally weigh an author's expertise or biases. See Chapter 15 to explore more about online reading.

2. *Id.*

meaningful his or her thoughts about a case can be. Also, experienced law students know full well that opinions have *not* been included in their casebooks merely to transmit objective information to the reader—and that reading cases passively as if they were just about "information" would be inappropriate. If casebook authors wanted to transmit "black letter rules,"[3] there would be much easier and more straightforward ways to do so.

Experienced law students know that cases are included in casebooks to give law students the opportunity to do what lawyers do in the real world—wrestle with the validity of the conclusions the court has drawn, question the characterization of the facts the court has adopted, wonder if the rules of law as stated are supported by the authorities cited. Reading law without evaluating it would be the last thing an exceptional lawyer would do.

When you read cases in your casebook, you can begin to evaluate what you're reading at four levels:

(1) Evaluate your thoughts and feelings about the reading *before* you actually start to read (as discussed in Chapter 8);

(2) Evaluate the judge's writing style as you read;

(3) Evaluate the judge's possible biases, assumptions, and perspectives;

(4) Evaluate the intellectual content of the reading.

A. Evaluate Your Thoughts and Feelings

As you have learned throughout this book, exceptional reading requires you to interact actively with a text, not to simply open your mind and have information poured into it. Your prior knowledge in the area of law you're reading about, your prior knowledge about the facts underlying a case you're reading about, your prior assumptions about premises the court may be adopting, and your prior knowledge about the socioeconomic and historical realities that existed at the time and place of decision all influ-

3. *See supra* Chapter 1, note 8.

ence what you can bring *to* your reading—and, hence, what you are able to take *from* your reading. The better you evaluate your prior knowledge (its accuracy, its influence on your ability to be open-minded, etc.), the more effective the results of your reading.

Similarly, your prior experiences and present beliefs create feelings about an area of law or a set of facts involved in your reading. How you *feel* when you read a case involving racial profiling will hinge largely on your politics, your belief system, and your life experiences. The better you evaluate your feelings—and the further ahead you can anticipate those feelings—the greater the chance that you will engage fully and will stay engaged with a case, or cluster of cases, you are reading. Unless you are fully engaged with the case as you read, you will not be fully informed by the case when you are done.[4]

B. Evaluate the Judge's Writing Style

George Gopen, Director of Writing at Duke University, tells a wonderful story.[5] He asks you to visualize yourself as a successful urban lawyer, commuting home from New York to Connecticut on a busy interstate in the days when change was tossed into baskets at toll booths. Approaching a toll booth, you enter the "exact change" lane. All signs indicate that you must deposit forty cents into the toll booth basket. Being a dutiful citizen, you pull out a quarter, a dime, and a nickel. When you reach the basket, you hurl all three coins enthusiastically at the toll basket. The quarter drops in,

4. PRESSLEY & AFFLERBACH, *supra* note 1, at 76. Interestingly, Pressley and Afflerbach note that having strong feelings about a text can predetermine how a reader will evaluate the text—as if readers "predecide" how they plan to react before they get very far in the reading itself.

5. I had the pleasure around 1990 of hearing Dr. Gopen tell this story in person. You can also find it in writing at George D. Gopen, *The State of Legal Writing: Res Ipsa Loquitur*, 86 MICH. L. REV. 333, 342–43 (1987). *See also* GEORGE D. GOPEN, EXPECTATIONS: TEACHING WRITING FROM THE READER'S PERSPECTIVE (2004) (asserting that clear communication requires that writers be aware of the needs of those who will read their work).

the dime drops in, but the nickel bounces off the basket on to the pavement. Are you entitled to drive through?

The answer, Dr. Gopen explains, depends on whether the driver's job is to *divest himself or herself* of forty cents (to be forty cents poorer) OR to enrich the State of Connecticut by forty cents. If the driver's job is to enrich the State of Connecticut by forty cents, the job is not yet done until the quarter, the dime, and the nickel are *all three* in the basket.

Dr. Gopen goes on to draw a parallel to the task of writing. Is it, he asks, the job of writers to simply *divest themselves* of the information in their heads by tossing it out in written form, or is it the job of writers to get that information into the heads of their readers? The point, of course, is that writing that does not inform—writing that misses the mark—is ineffective and a waste of the reader's time.

We have all been on the receiving end of ineffective writing. How many times do we put down a difficult text, or a poorly written text, or a boring text because the information is just not getting into our heads? Of course, communication is a two-way street. Among other things, I may miss an author's point because I'm too tired to be reading at all, or I may be reading something for which I do not have an adequate vocabulary, or I may be making wrong assumptions based on prior knowledge or old feelings. On the other hand, my lack of comprehension could well be the result of how the author has written the text I'm reading.

For busy law students, having to read a poorly written judicial opinion is like having to listen to nails scrape across a chalkboard. It's hard to imagine anything more irritating or less satisfying. The automatic (and healthy) reaction is to walk away—quickly! Of course, if you are responsible for understanding and mastering the text, walking away is not a good option.

The fact is, some opinions are poorly written, at least in the context of what we expect as readers today.[6] Particularly in the early days, court opin-

---

6. *See* Nancy A. Wanderer, *Writing Better Opinions: Communicating with Candor, Clarity, and Style,* 54 ME. L. REV. 47 (2002) (and articles cited therein).

ions were not written for wide distribution or for a wide audience. Rather, they were practical documents designed to efficiently inform parties and their attorneys of the results in a case. Moreover, judicial opinions aren't like classic movies—there are no "remakes" to update the language, content, and scenes to make them more accessible and engaging, or more politically correct and less offensive. They just are what they are (or were).

Being in the position of having to decipher a poorly written or presently offensive text is not pleasant. Law students are not like graduate students in history who are seeking out old documents for the purpose of decoding them to understand life in a bygone era. Rather, law students are reading cases to understand rules and principles of law—and the evolution of rules and principles of law. Reading the voluminous number of old cases—or cases from far-off state jurisdictions—frequently found in most casebooks can seem cumbersome at best, oppressive at worst.

An important way to exercise control of your reading is to evaluate the language and format of the text as you read it. Is this a well-written opinion? Is there language in it that just sings? Is there language in it that you could rewrite better? Is there offensive language that may be causing you to *dis*engage from the text? Are there words you don't understand that you need to look up? Are there words you don't understand that you can just skip over?

In addition to evaluating the quality of a judge's writing, you can also evaluate language (choice of words, syntax) as a way of predicting what's important to a judge (what are key, critical facts), where the judge is going in a case, and how the judge is going to justify a result. Evaluating words and syntax helps you develop and test a hypothesis about the reading.

Thus, assume a judge says, "This court regrets having to acknowledge the truth of the defendant's claim that her rights were blatantly ignored by the state." What's your best guess as to which way this case is going to come out? By using words such as "regrets" and "blatantly ignored" in association with the state, and words like "truth" and "rights" in relation to the defendant, the court is paving the way to rule for the defendant—and is expressing a strong reaction to what happened as well. Perhaps a better question would be, "How badly is the state going to lose this one?" What if, instead, the court had written: "Although the defendant claims that her 'rights' were ignored, this court finds it difficult to accept as a premise that the State was acting outside of the interests of the people." What result might you predict would follow this statement? What does it mean to you that the court put the word "rights" in quotation marks? What does it mean that the court capitalized the word "State" but not "people" or "defendant"? Does this court believe the state has an important status—perhaps more important than that of the defendant?

C. Evaluate the Judge's Possible Biases, Assumptions, Perspectives

Exceptional, engaged readers are invested in knowing the bias of an author. As the immediately prior paragraph illustrates, authors drop cues all over their writing that reveal their assumptions and perspectives. Such cues, when taken together, often create an over-arching tone or theme in the text. If you're alert, you'll spot these cues (and will be rewarded with a richer understanding of the author's meaning and possible flaws in the author's conclusions).

You have known for years that you don't have to believe everything you read. In fact, you absolutely shouldn't believe everything you read. Rather, thinking people look behind what they're reading to see what the author's point of view is, at whether the propositions in the writing are backed with legitimate facts and presumptions, at whether the writing is internally consistent.

Reading the law is no different. If there was ever a type of reading that called for skepticism, law is it. The need for skepticism arises precisely because all legal opinions are the end result of the adversarial process. In the adversarial process, each side has tried hard to persuade a listener of the truth of his or her position. The listener then decides which side will win. Where a written opinion is involved, the author (a judge) is invested in justifying the correctness (often morally as well as logically) of the result.

Judges are people, not dispassionate automatons. In reaching every result and then writing about it, a judge must make underlying assumptions about principles of law and justice, and often must make choices about which view of disputed facts to believe. Like good readers, good judges approach each new case with prior knowledge and experience. Also, like good readers, the best judges are alert to their prior knowledge and experience as well as to the impact their prior knowledge and experience might have on their thinking and on their writing.

D. Evaluate the Intellectual Content of the Reading

The best intellectual exercise a law student can engage in is to evaluate the intellectual content of a case before class, during class, and after class.

Many students make the mistake of thinking their primary task is to *understand* each case, like a consumer of information, as if each was brought down from the mountain on tablets. They weren't. As Professor and former Dean Ken Broun of the University of North Carolina School of Law used to say in class, "Written opinions are one judge's advice to the next judge." That's all they are.

Legal opinions are the written documentation of a court's reasoning in resolving a particular case in controversy. With high court decisions, such as those issued by the United States Supreme Court, especially since the latter half of the 20th century, decisions may have been written with the full awareness that they would "set precedent" (establish principles for lower courts and later courts to follow). Many other decisions were written for a much simpler purpose—to solve the exact controversy in front of the court under the exact circumstances under which that case arose.

You are reading these cases to get the hang of how courts reach such results (so that you can get a court to reach the result you want when you practice law) and to become familiar with widely recognized controlling principles of law. Thus, being able to figure out what the court actually decided is a critical skill and being able to figure out if a case makes sense is an equally critical skill. Could a case have been decided, rationally, some other way? Would a change in the socioeconomic environment of the times have brought a different result?

It takes time to develop the expertise and experience to think about your reading at this high a level.[7] In the beginning, it will be a struggle simply to find the result itself (really, what DID happen?). Later, you should strive to ask yourself whether the result made sense under the circumstances and whether it would still make sense today. You need to evaluate, eventually, whether other results would have been equally rational or perhaps even more rational. You need to ask yourself: "what would I have done if I had been the judge?" If you disagree with the court's result and are really on your game (and have time to do it), ask yourself (at least occasionally) *why* did I get to a different place? Do I see the *legal facts* or the *conflict facts* differently—or do I have a whole different set of underlying assumptions that is impacting the flow of my logic?

If you are not asking these kinds of questions, you are only skimming the surface of your reading. There may be times when skimming the surface is your immediate purpose, and that's okay occasionally. As a rule, however, reading law well demands enough investment in the cases before you, enough confidence in your reasoning abilities (which will grow with experience), and enough skepticism about the decision-making process to motivate you to read critically, evaluating the cases and their authors on many levels.

---

7. *See* Paula Lustbader, *Construction Sites, Building Types, and Bridging Gaps: A Cognitive Theory of the Learning Progression of Law Students*, 33 WILLAMETTE L. REV. 315 (1997) (describing four qualitatively distinct and progressive stages of legal reasoning experienced by students as they move through the study of law).

PRACTICE EXERCISES

The practice exercises for this chapter give you a rich opportunity to practice some of the reading skills you've been learning about in this and earlier chapters. The case included here, *Lindh v. Surman,* is long, but the facts and the law are interesting. Remember that you can visit caplaw.com/rll to see some of the responses I thought about as I wrote these practice exercise questions.

1. The following case, *Lindh v. Surman*, 560 Pa. 1, 742 A.2d 643 (1999), has been taken from *Property and Lawyering*, a first-year Property casebook by James L. Winokur, R. Wilson Freyermuth, and Jerome Organ. The case is included in the same section of the casebook that was explored in the Practice Exercises to Chapter 8 of this book: "Chapter 3: Transfer by Gift."

The first sentence of the case reads as follows: "In this appeal, we are asked to decide whether a donee of an engagement ring must return the ring or its equivalent value when the donor breaks the engagement."

Do you have any emotional reactions to that sentence? Have you been engaged, come close to being engaged, thought about being engaged, or been denied the opportunity by law to marry? Are you a romantic at heart? More practical than romantic about relationships? Is marriage an economic arrangement, at least in part? Do you think the tradition of a man giving a diamond ring to his fiancée is outdated? Inequitable? How do you think these prior experiences or beliefs might influence how you read this case?

2. Read the case below as reprinted (with additional edits) from the casebook:

Lindh v. Surman

Supreme Court of Pennsylvania 560 Pa. 1, 742 A.2d 643 (1999)[8]

NEWMAN, JUSTICE. In this appeal, we are asked to decide whether a donee of an engagement ring must return the ring or its equivalent value when the donor breaks the engagement.

The facts of this case depict a tumultuous engagement between Rodger Lindh (Rodger), a divorced, middle-aged man, and Janis Surman (Janis), the object of Rodger's inconstant affections. In August of 1993, Rodger proposed marriage to Janis. To that purpose, he presented her with a diamond engagement ring that he purchased for $17,400. Rodger testified that the price was less than the ring's market value because he was a "good customer" of the jeweler's, having previously purchased a $4,000 ring for his ex-wife and other expensive jewelry for his children. Janis, who had never been married, accepted his marriage proposal and the ring. Discord developed in the relationship between Rodger and Janis, and in October of 1993 Rodger broke the engagement and asked for the return of the ring. At that time, Janis obliged and gave Rodger the ring. Rodger and Janis attempted to reconcile. They succeeded, and Rodger again proposed marriage, and offered the ring, to Janis. For a second time, Janis accepted. In March of 1994, however, Rodger called off the engagement. He asked for the return of the ring, which Janis refused, and this litigation ensued.

Rodger filed a two-count complaint against Janis, seeking recovery of the ring or a judgment for its equivalent value. The case proceed-

8. Reprinted from JAMES L. WINOKUR, R. WILSON FREYERMUTH & JEROME M. ORGAN, PROPERTY AND LAWYERING 219–224 (2002) with permission of Thomson West (additional edits not included in the casebook).

ed to arbitration, where a panel of arbitrators awarded judgment for Janis. Rodger appealed to the Court of Common Pleas of Allegheny County, where a brief non-jury trial resulted in a judgment in favor of Rodger in the amount of $21,200. Janis appealed to the Superior Court, which affirmed the trial court. . .[and held] that the ring must be returned regardless of who broke the engagement, and irrespective of the reasons. . . .

We begin our analysis with the only principle on which all parties agree: that Pennsylvania law treats the giving of an engagement ring as a conditional gift. *See Pavlicic v. Vogtsberger*, 390 Pa. 502, 136 A.2d 127 (1957). In *Pavlicic*, the plaintiff supplied his ostensible fiancee with numerous gifts, including money for the purchase of engagement and wedding rings, with the understanding that they were given on the condition that she marry him. When the defendant left him for another man, the plaintiff sued her for recovery of these gifts. Justice Musmanno explained the conditional gift principle:

> A gift given by a man to a woman on condition that she embark on the sea of matrimony with him is no different from a gift based on the condition that the donee sail on any other sea. If, after receiving the provisional gift, the donee refuses to leave the harbor—if the anchor of contractual performance sticks in the sands of irresolution and procrastination—the gift must be restored to the donor. [*Id.* at 507, 136 A.2d at 130.]

Where the parties disagree, however, is: (1) what is the condition of the gift (*i.e.*, acceptance of the engagement or the marriage itself), and (2) whether fault is relevant to determining return of the ring. Janis argues that the condition of the gift is acceptance of the marriage proposal, not the performance of the marriage ceremony. She also contends that Pennsylvania law, which treats engagement gifts as implied-in-law conditional gifts, has never recognized a right of recovery in a donor who severs the engagement. In her view, we should not recognize such a right where the donor breaks off the engagement, because, if the condition of the gift is performance of the marriage ceremony, that would reward a donor who prevents the occurrence of the condition, which the donee was ready, willing, and eagerly waiting to perform.

Janis first argues that the condition of the gift is acceptance of the proposal of marriage, such that acceptance of the proposal vests absolute title in the donee. This theory is contrary to Pennsylvania's view of the engagement ring situation. In *Ruehling v. Hornung*, 98 Pa. Super. 535 (1929), the Superior Court provided what is still the most thorough Pennsylvania appellate court analysis of the problem:

> It does not appear whether the engagement was broken by plaintiff or whether it was dissolved by mutual consent. It follows that in order to permit a recovery by plaintiff, it would be necessary to hold that the gifts were subject to the implied condition that they would be returned by the donee to the donor whenever the engagement was dissolved. Under such a rule *the marriage would be a necessary prerequisite* to the passing of an absolute title to a Christmas gift made in such circumstances. We are unwilling to go that far, *except as to the engagement ring.* [*Id.* at 540 (emphasis added).]

This Court later affirmed that "[t]he promise to return an antenuptial gift made in contemplation of marriage *if the marriage does not take place* is a fictitious promise implied in law." *Semenza v. Alfano*, 443 Pa. 201, 204, 279 A.2d 29, 31 (1971) (emphasis added). Our caselaw clearly recognizes the giving of an engagement gift as having an implied condition that the marriage must occur in order to vest title in the donee; mere acceptance of the marriage proposal is not the implied condition for the gift.

Janis' argument that Pennsylvania law does not permit the donor to recover the ring where the donor terminates the engagement has some basis in the few Pennsylvania authorities that have addressed the matter. The following language from *Ruehling* implies that Janis' position is correct:

> We think that it [the engagement ring] is always given subject to the implied condition that if the marriage does not take place either because of the death, or a disability recognized by the law on the part of, either party, or by breach of the contract by the donee, or its dissolution by mutual consent, the gift shall be returned. [*Ruehling*, 98 Pa. Super. at 540.]

Noticeably absent from the recital by the court of the situations where the ring must be returned is when the donor breaks the engagement. Other Pennsylvania authorities also suggest that the donor cannot recover the ring when the donor breaks the engagement. *See* 7 Summary of Pennsylvania Jurisprudence 2d §15:29, p. 111 ("upon breach of the marriage engagement by the donee, the property may be recovered by the donor"); 17 Pennsylvania Law Encyclopedia, "Gifts," §9, p. 118 (citing to a 1953 common pleas court decision, "[i]f, on the other hand, the donor wrongfully terminates the engagement, he is not entitled to return of the ring").

This Court, however, has not decided the question of whether the donor is entitled to return of the ring where the donor admittedly ended the engagement. In the context of our conditional gift approach to engagement rings, the issue we must resolve is whether we will follow the fault-based theory, argued by Janis, or the no-fault rule advocated by Rodger. Under a fault-based analysis, return of the ring depends on an assessment of who broke the engagement, which necessarily entails a determination of why that person broke the engagement. A no-fault approach, however, involves no investigation into the motives or reasons for the cessation of the engagement and requires the return of the engagement ring simply upon the nonoccurrence of the marriage.

The rule concerning the return of a ring founded on fault principles has superficial appeal because, in the most outrageous instances of unfair behavior, it appeals to our sense of equity. Where one fiancee has truly "wronged" the other, depending on whether that person was the donor of the ring or the donee, justice appears to dictate that the wronged individual should be allowed to keep, or have the ring returned. However, the process of determining who is "wrong" and who is "right," when most modern relationships are complex circumstances, makes the fault-based approach less desirable. A thorough fault-based inquiry would not only end with the question of who terminated the engagement, but would also examine that person's reasons. In some instances the person who terminated the engagement may have been entirely justified in his or her actions. This kind of inquiry would invite the parties to stage the most bitter and unpleasant accusations against those whom they nearly made their spouse, and a court would have no clear guidance with regard to how to ascertain who was "at fault." The Supreme Court of Kansas recited the difficulties with the fault-based system:

> What is fault or the unjustifiable calling off of an engagement? By way of illustration, should courts be asked to determine which of the following grounds for breaking an engagement is fault or justified? (1) The parties have nothing in common; (2) one party cannot stand prospective in-laws; (3) a minor child of one of the parties is hostile to and will not accept the other party; (4) an adult child of one of the parties will not accept the other party; (5) the parties' pets do not get along; (6) a party was too hasty in proposing or accepting the proposal; (7) the engagement was a rebound situation which is now regretted; (8) one party

has untidy habits that irritate the other; or (9) the parties have religious differences. The list could be endless. [*Heiman v. Parrish*, 262 Kan. 926, 942 P.2d 631, 637 (Kan.1997).]

A ring-return rule based on fault principles will inevitably invite acrimony and encourage parties to portray their ex-fiancées in the worst possible light, hoping to drag out the most favorable arguments to justify, or to attack, the termination of an engagement. Furthermore, it is unlikely that trial courts would be presented with situations where fault was clear and easily ascertained and, as noted earlier, determining what constitutes fault would result in a rule that would defy universal application.

The approach that has been described as the modern trend is to apply a no-fault rule to engagement ring cases. *See Vigil v. Haber*, 888 P.2d at 455 (N.M.1994). Courts that have applied no-fault principles to engagement ring cases have borrowed from the policies of their respective legislatures that have moved away from the notion of fault in their divorce statutes. As described by the court in *Vigil*, this trend represents a move "towards a policy that removes fault-finding from the personal-relationship dynamics of marriage and divorce." *Vigil*, 888 P.2d at 457. Indeed, by 1986 . . . all fifty states had adopted some form of no-fault divorce. Pennsylvania, no exception to this trend, recognizes no-fault divorces. We agree with those jurisdictions that have looked towards the development of no-fault divorce law for a principle to decide engagement ring cases, and the inherent weaknesses in any fault-based system lead us to adopt a no-fault approach to resolution of engagement ring disputes.

Having adopted this no-fault principle, we still must address the original argument that the donor should not get return of the ring when the donor terminates the engagement. Such a rule would be consonant with a no-fault approach, it is argued, because it need not look

> at the reasons for termination of the engagement; if there is proof that the donor ended the relationship, then he has frustrated the occurrence of the condition and cannot benefit from that. In other words, we are asked to adopt a no-fault approach that would always deny the donor return of the ring where the donor breaks the engagement.
>
> We decline to adopt this modified no-fault position, and hold that the donor is entitled to return of the ring even if the donor broke the engagement. We believe that the benefits from the certainty of our rule outweigh its negatives, and that a strict no-fault approach is less flawed than a fault-based theory or modified no-fault position.

3. Can you state succinctly the "conflict" facts as you understand them? Do you think the court did a good job of presenting these facts objectively and clearly? Were you surprised, given how these facts were presented, with the result the court reached?

4. In the fourth paragraph, the court includes a lengthy quote from *Pavlicic v. Vogtsberger*, a 1957 case decided by the Pennsylvania Supreme Court. How did you react to that court's use of the "embarking on the sea of matrimony" image, including its conclusion that a woman's refusal to marry is analogous to a ship's "refusal to leave the harbor"? Do you think that is an appropriate image to invoke in 1999, when this case was decided? How about now? (Note that your answer to these questions are personal—there is no right or wrong answer to these questions).

5. In the fourth paragraph, the court states: "We begin our analysis with the only principle on which all parties agree: that Pennsylvania law treats the giving of an engagement ring as a conditional gift." Was this a helpful statement? Is it clearly written? Do you agree with the content of the statement?

6. Assuming all parties do agree that an engagement ring is a "conditional gift," what does the plaintiff (Mr. Lindh) think that condition is? What does Ms. Surman think that condition is? Do you personally, apart from the precedent for Pennsylvania included in the body of the opinion, agree with Mr. Lindh or with Ms. Surman (in other words, not knowing what the parties discussed between themselves, what would you personally think their agreement—assuming they even had an agreement—might have been)?

7. Near the middle of the opinion, the court notes that the "question of whether the donor is entitled to return of the ring where the donor admittedly ended the engagement" has not previously been decided in Pennsylvania. What rule does the court eventually adopt?

8. Why does the court believe the rule it adopted is the better rule?

9. Do you agree (a) with the result; and (b) with the court's reasoning in reaching this result?

10. If you had been a judge on this bench, would you have let Ms. Surman keep this ring or would you have required her to return it (or its value) to Mr. Lindh? What rule would you have adopted to support your decision? Were there any facts in this case that swayed you strongly one way or the other? Was there any precedent cited that strongly influenced you one way or the other?

11. This was apparently not an easy case even for seasoned judges to decide. There were two dissents filed in this case. If you are curious and would like to read them, go to caplaw.com/rll.

12. How long did it take you to read this case? Was this case easier or harder to read and understand than the San Francisco fire case you read in the Practice Exercise at the end of the last chapter?

CHAPTER 11

Review, Rephrase, Record

As we have learned, engaged, active, effective law students do not read mindlessly from the beginning of a case (or the beginning of a section in their casebook) to the end. Rather, they develop educated guesses (hypotheses) about what they will read and they repeatedly test their hypotheses against the text as they read. They ask questions of themselves (and maybe even others, if the opportunity arises). They pose hypotheticals that allow them to apply the guesses they're developing to new situations.

A. The Circularity of Expert Reading—It Doesn't Happen in a Straight Line

In addition to developing and testing hypotheses as they read, engaged, active, effective law readers loop back through what they're reading with frequency. Reading scholars refer to reading as a "recursive" (circular) intellectual activity. Expert legal readers review their ideas, testing a newly formed thought against the reality of the text. As they do so, they frequently rephrase (in their own words) what they're reading, and then test their paraphrase against the reality of the case as it unfolds.

When expert law students get to a difficult part in a case that appears to be inconsistent with the hypothesis they started with, they flip back to their earlier reading to review and question what's happening. "So," they ask themselves, "if the judge really meant that a defendant had to have obtained property legitimately in order for a plaintiff to have an action for 'conversion,' how can the court now be making light of the fact that this roommate took the other one's earrings without asking?"

Then, after looking back at the earlier parts of the reading, exceptional readers often clear up their own questions. Thus: "Oh, I see now. The court does agree that you have to have obtained the property legitimately to have 'converted' it. It's just that this court thinks that the first roommate actually *did* have the other's *unexpressed* permission to take the earrings because the roommates had a history of borrowing each other's jewelry. Hmmm.... I'm not sure I agree that this 'taking' occurred with the roommate's permission, but I see now where the court's coming from—and I understand that the main point of the case is that you have to have obtained property initially with permission in order to have converted it when you refuse to give it back."

B. Identifying Any "Magic" Words in the Text

One goal of this reviewing, rephrasing, revisiting cycle is to gain an increased appreciation for key words in a case. While paraphrasing is a valuable reading tool, it has a special application in legal reading. Part of the discourse of law is the special meaning of key words in any specialized area of law—words that have a rich history of case law behind them, developing their meaning beyond two dimensions and into a representation of reality itself.

I think of these key words that evolve over time as "magic words" in law. For example, there is a whole body of Property law that has established rules that allow someone to take the real property of someone by "adverse possession." When property is taken by "adverse possession," ownership is established through "open and notorious," "continuous" and "uninterrupted" use that is "adverse" to the other party for a legally defined period of time. In layman's terms, I can establish squatter's rights on someone else's land by using it openly in a manner that is contrary to the landowner's property interests for a prescribed period of time.

This final sentence of the preceding paragraph is a good paraphrase of the legal rule of adverse possession. That paraphrase is easier to follow and understand than much of the "legaleze" (heavy, cumbersome law-related words) that preceded it—but it doesn't capture the "magic words" the court uses. Each of the "magic words" in the court's description has a long history of case law behind it, case law that examines the boundaries of each term with care by applying the terms of the rule to actual facts in actual cases. Because of this long history, the "magic words" have special meaning to lawyers.

I could not fully understand a case (nor fully understand this area of law) if I abandon the magic words in favor of the paraphrase. The smart thing to do involves paraphrasing AND saving the "magic words." I can paraphrase to help straighten the rule out in my head, and then I can include a sentence or phrases incorporating the "magic words" (often in quotes—so I know they're magic) that have special meaning in this area of the law. For example: "I can establish title to someone else's property by 'adverse possession.' To establish title by 'adverse possession,' I have to use the land 'openly and notoriously' (conspicuously) in a manner that is contrary ('adverse') to the owner's interests. I have to maintain this adverse use 'continuously' and 'without interruption' for a legally prescribed period of time."

C. Where Memory Fits In

As you think about how many of these recursive internal dialogues an active reader maintains throughout the course of reading a day's assignments, you realize that it is critical for successful legal readers to use their working memories effectively. Working (short-term) memory is the part of our mind that we use to think about and process information.[1] Information

---

1. *See generally* Kenneth L. Higbee, Your Memory 19–22 (2d ed., Marlowe & Co. 1996) (providing an excellent overview of how memory works).

has to pass through working memory to ever have a chance of getting to long-term memory (and long term memory is where information has to be in order for you to pull it up later—like on an exam).

It is a waste of time, and counter-productive, to try to put unnecessary information into long-term memory. You won't be able to retrieve it all—and shouldn't have to. It is a much better idea to use your short-term memory to process information, come up with the "main idea" contained in your reading, and then choose to store that distilled main idea (not all the information that led up to it) in your long-term memory. Of course, you can't ever figure out the main idea if you don't have enough information in your short-term memory to allow you to think adequately about the topic at hand.

People attend to information better (getting it to stick in their short-term memories long enough to think about it) when they can make sense out of something.[2] Holding on to disconnected facts is almost impossible to do—especially if you're also trying to move those disconnected thoughts to long-term memory for retrieval later. Thus, the skill of paraphrasing while simultaneously connecting the "magic words" with the paraphrase is an enormously helpful reading tool for a law student. The paraphrase puts the "magic words" in a rational context, making both the words and the ideas they represent easier to think about (in your short-term memory) and then also easier to hold on to for later retrieval from your long-term memory.

Research on expertise teaches us that experts (true stars) in any field appear to have better "working memories" than less successful or less experienced individuals. Because they make discerning choices about what information to think about, experts have a lot more brain space available to "think" (process) with. Thus, it's no surprise that experts (the stars) use their short-term memories to think about information in their area of expertise more deeply and in a more meaningful way than non-experts do. When you're reading law, finding the main themes in a case and evaluating the

---

2. *Id.* at 46–67.

reasoning of the court are the kind of big-picture, challenging cognitive activities that require you to keep your short-term (working) memory uncluttered.

How can you keep your short-term, working memory uncluttered when there's so much to attend to in a case? How do the experts do it? Experts make maximum use of their short-term, working memories by "chunking" or clustering pieces of information together.[3] Thus, one classic study shows that expert chess players can move substantially quicker in a game of sixty-second chess than non-experts because they "chunk" chess pieces together in their mind when they view the chessboard (rather than looking at each piece separately) and the "chunks" of pieces helps the experts quickly evaluate all possible moves.[4]

Turning to a legal example, students who come to class having already discarded much of the extraneous information in the day's assigned cases and who have synthesized the history of the case, the germane conflict facts, and the legal rules will have more working memory available to process new information that comes to light during class. They won't be bringing extraneous information (for example, the middle name of the plaintiff) to class to clutter their minds and will therefore be better able to think deeply about the more complex questions raised in the class discussion.

At the end of class, those same students can modify the chunks of information they brought with them to class and decide—then and there—what is worth storing in long-term memory. Being able to make those long-term storage decisions on the spot is tough. Most students find that taking good notes helps.

---

3. Higbee, *supra* note 1. *See generally* The Nature of Expertise (Michelene T. H. Chi et al. eds., 1988).

4. Chi et al., *supra* note 3, at xv–xvi (citing numerous early studies of artificial intelligence focusing on the thinking patterns of chess players).

D. Taking Notes to Improve Your Working Memory

Expert readers of law can take full advantage of their working memories by "chunking" appropriate information into rational groupings as they read background information, cases, and clusters of cases in their casebooks. Rather than trying to hold on to information (much of which is new) all at one time in working memory—causing a gridlock or overflow of information—wise readers write down what they're thinking (their evaluation of their prior knowledge as it becomes relevant, their reactions to the author's writing style, questions that arise from ambiguities in the text, summaries or paraphrases of an important point) in the margin of their book or the margins of their case briefs. In the margin, right next to where they're thinking it.

Having written down their important thoughts and reactions as they move through a text, wise readers can then go back and review the case by skimming the text and their comments, chunking related thoughts together. So, a good legal reader might go back at the end of a case and summarize, like this, "This plaintiff was surprisingly ahead of her times. Her demand for equal pay for equal work, while poorly expressed, was pretty forward-thinking." That thought, the summary of lots of other smaller observations, might be just one of several other reactions to the case. For example, the reader might also note, "The court is having trouble getting around precedent that establishes firmly that the earnings of wives belong to their husbands. Wow. Hard to believe that was ever the law." Putting all this together, the reader might decide that the main idea of the case is this: "'Similarly situated' people are to be treated 'similarly' under constitutional principles—but the trick at any given point in history is how a court decides who is 'similarly situated.'"

Without recording notes to keep his or her mind clear, the reader might not have enough working memory to take on new (and important) ideas as he or she moves through a case (or might "dump" earlier—important—ideas to make room for the new ones). By taking contemporaneous notes as they read, however, readers can "hold on" to ideas without clogging up their minds. By going back to review and rephrase these earlier thoughts, readers can then "chunk" information together, holding it in working memory in a manageable form.[5]

With a mind full of good, well-clustered ideas, the reader is then free to begin the challenging work of advanced case reading—he or she can begin to evaluate the content of the case and think about what might constitute the "main idea" of the text.

It is tempting, but a mistake, simply to move through assigned reading with a highlighter in your hand. It is equally misguided to read with your keyboard at your fingertips, ready to be used to write a brief summarizing only the parts of a case that go into a case brief.

Both of these actions—indiscriminate highlighting and routine computer briefing (without more)—will hold you back. When you highlight, you are trying to efficiently piggy-back on what has already been written by marking it so it will stand out when you go back to review later. It's certainly possible—even probable—that much of what you read in your casebook, including in cases, is valuable and would be helpful if you highlight it and review it later. However, highlighting is not ALL you should be doing. The best highlighting in the world can only capture the author's words. You also need to read with a pen or pencil at your side so that you capture your *own* thoughts and reactions to what you are reading.

Similarly, typing up a summary of a case *after* you've read a case, without more, is not your best tool for effective reading. While typing up a summary is a good way to organize (chunk) your thoughts, ONLY typing up a summary will not maximize your learning. It's even better to write contemporaneous remarks in the book next to the text that spawned your idea, and then use those remarks and your memory of the case to type up a short case brief or other synthesized notes capturing the main idea of the case.

---

5. One of the important keys to effective on-screen reading is finding a way to take notes that works for you. Chapter 15 discusses this challenge and other aspects of on-screen reading.

E. To Brief or Not to Brief?

We have established that experts have systems for chunking information in rational groups. Once clumped into manageable groups, the same amount of information takes up less storage space in working memory—thus freeing more space in working memory for the challenging task of actually thinking about the material. It's like creating computer files in your mind rather than trying to store everything you create as its own document—risking a meltdown.

Traditional case briefing, as described in Chapter 2, is a useful "chunking" tool. It is a way that experienced law students, law professors, and lawyers have found they can take apart a case and recluster the information contained in it in a manageable way. There are probably lots of ways that information in cases could be rationally "chunked," but case briefs are so widely used that they provide a language common to all lawyers, all law professors, and all judges. Hence, they're a great "thinking" shortcut for all these people who frequently have to interact with each other about the main idea of a particular case or group of cases.

Rhetoric theorists and educators agree that "you can't separate thinking, speaking, and writing."[6] Hence, the best way to use a case brief to forward your understanding of an area of law is to write it out by hand (or type it out on your computer if you don't have to "feel" yourself write to stay in touch with your thinking). Writing out your thoughts forces you to bring them to a conscious level and identify what you don't yet understand. You can (and should) edit this initial brief as you learn more in class about the case and the law behind it.

As the semester wears on, some students find that writing out briefs is taking too much time. After the first weeks of class, actually writing out

---

6. I am indebted to Dr. Edward M. Neal, Director of Faculty Development for the Center for Teaching and Learning at the University of North Carolina, for sharing these thoughts at an informal training session at The University of North Carolina School of Law in the early 1990s.

the brief should take no more than about five minutes. If it is taking longer than that, you have your task defined wrong. Writing the brief is an aid to reading and an aid to class participation. It is a way of "chunking" information to free up working memory so you can think about the main idea of a case (or group of cases). It is not an end in itself. If briefing is taking too long, try these tips: (1) write your brief *as* (not after) you read, filling it in as you come to the relevant parts of the case; (2) write the brief in the margin of your casebook; (3) cut down on the fact section, including either the relevant facts only and/or a "movie title" that will help you replay the facts of the movie you created in your imagination as you read the case; (4) read more actively so you become curious enough about the case to want to read for the main idea rather than focusing on the components of the brief as if these component parts *actually were* the main idea.

You might also consider trying a multi-colored highlighter method of briefing (often called "book briefing"). Students who are hung-up on writing and don't like to or won't write fast often respond well to using highlighters of various colors to highlight the parts of the brief in their book. To be effective, the system requires that you use the same color for each part of the brief every time. Thus, you might always highlight the heading in green, the procedural history in orange, the facts in yellow, etc. Students who use this technique report that, if you get good at it, it helps them read selectively because it motivates them to skim for the part of the case where the information they're seeking is contained.

Courts, over ages, have used many of the same transitional words and phrases to alert readers to the "part" of the case they're getting to (e.g., "This court holds . . ."; or "On appeal, the appellee asks . . ."), so skimming for those transitions can speed up your reading. If you decide to book brief in color, it would be wise to *also* keep a pen or pencil at your side to write down your *own* thoughts that can't be captured by highlighting only the words of the court. Once you have color-briefed the case, remember to think about the "chunks" of information you've identified and reach an independent conclusion about the deeper meaning of the case within the context of your course. Some students can successfully "book brief" without even using multi-colored highlighters. These students develop a consistent system for making margin notes identifying the various "chunks" of information within the case itself, sometimes supplementing the court's words with their own paraphrase in the casebook margins.

F. Beyond Briefing

Briefing, in any form, is a good thing when it focuses your thinking and streamlines your reading. Briefing, in any form, is a bad thing when it becomes an end in itself, serving as a substitute for reading actively or for thinking independently. The only exception to this rule is in the rare instance when you are so pressed for time that you make the conscious decision to cut corners and read *solely* to get by in class and/or to bring enough of a working knowledge of the cases to class so that you can glean something from the class discussion. Of course reading only to prepare for class is not a productive strategy over the long haul, but if you know that is your purpose, it is not irrational to gear your reading towards accomplishing that goal (once in awhile). Ultimately, like all experts, you should celebrate when your thoughts turn to larger issues such as the themes and patterns that are emerging from the details of the cases you read.

PRACTICE EXERCISES

These practice exercises will give you the opportunity to read a very long case, which is read by almost every first-year law student in the country, while taking margin notes to identify the conflict facts, the legal facts, and your own emotional reactions about the case. Remember that you can visit caplaw.com/rll to see some of the responses I thought about as I wrote these practice exercise questions.

1. Read the following case in its entirety, keeping notes in the margin of the book as you read. In your margin notes, try to include any spontaneous emotional reactions you have to the facts or the court's reasoning and any value judgments you make about the court's language or reasoning, or about the positions of the parties. Pay attention to whether you are clearly and accurately visualizing the "conflict facts" and the "legal facts" discussed in Chapter 9. Before you begin, assume that this case appears in a Contracts casebook in a section concerning "offer" and, more specifically, in a subsection concerning when an offer is sufficiently firm that it binds the person making the offer to a contract if the offer is accepted.

Leonard v. Pepsico, Inc.

88 F. Supp. 2d 116 (1999)

Plaintiff brought this action seeking, among other things, specific performance of an alleged offer of a Harrier Jet, featured in a television advertisement for defendant's "Pepsi Stuff" promotion. Defendant has moved for summary judgment pursuant to Federal Rule of Civil Procedure 56. For the reasons stated below, defendant's motion is granted.

I. Background

This case arises out of a promotional campaign conducted by defendant, the producer and distributor of the soft drinks Pepsi and Diet Pepsi. The promotion, entitled "Pepsi Stuff," encouraged consumers to collect "Pepsi Points" from specially marked packages of Pepsi or Diet Pepsi and redeem these points for merchandise featuring the Pepsi logo. Before introducing the promotion nationally, defendant conducted a test of the promotion in the Pacific Northwest from October 1995 to March 1996. A Pepsi Stuff catalog was distributed to consumers in the test market, including Washington State. Plaintiff is a resident of Seattle, Washington. While living in Seattle, plaintiff saw the Pepsi Stuff commercial that he contends constituted an offer of a Harrier Jet.

A. *The Alleged Offer*

Because whether the television commercial constituted an offer is the central question in this case, the Court will describe the commercial in detail. The commercial opens upon an idyllic, suburban morning, where the chirping of birds in sun-dappled trees welcomes a paperboy on his morning route. As the newspaper hits the stoop of a conventional two-story house, the tattoo of a military drum introduces the subtitle, "MONDAY 7:58 AM." The stirring strains of a martial air mark the appearance of a well-coiffed teenager preparing to leave for school, dressed in a shirt emblazoned with the Pepsi logo, a red-white-and-blue ball. While the teenager confidently preens, the military drumroll again sounds as the subtitle "T-SHIRT 75 PEPSI POINTS" scrolls across the screen. Bursting from his room, the teenager strides down the hallway wearing a leather jacket. The drumroll sounds again, as the subtitle "LEATHER JACKET 1450 PEPSI POINTS" appears. The teenager opens the door of his house and, unfazed by the glare of the early morning sunshine, puts on a pair of sunglasses. The drumroll then accompanies the subtitle "SHADES 175 PEPSI POINTS." A voiceover then intones, "Introducing the new Pepsi Stuff catalog," as the camera focuses on the cover of the catalog. (*See* Defendant's Local Rule 56.1 Stat., Exh. A (the "Catalog").)[2]

The scene then shifts to three young boys sitting in front of a high school building. The boy in the middle is intent on his Pepsi Stuff Catalog, while the boys on either side are each drinking Pepsi. The three oys gaze in awe at an object rushing overhead, as the military march builds to a crescendo. The Harrier Jet is not yet visible, but the observer senses the presence of a mighty plane as the extreme winds generated by its flight create a paper maelstrom in a classroom devoted to an otherwise dull physics lesson. Finally, the Harrier Jet swings into view and lands by the side of the school building, next to a bicycle rack. Several students run for cover, and the velocity of the wind strips one hapless faculty member down to his underwear. While the faculty member is being deprived of his dignity, the voice-over announces: "Now the more Pepsi you drink, the more great stuff you're gonna get."

The teenager opens the cockpit of the fighter and can be seen, helmetless, holding a Pepsi. "[L]ooking very pleased with himself," the teenager exclaims, "Sure beats the bus," and chortles. The military drumroll sounds a final time, as the following words appear: "HARRIER FIGHTER 7,000,000 PEPSI POINTS." A few seconds later, the following appears in more stylized script: "Drink Pepsi—Get Stuff." With that message, the music and the commercial end with a triumphant flourish.

Inspired by this commercial, plaintiff set out to obtain a Harrier Jet. Plaintiff explains that he is "typical of the 'Pepsi Generation' . . . he is

---

2. At this point, the following message appears at the bottom of the screen: "Offer not available in all areas. See details on specially marked packages."

young, has an adventurous spirit, and the notion of obtaining a Harrier Jet appealed to him enormously." Plaintiff consulted the Pepsi Stuff Catalog. The Catalog features youths dressed in Pepsi Stuff regalia or enjoying Pepsi Stuff accessories, such as "Blue Shades" ("As if you need another reason to look forward to sunny days."), "Pepsi Tees" ("Live in 'em. Laugh in 'em. Get in 'em."), "Bag of Balls" ("Three balls. One bag. No rules."), and "Pepsi Phone Card" ("Call your mom!"). The Catalog specifies the number of Pepsi Points required to obtain promotional merchandise. (*See* Catalog, at rear foldout pages.) The Catalog includes an Order Form which lists, on one side, fifty-three items of Pepsi Stuff merchandise redeemable for Pepsi Points (*see id.* (the "Order Form")). Conspicuously absent from the Order Form is any entry or description of a Harrier Jet. (*See id.*) The amount of Pepsi Points required to obtain the listed merchandise ranges from 15 (for a "Jacket Tattoo" ("Sew 'em on your jacket, not your arm.")) to 3300 (for a "Fila Mountain Bike" ("Rugged. All-terrain. Exclusively for Pepsi.")). It should be noted that plaintiff objects to the implication that because an item was not shown in the Catalog, it was unavailable.

The rear foldout pages of the Catalog contain directions for redeeming Pepsi Points for merchandise. (*See* Catalog, at rear foldout pages.) These directions note that merchandise may be ordered "only" with the original Order Form. (*See id.*) The Catalog notes that in the event that a consumer lacks enough Pepsi Points to obtain a desired item, additional Pepsi Points may be purchased for ten cents each; however, at least fifteen original Pepsi Points must accompany each order. (*See id.*)

Although plaintiff initially set out to collect 7,000,000 Pepsi Points by consuming Pepsi products, it soon became clear to him that he "would not be able to buy (let alone drink) enough Pepsi to collect the necessary Pepsi Points fast enough." Reevaluating his strategy, plaintiff "focused for the first time on the packaging materials in the

Pepsi Stuff promotion," and realized that buying Pepsi Points would be a more promising option. Through acquaintances, plaintiff ultimately raised about $700,000.

B. *Plaintiff's Efforts to Redeem the Alleged Offer*

On or about March 27, 1996, plaintiff submitted an Order Form, fifteen original Pepsi Points, and a check for $700,008.50. Plaintiff appears to have been represented by counsel at the time he mailed his check; the check is drawn on an account of plaintiff's first set of attorneys. At the bottom of the Order Form, plaintiff wrote in "1 Harrier Jet" in the "Item" column and "7,000,000" in the "Total Points" column. In a letter accompanying his submission, plaintiff stated that the check was to purchase additional Pepsi Points "expressly for obtaining a new Harrier jet as advertised in your Pepsi Stuff commercial."

On or about May 7, 1996, defendant's fulfillment house rejected plaintiff's submission and returned the check, explaining that:

> The item that you have requested is not part of the Pepsi Stuff collection. It is not included in the catalogue or on the order form, and only catalogue merchandise can be redeemed under this program.
>
> The Harrier jet in the Pepsi commercial is fanciful and is simply included to create a humorous and entertaining ad. We apologize for any misunderstanding or confusion that you may have experienced and are enclosing some free product coupons for your use.

Plaintiff's previous counsel responded on or about May 14, 1996, as follows:

> Your letter of May 7, 1996 is totally unacceptable. We have reviewed the video tape of the Pepsi Stuff commercial . . . and it

> clearly offers the new Harrier jet for 7,000,000 Pepsi Points. Our client followed your rules explicitly. . . .
>
> This is a formal demand that you honor your commitment and make immediate arrangements to transfer the new Harrier jet to our client. If we do not receive transfer instructions within ten (10) business days of the date of this letter you will leave us no choice but to file an appropriate action against Pepsi. . . .

. . . The present motion . . . follows three years of jurisdictional and procedural wrangling.

II. Discussion

A. *The Legal Framework*

1. *Standard for Summary Judgment*

. . .

The question of whether or not a contract was formed is appropriate for resolution on summary judgment. As the Second Circuit has recently noted, "Summary judgment is proper when the 'words and actions that allegedly formed a contract [are] so clear themselves that reasonable people could not differ over their meaning.'" *Krumme v. Westpoint Stevens, Inc.*, 143 F.3d 71, 83 (2d Cir.1998) (quoting *Bourque v. FDIC*, 42 F.3d 704, 708 (1st Cir.1994)) (further citations omitted); *see also Wards Co. v. Stamford Ridgeway Assocs.*, 761 F.2d 117, 120 (2d Cir.1985) (summary judgment is appropriate in contract case where interpretation urged by non-moving party is not "fairly reasonable"). Summary judgment is appropriate in such cases because there is "sometimes no genuine issue as to whether the parties' conduct implied a 'contractual understanding.' . . . In such cases, 'the judge must decide the issue himself, just as he decides any factual issue in respect to which reasonable people cannot differ.'" *Bourque*, 42 F.3d at 708 (quoting *Boston Five Cents Sav. Bank v. Secretary of Dep't of Housing & Urban Dev.*, 768 F.2d 5, 8 (1st Cir.1985)).

. . .

B. *Defendant's Advertisement Was Not an Offer*

1. *Advertisements as Offers*

The general rule is that an advertisement does not constitute an offer. The *Restatement (Second) of Contracts* explains that:

> Advertisements of goods by display, sign, handbill, newspaper, radio or television are not ordinarily intended or understood as offers to sell. The same is true of catalogues, price lists and circulars, even though the terms of suggested bargains may be stated in some detail. It is of course possible to make an offer by an advertisement directed to the general public (see § 29), but there must ordinarily be some language of commitment or some invitation to take action without further communication.

Restatement (Second) of Contracts § 26 cmt. b (1979). Similarly, a leading treatise notes that:

> It is quite possible to make a definite and operative offer to buy or sell goods by advertisement, in a newspaper, by a handbill, a catalog or circular or on a placard in a store window. *It is not customary to do this, however; and the presumption is the other way.* . . .
>
> Such advertisements are understood to be mere requests to consider and examine and negotiate; and no one can reasonably regard them as otherwise unless the circumstances are exceptional and the words used are very plain and clear.

. . .

An advertisement is not transformed into an enforceable offer merely by a potential offeree's expression of willingness to accept the offer through, among other means, completion of an order form. In *Mesaros v. United States*, 845 F.2d 1576 (Fed.Cir.1988), for example, the plaintiffs sued the United States Mint for failure to deliver a number of Statue of Liberty commemorative coins that they had ordered. When demand for the coins proved unexpectedly robust, a number of individuals who had sent in their orders in a timely fashion were left empty-handed. *See id.* at 1578–80. The court began by noting the "well-established" rule that advertisements and order forms are "mere notices and solicitations for offers which create no power of acceptance in the recipient." *Id.* at 1580. . . . The spurned coin collectors could not maintain a breach of contract action because no contract would be formed until the advertiser accepted the order form and processed payment. *See id.* at 1581; *see also Alligood v. Procter & Gamble,* 72 Ohio App.3d 309, 594 N.E.2d 668 (1991) (finding that no offer was made in promotional campaign for baby diapers, in which consumers were to redeem teddy bear proof-of-purchase symbols for catalog merchandise). . . .

The exception to the rule that advertisements do not create any power of acceptance in potential offerees is where the advertisement is "clear, definite, and explicit, and leaves nothing open for negotiation," in that circumstance, "it constitutes an offer, acceptance of which will complete the contract." *Lefkowitz v. Great Minneapolis Surplus Store,* 251 Minn. 188, 86 N.W.2d 689, 691 (1957). In *Lefkowitz,* defendant had published a newspaper announcement stating: "Saturday 9 AM Sharp, 3 Brand New Fur Coats, Worth to $100.00, First Come First Served $1 Each." *Id.* at 690. Mr. Morris Lefkowitz arrived at the store, dollar in hand, but was informed that under defendant's "house rules," the offer was open to ladies, but not gentlemen. *See id.* The court ruled that because plaintiff had fulfilled all of the terms of the advertisement and the advertisement was specific and left nothing open for negotiation, a contract had been formed. *See id.; see also Johnson v. Capital City Ford Co.,* 85 So.2d 75, 79 (La.Ct. App.1955) (finding that newspaper advertisement was sufficiently certain and definite to constitute an offer).

The present case is distinguishable from *Lefkowitz.* First, the commercial cannot be regarded in itself as sufficiently definite, because it specifically reserved the details of the offer to a separate writing, the Catalog. The commercial itself made no mention of the steps a potential offeree would be required to take to accept the alleged offer of a Harrier Jet. The advertisement in *Lefkowitz,* in contrast, "identified the person who could accept." Corbin, *supra,* § 2.4, at 119. *See generally United States v. Braunstein,* 75 F.Supp. 137, 139 (S.D.N.Y.1947) ("Greater precision of expression may be required, and less help from the court given, when the parties are merely at the threshold of a contract."); Farnsworth, *supra,* at 239 ("The fact that a proposal is very detailed suggests that it is an offer, while omission of many terms suggests that it is not."). Second, even if the Catalog had included a Harrier Jet among the items that could be obtained by redemption of Pepsi Points, the advertisement of a Harrier Jet by both television commercial and catalog would still not constitute an offer. As the *Mesaros* court explained, the absence of any words of limitation such as "first come, first served," renders the alleged offer sufficiently indefinite that no contract could be formed. *See Mesaros,* 845 F.2d at 1581. "A customer would not usually have reason to believe that the shopkeeper intended exposure to the risk of a multitude of acceptances resulting in a number of contracts exceeding the shopkeeper's inventory." Farnsworth, *supra,* at 242. There was no such danger in *Lefkowitz,* owing to the limitation "first come, first served."

The Court finds, in sum, that the Harrier Jet commercial was merely an advertisement. The Court now turns to the line of cases upon which plaintiff rests much of his argument.

. . .

In the present case, the Harrier Jet commercial did not direct that anyone who appeared at Pepsi headquarters with 7,000,000 Pepsi Points on the Fourth of July would receive a Harrier Jet. Instead, the commercial urged consumers to accumulate Pepsi Points and to refer to the Catalog to determine how they could redeem their Pepsi Points. The commercial sought a reciprocal promise, expressed through acceptance of, and compliance with, the terms of the Order Form. As noted previously, the Catalog contains no mention of the Harrier Jet. Plaintiff states that he "noted that the Harrier Jet was not among the items described in the catalog, but this did not affect [his] understanding of the offer." (Pl. Mem. at 4.) It should have.

. . .

. . . Because the alleged offer in this case was, at most, an advertisement to receive offers rather than an offer of reward, plaintiff cannot show that there was an offer made in the circumstances of this case.

C. *An Objective, Reasonable Person Would Not Have Considered the Commercial an Offer*

Plaintiff's understanding of the commercial as an offer must also be rejected because the Court finds that no objective person could reasonably have concluded that the commercial actually offered consumers a Harrier Jet.

1. *Objective Reasonable Person Standard*

In evaluating the commercial, the Court must not consider defendant's subjective intent in making the commercial, or plaintiff's subjective view of what the commercial offered, but what an objective, reasonable person would have understood the commercial to convey. *See Kay-R Elec. Corp. v. Stone & Webster Constr. Co.,* 23 F.3d 55, 57 (2d Cir.1994) ("[W]e are not concerned with what was going through the heads of the parties at the time [of the alleged contract]. Rather, we are talking about the objective principles of contract law."); *Mesaros,* 845 F.2d at 1581 ("A basic rule of contracts holds that whether an offer has been made depends on the objective reasonableness of the alleged offeree's belief that the advertisement or solicitation was intended as an offer."); Farnsworth, *supra,* § 3.10, at 237; Williston, *supra,* § 4:7 at 296–97.

If it is clear that an offer was not serious, then no offer has been made: . . .

. . .On the other hand, if there is no indication that the offer is "evidently in jest," and that an objective, reasonable person would find that the offer was serious, then there may be a valid offer. *See Barnes,* 549 P.2d at 1155 ("[I]f the jest is not apparent and a reasonable hearer would believe that an offer was being made, then the speaker risks the formation of a contract which was not intended."); *see also Lucy v. Zehmer,* 196 Va. 493, 84 S.E.2d 516, 518, 520 (1954) (ordering specific performance of a contract to purchase a farm despite defendant's protestation that the transaction was done in jest as "'just a bunch of two doggoned drunks bluffing'").

2. *Necessity of a Jury Determination*

Plaintiff also contends that summary judgment is improper because the question of whether the commercial conveyed a sincere offer can be answered only by a jury. Relying on dictum from *Gallagher v. Delaney,* 139 F.3d 338 (2d Cir. 1998), plaintiff argues that a federal judge comes from a "narrow segment of the enormously broad American socioeconomic spectrum," *id.* at 342, and, thus, that the question whether the commercial constituted a serious offer must be decided by a jury composed of, *inter alia,* members of the "Pepsi Generation," who are, as plaintiff puts it, "young, open to adventure, willing to do the unconventional." Plaintiff essentially argues that a federal judge would view his claim differently than fellow members of the "Pepsi Generation."

Plaintiff's argument that his claim must be put to a jury is without merit. *Gallagher* involved a claim of sexual harassment in which the defendant allegedly invited plaintiff to sit on his lap, gave her inappropriate Valentine's Day gifts, told her that "she brought out feelings that he had not had since he was sixteen," and "invited her to help him feed the ducks in the pond, since he was 'a bachelor for the evening.'" *Gallagher,* 139 F.3d at 344. The court concluded that a jury determination was particularly appropriate because a federal judge lacked "the current real-life experience required in interpreting subtle sexual dynamics of the workplace based on nuances, subtle perceptions, and implicit communications." *Id.* at 342. This case, in contrast, presents a question of whether there was an offer to enter into a contract, requiring the Court to determine how a reasonable, objective person would have understood defendant's commercial. Such an inquiry is commonly performed by courts on a motion for summary judgment. *See Krumme,* 143 F.3d at 83; *Bourque,* 42 F.3d at 708; *Wards Co.,* 761 F.2d at 120.

3. *Whether the Commercial Was "Evidently Done In Jest"*

Plaintiff's insistence that the commercial appears to be a serious offer requires the Court to explain why the commercial is funny. Explaining why a joke is funny is a daunting task; as the essayist

E.B. White has remarked, "Humor can be dissected, as a frog can, but the thing dies in the process. . . ."[11] The commercial is the embodiment of what defendant appropriately characterizes as "zany humor."

First, the commercial suggests, as commercials often do, that use of the advertised product will transform what, for most youth, can be a fairly routine and ordinary experience. The military tattoo and stirring martial music, as well as the use of subtitles in a Courier font that scroll terse messages across the screen, such as "MONDAY 7:58 AM," evoke military and espionage thrillers. The implication of the commercial is that Pepsi Stuff merchandise will inject drama and moment into hitherto unexceptional lives. The commercial in this case thus makes the exaggerated claims similar to those of many television advertisements: that by consuming the featured clothing, car, beer, or potato chips, one will become attractive, stylish, desirable, and admired by all. A reasonable viewer would understand such advertisements as mere puffery, not as statements of fact, *see, e.g., Hubbard v. General Motors Corp.,* 95 Civ. 4362(AGS), 1996 WL 274018, at *6 (S.D.N.Y. May 22, 1996) (advertisement describing automobile as

"Like a Rock," was mere puffery, not a warranty of quality); *Lovett*, 207 N.Y.S. at 756; and refrain from interpreting the promises of the commercial as being literally true.

Second, the callow youth featured in the commercial is a highly improbable pilot, one who could barely be trusted with the keys to his parents' car, much less the prize aircraft of the United States Marine Corps. Rather than checking the fuel gauges on his aircraft, the teenager spends his precious preflight minutes preening. The youth's concern for his coiffure appears to extend to his flying without a helmet. Finally, the teenager's comment that flying a Harrier Jet to school "sure beats the bus" evinces an improbably insouciant attitude toward the relative difficulty and danger of piloting a fighter plane in a residential area, as opposed to taking public transportation.

Third, the notion of traveling to school in a Harrier Jet is an exaggerated adolescent fantasy. In this commercial, the fantasy is underscored by how the teenager's schoolmates gape in admiration, ignoring their physics lesson. The force of the wind generated by the Harrier Jet blows off one teacher's clothes, literally defrocking an authority figure. As if to emphasize the fantastic quality of having a Harrier Jet arrive at school, the Jet lands next to a plebeian bike rack. This fantasy is, of course, extremely unrealistic. No school would provide landing space for a student's fighter jet, or condone the disruption the jet's use would cause.

. . .

Plaintiff argues that a reasonable, objective person would have understood the commercial to make a serious offer of a Harrier Jet because there was "absolutely no distinction in the manner" in which the items in the commercial were presented. Plaintiff also relies upon a press release highlighting the promotional campaign, issued by defendant, in which "[n]o mention is made by [defendant] of humor, or anything of the sort." These arguments suggest merely that the humor of the promotional campaign was tongue in cheek. Humor

> is not limited to what Justice Cardozo called "[t]he rough and boisterous joke . . . [that] evokes its own guffaws." *Murphy v. Steeplechase Amusement Co.*, 250 N.Y. 479, 483, 166 N.E. 173, 174 (1929). In light of the obvious absurdity of the commercial, the Court rejects plaintiff's argument that the commercial was not clearly in jest.

2. What year did this ad campaign hit the airwaves? ______ How old were you at that time, or were you even born? Can you think of anyone in your family who might remember seeing or hearing about any of the "Pepsi Generation" ads? Out of curiosity, you might see if that person remembers seeing *this* Pepsi Generation ad. Even if you are too young to remember this ad campaign, can you relate to what it must have meant to be a member of the "Pepsi Generation"? How might these personal perceptions (or the lack of them) impact how you read the case?

3. Do you think there's any merit to the plaintiff's argument that his case should be heard by a jury of his "peers" (other members of the Pepsi Generation)? Do you think there's any merit to the plaintiff's contention that a federal judge is not a member of the audience targeted by this ad campaign and therefore could not evaluate whether it would be perceived of as an "offer" by the target audience? Did the judge directly address this contention or side-step it?

4. Do you think the plaintiff in this case really believed he had been given an offer to purchase a Harrier Jet? Do you think the court thought he believed it? Can you point to what parts of the text caused you to think that

the court did or didn't believe that Mr. Leonard really thought the Pepsi Co. was making a contract offer?

5. Please "book brief" this case in this book or write out a more traditional brief in the space below, paying attention to the parts of a brief you read about in Chapter 2.

6. Assume you read this case for a contracts class that you know would be introducing the notion of what constitutes a firm offer which, if accepted, would form a binding contract. What do you think is the "main idea" presented by this case? Are there other secondary main ideas that are also important? What "working hypothesis" about this case and about "offer" might you take to class after reading this opinion?

7. How long did it take you to read this case, take notes while you read, and brief the case?

8. When you are finished reading and briefing this case, turn the page over and you can see some of the thoughts I preserved in the margins as I read this case. **Any comments in parentheses are things I would have thought to myself but probably wouldn't have written down. I probably would have written everything else down in the margins as I read.**

You will also see the short brief I might have taken to class with me. Remember that no two readers *ever* think exactly the same thing even when they are reading exactly the same material. We all bring in our prior experience, our presuppositions, and our own energy to the reading task as we respond to the text and create new knowledge from what we've read.

Leonard v. Pepsico, Inc.

88 F. Supp. 2d 116 (1999)

In other words, Π wants the court to make Δ follow through on something (maybe a contract?)

The court is skeptical about this being an offer.

This is going to be interesting.

Δ wants to avoid trial & thinks the court can decide this case as a matter of law.

Plaintiff brought this action seeking, among other things, specific performance of an alleged offer of a Harrier Jet, featured in a television advertisement for defendant's "Pepsi Stuff" promotion. Defendant has moved for summary judgment pursuant to Federal Rule of Civil Procedure 56. For the reasons stated below, defendant's motion is granted.

I. Background

I.e., Pepsi—Δ

This case arises out of a promotional campaign conducted by defendant, the producer and distributor of the soft drinks Pepsi and Diet Pepsi. The promotion, entitled "Pepsi Stuff," encouraged consumers to collect "Pepsi Points" from specially marked packages of Pepsi or Diet Pepsi and redeem these points for merchandise featuring the Pepsi logo. Before introducing the promotion nationally, defendant conducted a test of the promotion in the Pacific Northwest from October 1995 to March 1996. A Pepsi Stuff catalog was distributed to consumers in the test market, including Washington State. Plaintiff is a resident of Seattle, Washington. While living in Seattle, plaintiff saw the Pepsi Stuff commercial that he contends constituted an offer of a Harrier Jet.

But maybe didn't get the catalog that was distributed?

A. *The Alleged Offer*

This is the key Q here: is this ad an offer to enter a contract?

Looks like the opening scene of a "Leave It To Beaver" episode

("Martial air"? don't know that phrase. Must be music because they talk about "stirring strains." Military music?)

Because whether the television commercial constituted an offer is the central question in this case, the Court will describe the commercial in detail. The commercial opens upon an idyllic, suburban morning, where the chirping of birds in sun-dappled trees welcomes a paperboy on his morning route. As the newspaper hits the stoop of a conventional two-story house, the tattoo of a military drum introduces the subtitle, "MONDAY 7:58 AM." The stirring strains of a martial air mark the appearance of a well-coiffed teenager preparing to leave for school, dressed in a shirt emblazoned with the Pepsi logo, a red-white-and-blue ball. While the teenager confidently preens, the military drumroll again sounds as the subtitle "T-SHIRT

75 PEPSI POINTS" scrolls across the screen. Bursting from his room, the teenager strides down the hallway wearing a leather jacket. The drumroll sounds again, as the subtitle "LEATHER JACKET 1450 PEPSI POINTS" appears. The teenager opens the door of his house and, unfazed by the glare of the early morning sunshine, puts on a pair of sunglasses. The drumroll then accompanies the subtitle "SHADES 175 PEPSI POINTS." A voiceover then intones, "Introducing the new Pepsi Stuff catalog," as the camera focuses on the cover of the catalog.[2]

Nice image!
(I wonder if the judge or the judge's clerk wrote all this!)

The scene then shifts to three young boys sitting in front of a high school building. The boy in the middle is intent on his Pepsi Stuff Catalog, while the boys on either side are each drinking Pepsi. The three boys gaze in awe at an object rushing overhead, as the military march builds to a crescendo. The Harrier Jet is not yet visible, but the observer senses the presence of a mighty plane as the extreme winds generated by its flight create a paper maelstrom in a classroom devoted to an otherwise dull physics lesson. Finally, the Harrier Jet swings into view and lands by the side of the school building, next to a bicycle rack. Several students run for cover, and the velocity of the wind strips one hapless faculty member down to his underwear. While the faculty member is being deprived of his dignity, the voiceover announces: "Now the more Pepsi you drink, the more great stuff you're gonna get."

(How young can they be if this is outside a h.s.?)

Again, the catalog. Must be significant.

(Cute turn of phrase)

The teenager opens the cockpit of the fighter and can be seen, helmetless, holding a Pepsi. "[L]ooking very pleased with himself," the teenager exclaims, "Sure beats the bus," and chortles. The military drumroll sounds a final time, as the following words appear: "HARRIER FIGHTER 7,000,000 PEPSI POINTS." A few seconds later, the following appears in more stylized script: "Drink Pepsi—Get Stuff." With that message, the music and the commercial end with a triumphant flourish.

(The point is, he didn't really fly it. He's a h.s. kid)

I.e., for 7,000,000 points, I can get a jet!? Probably not!

(The facts end here.)

2. At this point, the following message appears at the bottom of the screen: "Offer not available in all areas. See details on specially marked packages."

Inspired by this commercial, plaintiff set out to obtain a Harrier Jet. Plaintiff explains that he is "typical of the 'Pepsi Generation' . . . he is young, has an adventurous spirit, and the notion of obtaining a Harrier Jet appealed to him enormously." Plaintiff consulted the Pepsi Stuff Catalog. The Catalog features youths dressed in Pepsi Stuff regalia or enjoying Pepsi Stuff accessories, such as "Blue Shades" ("As if you need another reason to look forward to sunny days."), "Pepsi Tees" ("Live in 'em. Laugh in 'em. Get in 'em."), "Bag of Balls" ("Three balls. One bag. No rules."),[[MR 24]] and "Pepsi Phone Card" ("Call your mom!"). The Catalog specifies the number of Pepsi Points required to obtain promotional merchandise. (*See* Catalog, at rear foldout pages.) The Catalog includes an Order Form which lists, on one side, fifty-three items of Pepsi Stuff merchandise redeemable for Pepsi Points (*see id.* (the "Order Form")). Conspicuously absent from the Order Form is any entry or description of a Harrier Jet. (*See id.*) The amount of Pepsi Points required to obtain the listed merchandise ranges from 15 (for a "Jacket Tattoo" ("Sew 'em on your jacket, not your arm.")) to 3300 (for a "Fila Mountain Bike" ("Rugged. All-terrain. Exclusively for Pepsi.")). It should be noted that plaintiff objects to the implication that because an item was not shown in the Catalog, it was unavailable.

Details about how to order from the catalog. (I can come back to this later)

The rear foldout pages of the Catalog contain directions for redeeming Pepsi Points for merchandise. (*See* Catalog, at rear foldout pages.) These directions note that merchandise may be ordered "only" with the original Order Form. (*See id.*) The Catalog notes that in the event that a consumer lacks enough Pepsi Points to obtain a desired item, additional Pepsi Points may be purchased for ten cents each; however, at least fifteen original Pepsi Points must accompany each order. (*See id.*)

Although plaintiff initially set out to collect 7,000,000 Pepsi Points by consuming Pepsi products, it soon became clear to him that he "would not be able to buy (let alone drink) enough Pepsi to collect the necessary Pepsi Points fast enough." Reevaluating his strategy, plaintiff "focused for the first time on the packaging materials in the Pepsi Stuff promotion," and realized that buying Pepsi Points would be a more promising option. Through acquaintances, plaintiff ultimately raised about $700,000.

Enough to "buy" the jet.

B. *Plaintiff's Efforts to Redeem the Alleged Offer*

On or about March 27, 1996, plaintiff submitted an Order Form, fifteen original Pepsi Points, and a check for $700,008.50. Plaintiff appears to have been represented by counsel at the time he mailed his check; the check is drawn on an account of plaintiff's first set of attorneys. At the bottom of the Order Form, plaintiff wrote in "1 Harrier Jet" in the "Item" column and "7,000,000" in the "Total Points" column. (*See id.*) In a letter accompanying his submission, plaintiff stated that the check was to purchase additional Pepsi Points "expressly for obtaining a new Harrier jet as advertised in your Pepsi Stuff commercial."

Technically, all he needed to get the jet (if the ad was really an offer).

On or about May 7, 1996, defendant's fulfillment house rejected plaintiff's submission and returned the check, explaining that:

> The item that you have requested is not part of the Pepsi Stuff collection. It is not included in the catalogue or on the order form, and only catalogue merchandise can be redeemed under this program.
>
> The Harrier jet in the Pepsi commercial is fanciful and is simply included to create a humorous and entertaining ad. We apologize for any misunderstanding or confusion that you may have experienced and are enclosing some free product coupons for your use.

(I wonder if their legal staff was alarmed at this point!?)

Plaintiff's previous counsel responded on or about May 14, 1996, as follows:

> Your letter of May 7, 1996 is totally unacceptable. We have reviewed the video tape of the Pepsi Stuff commercial . . . and it clearly offers the new Harrier jet for 7,000,000 Pepsi Points. Our client followed your rules explicitly. . . .
>
> This is a formal demand that you[[MR 28]] honor your commitment and make immediate arrangements to transfer the new Harrier jet to our client. If we do not receive transfer instructions within ten (10) business days of the date of this letter you will leave us no choice but to file an appropriate action against Pepsi. . . .

Uh-oh. If Pepsi's lawyers weren't alarmed before, they are now.

... The present motion ... follows three years of jurisdictional and procedural wrangling.

II. Discussion

A. *The Legal Framework*

1. *Standard for Summary Judgment*

...

(The court will decide this case without a trial)

The question of whether or not a contract was formed is appropriate for resolution on summary judgment. As the Second Circuit has recently noted, "Summary judgment is proper when the 'words and actions that allegedly formed a contract [are] so clear themselves that reasonable people could not differ over their meaning.'" *Krumme v. Westpoint Stevens, Inc.*, 143 F.3d 71, 83 (2d Cir.1998) (quoting *Bourque v. FDIC*, 42 F.3d 704, 708 (1st Cir.1994)) (further citations omitted); *see also Wards Co. v. Stamford Ridgeway Assocs.*, 761 F.2d 117, 120 (2d Cir.1985) (summary judgment is appropriate in contract case where interpretation urged by non-moving party is not "fairly reasonable"). Summary judgment is appropriate in such cases because there is "sometimes no genuine issue as to whether the parties' conduct implied a 'contractual understanding.' ... In such cases, 'the judge must decide the issue himself, just as he decides any factual issue in respect to which reasonable people cannot differ.'" *Bourque*, 42 F.3d at 708 (quoting *Boston Five Cents Sav. Bank v. Secretary of Dep't of Housing & Urban Dev.*, 768 F.2d 5, 8 (1st Cir.1985)).

...

The court has characterized this whole transaction as an "advertisement," and therefore NOT an offer. This section will explain why this ad wasn't a contract "offer."

B. *Defendant's Advertisement Was Not an Offer*

1. *Advertisements as Offers*

The general rule is that an advertisement does not constitute an offer. The *Restatement (Second) of Contracts* explains that:

> Advertisements of goods by display, sign, handbill, newspaper, radio or television are not ordinarily intended or understood as offers to sell. The same is true of catalogues, price lists and circulars, even though the terms of suggested bargains may be stated in some detail.

> It is of course possible to make an offer by an advertisement directed to the general public (see § 29), but there must ordinarily be some language of commitment or some invitation to take action without further communication.

Restatement (Second) of Contracts § 26 cmt. b (1979). Similarly, a leading treatise notes that:

> It is quite possible to make a definite and operative offer to buy or sell goods by advertisement, in a newspaper, by a handbill, a catalog or circular or on a placard in a store window. *It is not customary to do this, however; and the presumption is the other way. . . .*
>
> Such advertisements are understood to be mere requests to consider and examine and negotiate; and no one can reasonably regard them as otherwise unless the circumstances are exceptional and the words used are very plain and clear.

Most ads do not constitute a definite offer—they are only "requests to consider" a purchase.

. . .

An advertisement is not transformed into an enforceable offer merely by a potential offeree's expression of willingness to accept the offer through, among other means, completion of an order form. In *Mesaros v. United States,* 845 F.2d 1576 (Fed.Cir.1988), for example, the plaintiffs sued the United States Mint for failure to deliver a number of Statue of Liberty commemorative coins that they had ordered. When demand for the coins proved unexpectedly robust, a number of individuals who had sent in their orders in a timely fashion were left empty-handed. *See id.* at 1578–80. The court began by noting the "well-established" rule that advertisements and order forms are "mere notices and solicitations for offers which create no power of acceptance in the recipient." *Id.* at 1580. . . . The spurned coin collectors could not maintain a breach of contract action because no contract would be formed until the advertiser accepted the order form and processed payment. *See id.* at 1581; *see also Alligood v. Procter & Gamble,* 72 Ohio App.3d 309, 594 N.E.2d 668 (1991) (finding that no offer was made in promotional

I can't turn an ad into a binding offer just by indicating I want to buy whatever was advertised.

campaign for baby diapers, in which consumers were to redeem teddy bear proof-of-purchase symbols for catalog merchandise). . . .

An ad CAN be an offer if it's so definite as to be non-negotiable.

The exception to the rule that advertisements do not create any power of acceptance in potential offerees is where the advertisement is "clear, definite, and explicit, and leaves nothing open for negotiation," in that circumstance, "it constitutes an offer, acceptance of which will complete the contract." *Lefkowitz v. Great Minneapolis Surplus Store,* 251 Minn. 188, 86 N.W.2d 689, 691 (1957). In *Lefkowitz,* defendant had published a newspaper announcement stating: "Saturday 9 AM Sharp, 3 Brand New Fur Coats, Worth to $100.00, First Come First Served $1 Each." *Id.* at 690. Mr. Morris Lefkowitz arrived at the store, dollar in hand, but was informed that under defendant's "house rules," the offer was open to ladies, but not gentlemen. *See id.* The court ruled that because plaintiff had fulfilled all of the terms of the advertisement and the advertisement was specific and left nothing open for negotiation, a contract had been formed. *See id.; see also Johnson v. Capital City Ford Co.,* 85 So.2d 75, 79 (La.Ct. App.1955) (finding that newspaper advertisement was sufficiently certain and definite to constitute an offer).

The present case is distinguishable from *Lefkowitz.* First, the commercial cannot be regarded in itself as sufficiently definite, because it specifically reserved the details of the offer to a separate writing, the Catalog. The commercial itself made no mention of the steps a potential offeree would be required to take to accept the alleged offer of a Harrier Jet. The advertisement in *Lefkowitz,* in contrast, "identified the person who could accept." Corbin, *supra,* § 2.4, at 119. *See generally United States v. Braunstein,* 75 F.Supp. 137, 139 (S.D.N.Y.1947) ("Greater precision of expression may be required, and less help from the court given, when the parties are merely at the threshold of a contract."); Farnsworth, *supra,* at 239 ("The fact that a proposal is very detailed suggests that it is an offer, while omission of many terms suggests that it is not."). Second, even if the Catalog had included a Harrier Jet among the items that could be obtained by redemption of Pepsi Points, the advertisement of a Harrier Jet by both television commercial and catalog would still not constitute an offer. As the *Mesaros* court explained, the absence of any words of limitation such as "first come, first served," renders the alleged offer sufficiently indefinite that no contract could be formed. *See Mesaros,* 845 F.2d at 1581. "A customer would not usually have reason to believe that the shopkeeper intended exposure to the risk of a multitude of acceptances resulting in a number of contracts exceeding the shopkeeper's inventory." Farnsworth, *supra,* at 242. There was no such danger in *Lefkowitz,* owing to the limitation "first come, first served."

Definiteness alone doesn't seem to be enough. It has to be limited so the advertiser could limit exposure.

... and, more importantly, limited to only 3 coats!

The Court finds, in sum, that the Harrier Jet commercial was merely an advertisement. The Court now turns to the line of cases upon which plaintiff rests much of his argument.

...

In the present case, the Harrier Jet commercial did not direct that anyone who appeared at Pepsi headquarters with 7,000,000 Pepsi Points on the Fourth of July would receive a Harrier Jet. Instead, the commercial urged consumers to accumulate Pepsi Points and to refer to the Catalog to determine how they could redeem their Pepsi Points. The commercial sought a reciprocal promise, expressed through acceptance of, and compliance with, the terms of the Order Form. As noted previously, the Catalog contains no mention of the Harrier Jet. Plaintiff states that he "noted that the Harrier Jet was not among the items described in the catalog, but this did not affect [his] understanding of the offer." It should have.

Whoa! (Tough language. The court is definitely not pleased with the Π.)

...

... Because the alleged offer in this case was, at most, an advertisement to receive offers rather than an offer of reward, plaintiff cannot show that there was an offer made in the circumstances of this case.

C. *An Objective, Reasonable Person Would Not Have Considered the Commercial an Offer*

Plaintiff's understanding of the commercial as an offer must also be rejected because the Court finds that no objective person could reasonably have concluded that the commercial actually offered consumers a Harrier Jet.

So, in addition to this being an ad, it's also not a binding "offer" because no reasonable person would have believed it.

1. *Objective Reasonable Person Standard*

What the parties believe an offer to be doesn't matter to this court (even if the parties agree). It's what reasonable people would believe the words of the offer to intend that matters.

In evaluating the commercial, the Court must not consider defendant's subjective intent in making the commercial, or plaintiff's subjective view of what the commercial offered, but what an objective, reasonable person would have understood the commercial to convey. *See Kay-R Elec. Corp. v. Stone & Webster Constr. Co.*, 23 F.3d 55, 57 (2d Cir.1994) ("[W]e are not concerned with what was going through the heads of the parties at the time [of the alleged contract]. Rather, we are talking about the objective principles of contract law."); *Mesaros*, 845 F.2d at 1581 ("A basic rule of contracts holds that whether an offer has been made depends on the objective reasonableness of the alleged offeree's belief that the advertisement or solicitation was intended as an offer."); Farnsworth, *supra*, § 3.10, at 237; Williston, *supra*, § 4:7 at 296–97.

A joke can't ever be an offer because reasonable people would understand it was a joke.

If it is clear that an offer was not serious, then no offer has been made: . . .

. . . On the other hand, if there is no indication that the offer[[MR 39]] is "evidently in jest," and that an objective, reasonable person would find that the offer was serious, then there may be a valid offer. *See Barnes*, 549 P.2d at 1155 ("[I]f the jest is not apparent and a reasonable hearer would believe that an offer was being made, then the speaker risks the formation of a contract which was not intended."); *see also Lucy v. Zehmer*, 196 Va. 493, 84 S.E.2d 516, 518, 520 (1954) (ordering specific performance of a contract to purchase a farm despite defendant's protestation that the transaction was done in jest as "'just a bunch of two doggoned drunks bluffing'").

2. *Necessity of a Jury Determination*

Plaintiff also contends that summary judgment is improper because the question of whether the commercial conveyed a sincere offer can be answered only by a jury. Relying on dictum from *Gallagher v. Delaney*, 139 F.3d 338 (2d Cir. 1998), plaintiff argues that a federal judge comes from a "narrow segment of the enormously broad American socio-economic spectrum," *id.* at 342, and, thus, that the question whether the commercial constituted a serious offer must be decided by a jury composed of, *inter alia*, members of the "Pepsi Generation," who are, as plaintiff puts it, "young, open to adventure, willing to do the unconventional." Plaintiff essentially argues that a federal judge would view his claim differently than fellow members of the "Pepsi Generation."

Plaintiff's argument that his claim must be put to a jury is without merit. *Gallagher* involved a claim of sexual harassment in which the defendant allegedly invited plaintiff to sit on his lap, gave her inappropriate Valentine's Day gifts, told her that "she brought out feelings that he had not had since he was sixteen," and "invited her to help him feed the ducks in the pond, since he was 'a bachelor for the evening.'" *Gallagher,* 139 F.3d at 344. The court concluded that a jury determination was particularly appropriate because a federal judge lacked "the current real-life experience required in interpreting subtle sexual dynamics of the workplace based on nuances, subtle perceptions, and implicit communications." *Id.* at 342. This case, in contrast, presents a question of whether there was an offer to enter into a contract, requiring the Court to determine how a reasonable, objective person would have understood defendant's commercial. Such an inquiry is commonly performed by courts on a motion for summary judgment. *See Krumme,* 143 F.3d at 83; *Bourque,* 42 F.3d at 708; *Wards Co.,* 761 F.2d at 120.

3. *Whether the Commercial Was "Evidently Done In Jest"*

I wonder why this section is here and not up earlier, when the judge says a joke can't be an offer?)

Plaintiff's insistence that the commercial appears to be a serious offer requires the Court to explain why the commercial is funny. Explaining why a joke is funny is a daunting task; as the essayist

E.B. White has remarked, "Humor can be dissected, as a frog can, but the thing dies in the process. . . ."[11] The commercial is the embodiment of what defendant appropriately characterizes as "zany humor." (Def. Mem. at 18.)

First, the commercial suggests, as commercials often do, that use of the advertised product will transform what, for most youth, can be a fairly routine and ordinary experience. The military tattoo and stirring martial music, as well as the use of subtitles in a Courier font that scroll terse messages across the screen, such as "MONDAY 7:58 AM," evoke military and espionage thrillers. The implication of the commercial is that Pepsi Stuff merchandise will inject drama and moment into hitherto unexceptional lives. The commercial in this case thus makes the exaggerated claims similar to those of many television advertisements: that by consuming the featured clothing, car, beer, or potato chips, one will become attractive, stylish, desirable, and admired by all. A reasonable viewer would understand such advertisements as mere puffery, not as statements of fact, *see, e.g., Hubbard v. General Motors Corp.*, 95 Civ. 4362(AGS), 1996 WL 274018, at *6 (S.D.N.Y. May 22, 1996) (advertisement describing automobile as "Like a Rock," was mere puffery, not a warranty of quality); *Lovett,* 207 N.Y.S. at 756; and refrain from interpreting the promises of the commercial as being literally true.

Second, the callow youth featured in the commercial is a highly improbable pilot, one who could barely be trusted with the keys to his parents' car, much less the prize aircraft of the United States Marine Corps. Rather than checking the fuel gauges on his aircraft, the teenager spends his precious preflight minutes preening. The youth's concern for his coiffure appears to extend to his flying without a helmet. Finally, the teenager's comment that flying a Harrier Jet to school "sure beats the bus" evinces an improbably insouciant attitude toward the relative difficulty and danger of piloting a fighter plane in a residential area, as opposed to taking public transportation.

Third, the notion of traveling to school in a Harrier Jet is an exaggerated adolescent fantasy. In this commercial, the fantasy is underscored by how the teenager's schoolmates gape in admiration, ignoring their physics lesson. The force of the wind generated by the Harrier Jet blows off one teacher's clothes, literally defrocking an authority figure. As if to emphasize the fantastic quality of having a Harrier Jet arrive at school, the Jet lands next to a plebeian bike rack. This fantasy is, of course, extremely unrealistic. No school would provide landing space for a student's fighter jet, or condone the disruption the jet's use would cause.

...

Plaintiff argues that a reasonable, objective person would have understood the commercial to make a serious offer of a Harrier Jet because there was "absolutely no distinction in the manner" in which the items in the commercial were presented. Plaintiff also relies upon a press release highlighting the promotional campaign, issued by defendant, in which "[n]o mention is made by [defendant] of humor, or anything of the sort." These arguments suggest merely that the humor of the promotional campaign was tongue in cheek. Humor is not limited to what Justice Cardozo called "[t]he rough and boisterous joke . . . [that] evokes its own guffaws." *Murphy v. Steeplechase Amusement Co.,* 250 N.Y. 479, 483, 166 N.E. 173, 174 (1929). In light of the obvious absurdity of the commercial, the Court rejects plaintiff's argument that the commercial was not clearly in jest.

Pepsi wins—there was no offer and no contract.

Case Brief

Leonard v. Pepsico
88 F. Supp. 2d 116 (S.D.N.Y 1999)

Π: Leonard (a young man?)

Δ: Pepsico (the Pepsi corporation)

PH: (1) Π filed suit for specific performance;
(2) Δ filed for summary judgment;
(3) This Federal District (trial) court granted Δ 's summary judgment motion.

F: Π saw Pepsi's "Pepsi Points" commercial that ended (with a flourish) with a teenager flying a Harrier Jet to school, followed by the statement, "Harrier Jet—7,000,000 Pepsi Points" (roughly $700,000 worth). The ad also said "see the Pepsi Points catalog for details." Π raised $700,000 and tried to cash in. Pepsi said there was no offer. Π sued to get the jet.

Q: (1) Was this ad an enforceable offer" (which, if accepted, would bind the Δ to exchange the jet for the proferred Pepsi Points)?; and
(2) More generally, when is an ad an enforceable offer?

Holding: This ad was not an enforceable offer and Pepsi didn't have to exchange its Pepsi Points for a Harrier Jet.

Rule: An advertisement is presumptively NOT an offer, but rather only an offer to enter into negotiations or further discussions. There is an exception to this rule when an ad is sufficiently specific (with limiting language to protect the offeror) that reasonable people would assume it was a concrete (and therefore enforceable) offer to contract.

Reasoning: If an offer is made, the offeror is bound to a contract if the offer is accepted. The court here adopts an "objective" standard to determine when an advertisement might constitute a binding offer, finding that it doesn't matter what the parties themselves (or any one party) actually believed to be going on. The court will only find an offer if reasonable people would believe an offer was made. Hence, jokes don't count—but something intended to be a joke that reasonable people would take seriously *would* constitute an offer. Also, I guess that's why advertisements don't usually count (because most people would realize that a store could quickly get in over its head if everyone they were reaching responded, thinking they were entitled to the product advertised).

After you've looked over my notes and brief, use the space below to compare what I was thinking with your own thoughts. Could we have learned anything from each other? Would we have things we could discuss in class to help each of us understand what constitutes a sufficiently "firm" offer to support a claim that a contract is formed if the "offer" is accepted?

CHAPTER 12

Casebook Reading

A Summary

You are now at the end of Part II and have learned a lot about the behaviors you can adopt to be a powerful, exceptionally successful reader of law.

You've learned that expert law students, students who have experience and excel, share some common approaches to their assigned reading. Like experts in other fields, their expertise is not simply a matter of having more information at their fingertips—rather, their expertise is also the result of strategies they employ as they engage in the most fundamental of all law student activities: reading the law.

As you've read these preceding seven chapters, you've learned some things NOT to do:

(1) Don't read to impress your peers or to avoid embarrassment in class;

(2) Don't read to anticipate the answer to every question your professor might ask in a Socratic dialogue in class (unless there's a good chance you're the student who will be called on that day to help "carry the ball" for the class discussion);

(3) Don't highlight as your only means of taking notes;

(4) Don't write a brief as an end in itself;

(5) Don't let your feelings about a case keep you from understanding it;

(6) Don't read passively, expecting to be taught some "truth" by each case;

(7) Don't try to save time by reading only the cases, rather than the supporting background information and "Notes & Problems" provided by your casebook author;

(8) Don't read when you're too tired to engage effectively.

Happily, you've also learned many things that you SHOULD be doing as you read cases:

(1) Do engage in a dialogue with the judge who authored the case you're reading—interact with the judge in your mind to develop a rich understanding (within the context of your course) of what happened, what was decided, and why. Let the judge "talk" to you—and respond.

(2) Do read actively. Monitor yourself as you read. Develop a hypothesis about the case as you begin to read (based on cues within the casebook and the course, and based on your own past knowledge and experience). Check out whether your original hypothesis about your reading still makes sense as you read through the case. Look up words you don't understand. Track down the legal facts and the conflict facts. Keep an eye on the clock, saving enough time for other important study tasks. Make sure you have enough energy to keep reading (or take a break).

(3) Do know the purpose of your reading. Read because you want to understand the prevailing principles and rules that a court might follow to resolve conflicts in this area of law—especially if there is a high probability that these principles will be covered by your professor on an exam. Also, as a recurring theme, read because

you want to learn how lawyers use cases about past conflicts to figure out what courts will do with a present conflict.

(4) Do modify your reading purpose to match the time you have available, the likelihood that you'll be called on in class, and the relative importance of the material assigned. Always go to class with at least a cursory hypothesis about the meaning of a case (even if, in an emergency, that means asking someone else or using an outside study aid).

(5) Do pay attention to what you do and don't know about the subject of the case. Use your prior knowledge to accelerate your "visualization" of the action in the case and your understanding of the court's language and reasoning. Be flexible. Recognize that the court may not know (or may not accept) what you know.

(6) Do pay attention to what you do and don't know about legal reasoning. Especially in the first weeks of class, try to learn as much as you can about how courts function and how judges write opinions. You can learn these things through your reading and by paying careful attention in class. You want to have a lot of "ah-hah" moments about information that is foundational to the legal decision-making process. The more you learn about this kind of fundamental, foundational information, the more free you will be to fold that information into your thinking as you read subsequent cases—and the more accurate your hypotheses about the meaning of cases will become. You will also be able to read subsequent cases much more quickly, without sacrificing comprehension.

(7) Do use case-briefing as a tool to help you "chunk" information into useful clusters and to help you focus your reading quickly on the "who, what, when, where, and why" that is important to lawyers reading cases. Remember that a rule of law taken out of the context of the facts of a case is like the shell of a building with no infra-structure. It may look good, but it has little use.

(8) Do have an opinion about what you're reading (the author's style, the logic of the case, the morality of the result), and then go the extra mile to rephrase your opinion about the result of the case as a logic syllogism (see Chapter 3) that will make sense to lawyers. Remember, you could be wrong about the law (although you can't ever be wrong about your *opinion*). If you're wrong about the law, that's okay (as long as you eventually correct any erroneous assumptions). You'll learn more about what is *right* (and you'll hold on to it longer) if you ventured a guess in the first place than if you waited silently for the right answer to fall in your lap.

(9) Do be flexible as you read. Frequently review what you've read when new information raises questions about what you were thinking just a few pages or paragraphs back. Flip to the result of the case so you can anticipate where the court is going. Read selectively, focusing more attention on what is important and buzzing through unimportant text.

(10) Do rephrase difficult passages better in your own words, paying attention to which words in a case might be "magic" words with special meaning in this area of the law. Try writing paraphrases down in the margins of the case, particularly highlighting the "magic" words. If you can't explain a concept in your own words, you don't really understand it. Review your comments at the end of your reading and cluster your ideas in useful chunks that summarize the things you want to hold on to about this case.

(11) Do take advantage of what you know about memory. Don't clutter your short-term (working) memory with disconnected information. Instead, group information into manageable chunks and write things down to help you hold on to interim information (micropropositions) that will eventually help you reach meaningful conclusions (macropropositions). Use your written notes to help trigger your thoughts as you think about the sweeping issues raised by a case or cluster of cases.

(12) Do use the details contained in cases to lead you to the larger picture. Don't assume that the details ARE the larger picture. They're not. The larger picture emerges from the sweeping principles applied by courts wrestling with conflicts arising in any area of law. An understanding of these sweeping principles emerges from studying case after case, posing hypothetical after hypothetical, examining why the court went one way and not another this time—but, perhaps, not the last time.

You now have the inside scoop on casebook reading in law school. Be inquisitive. Be engaged. Be yourself. Think hard. Be open to new ideas. Take risks. Make mistakes. Learn. If you read with energy and enthusiasm, strategically taking advantage of the time available to you to develop a working hypothesis about each case to take to class, you will be well down the road to developing a more thorough understanding of the things you will need to reproduce on exams. That thorough understanding doesn't occur *just* from strong reading—but it sure can't occur *without* strong reading. Skilled legal thinking emerges as you invest in your reading, projecting what you already know onto this new material, and then carrying your best ideas about the reading to class for further exploration and refinement.

The common denominator in this learning process—the process that begins as you start to read, continues through your reading, and follows you into class—is you. Not the judges who wrote the opinions. Not your peers in class (who may, or may not, know the same things you do about a case). Not your professor. Reading—like thinking—is an intensely personal experience, unique to each of us.

Take the ideas presented in this section and make them your own. You'll be an expert before you know it.

PART III

Moving Beyond the Casebook

CHAPTER 13

Reading Statutes[1]

No matter how you slice it, reading statutes—especially for a beginner—is just not easy. Statutes aren't written like narrative text, in neat paragraphs with opening sentences and helpful transitional phrases that we have all, as experienced readers, come to expect in much of what we read. Rather, reading statutes requires you to learn about new reading cues and conventions.

Your ability to read statutes effectively and efficiently will improve as you become more familiar with the layout common to most statutes. Your ability to read statutes well will also improve as you learn more about the influence court decisions have on the meaning of statutes as courts resolve disputes that arise under them. Finally, your ability to read statutes well will improve with practice—especially if you aren't afraid to engage with the text, to be corrected by any and all experts you can find who are willing to help you interpret the text you are reading, and to learn from the mistakes you will make along the way.

---

1. I am heavily indebted to Jeff W. Hudson, Director of the Legislative Analysis Division for the North Carolina General Assembly, for sharing his considerable wisdom on this topic with me.

This chapter is divided into three sections that will teach you what you need to know to begin the lifelong task of developing exceptional statutory reading skills. In Section A below, you will learn about how most statutes are organized—in essence, what you can expect a statute to look like and what kinds of reading cues a typical statute might contain. In Section B below, you will learn about the outside factors that influence the meaning of a statute—how the decisions of courts, the practices in the field addressed by the statute, and the use of terms in other sections of the same or related statutes can determine the meaning of a word or phrase used in a statute. Finally, in Section C below, you will learn how the same reading skills that make for exceptional reading in general and for exceptional reading in case law can also help make you an exceptional reader of statutes.

A. How Statutes Are Often Organized

Modern rhetoric (language/communications) theory suggests that reading and writing are interactive processes. The writer of a text is writing to communicate information and ideas; the reader is attempting to understand what is being communicated.

At a highly academic level, there is much debate over whether the meaning of any text has a life of its own (that the reader should "take in") or whether the meaning of a text is itself the result of *interaction* between the writer's thoughts and words on the one hand, and the reader's ideas and reactions on the other.[2] All that we need to take from this challenging dialogue is the fact that the best writers write with an awareness of the purpose of their writing and of the audience that will read it. Similarly, the best readers read with an awareness of the author's perspective and intent as well as of the reader's own knowledge and limitations.

---

2. *See generally, e.g.*, MICHAEL PRESSLEY, READING INSTRUCTION THAT WORKS (4th ed. 2014) (exploring multiple theories of reading instruction).

The best statutes are written so that legislators, judges, and lay people can all understand them. The idea for legislation may be born from a grassroots movement (or initiated by one individual), then may be discussed initially in the halls of the legislature, and eventually proposed by an elected official who sponsors a bill through committee and onto the floor of the elected body that ultimately passes the statute.

In many cases, the responsibility for drafting the actual language of a statute in its original and final forms rests on individual legislative drafters who are employed for the express purpose of drafting and revising legislation so that it ultimately puts into action the plan of the legislators sponsoring it and the majority voting in favor of it. These drafting efforts are the result of much collaborative work, discussion, rewriting, editing, and thought.

B. The Challenge of Writing Clear Statutes

It helps to read statutes by thinking of them first as a writing challenge. Most legislative acts manage or regulate complex behavior. Clarity before a wide and varied audience is critical. As a result of this need to take what is inherently complex and make it as simple and orderly as possible, today's statutes that make more than a simple one-sentence or one-paragraph statement are most often written in outline form, with each section of the outline covering one distinct part of the legislation and all sections together comprising a coherent whole.[3]

Following traditional outline format, statutes today often include titles for all main headings to help the reader anticipate what is contained

3. Formatting cues are indispensable reading aids where statutes and other legislative actions are involved. The benefits of that structure can get lost easily when you read those same materials on a screen where we have the ability to move around quickly within a long piece of legislation or a complex set of administrative regulations. To read statutes and regulations effectively on a screen, it's critical to stay tuned into the structural cues that the drafters supplied in the original format. Chapter 15 offers more discussion about on-screen reading.

in that section. Large sections are frequently subdivided, in outline form, into component parts. These subdivisions may contain clarifying titles or headings as well. These outline headings and subheadings will often appear at the beginning of a chapter or act in a kind of Table of Contents and are a very useful tool to help the reader get an overview for the act as a whole. They can also help a reader isolate which sections of an act might be the best to read in detail, given the reader's specific reading purpose.

C. What's Up with All Those Lists?

Within the sections and subsections of a typical statute, information that can be chunked or grouped into coherent clusters are often written as a tabulation. A tabulation is a writing tool that helps the author save space and avoid potential confusion by beginning a list with a common lead-in (root) phrase and bulleting the related concepts beneath it. For example:

When I go to the store, I will buy:

(a) apples;

(b) oranges; and

(c) other fruit.

When reading a bulleted phrase included in a tabulation, you should always read it as its own sentence, which will always begin with the lead-in phrase at the beginning of the list. Each phrase, when read together with the preceding lead-in phrase, will make its own grammatically correct sentence (if the statute's author has written the tabulation correctly). Thus, here, there are actually three sentences: "When I go to the store, I will buy apples. When I go to the store, I will also by oranges. When I go to the store, I will buy other fruit, too."

In a tabulated list, the connecting phrase just before the end of the tabulated list is critical to the meaning of the entire tabulation. Thus, if the connecting phrase in the example above had been "or" (instead of "and"), my three sentences would have been very different: "When I go to the store, I might buy some apples. Alternatively, when I go to the store, I might buy some oranges. On the other hand, when I go to the store, I could end up buying some other fruit. I know I will buy one of the three."

When listing information, legislative drafters must also be careful about whether they are listing illustrations that leave the door open for other examples or setting down an exclusive list of all possibilities. For example, if a legislature passes a bill giving "all teachers (practice teachers, certified teachers, part-time teachers, and substitute teachers)" an extra week of vacation, does a teacher's aid get the extra week of vacation? Arguments could be made both ways. One argument would be that the list was "exclusive" and, because teacher's aids weren't expressly included on the list, they are expressly excluded from getting the extra week's vacation. On the other hand, it might be that the list was only illustrative and if a teacher's aid is considered a teacher for other purposes within the act or in the school, then he or she could start packing for an extra week at the beach.

When faced with the question of whether a list is inclusive or illustrative, look for cue words such as "for example" or "and similar employees" to help clarify the meaning of the statute. What if the drafter in the example above had written, "all teachers, including but not limited to practice teachers, certified teachers, part-time teachers, and substitute teachers" have an extra week of vacation? Would the teacher's aid now have a stronger argument that he or she was entitled to the extra time off?

Just as the exact word used to connect a list is important and the inclusive or exclusive nature of a list matters, words indicating permission to act or not act versus a mandate (requirement) to act or not act are critical to an accurate understanding of the meaning of a statute. When reading statutes, pay careful attention to key words such as "may" or "must"; "shall" or "can"; "is permitted to" or "is required to." Consider, for example, the difference between a statement like "the judge may consider the income of the parties" and a statement like "the judge must consider the income of the parties." In the first instance, a judge's decision NOT to consider the parties' income is okay (although the judge's decision TO consider the income would be okay, too). In the second instance, a judge's decision not to consider the parties' income would be a direct violation of the statute.

D. Reading Related Statutes Together, Like a Family

Statutes are part of a larger whole and must be read in context, not in isolation. In a sense, all statutes within any jurisdiction are part of the whole codified body of law for that jurisdiction. More commonly, however, individual statutes are part of a related chapter or act and should be read within the context of that act. Thus, a purpose section appearing at the beginning of a large act states the purpose for all subsections of the act as well. Similarly, a definitions section for an act covers the terms used within all subsections of the act (unless there's language someplace in a subsection that would cause you to believe that those general definitions don't apply there).

Cross-references to sections or acts outside of the statute you are reading, or to other subsections within the act you are reading, or to administrative regulations implementing parts of the act you are reading, are critical cues to meaning. They are like a bright yellow caution flag that you should pay attention to. As one legislative drafter put it, "cross-references are to be ignored at your peril." If you think again about the interaction between author and reader, you'll see why a cross-reference within a statute is such a big deal. For a drafter (the author) to include it requires the drafter to ensure that the reference and cite are absolutely accurate and that any future changes to the code involving the cross-referenced section will be accurately reflected. Thus, a legislative drafter would only go to the trouble of referring to another section if such a cross-reference was critical to a complete understanding of the statute at hand.

E. What Does "Notwithstanding" Mean?

Finally, there is one term that appears frequently enough in statutes, but rarely anyplace else, to warrant your attention. If you see the word "notwithstanding" as you read a statute, slow down and pay attention. "Notwithstanding," in effect, means that whatever immediately follows that word is about to be trumped by the action supported in the rest of the sentence. For example:

> "Notwithstanding the other requirements or restrictions concerning corporal punishment listed in this Act, teachers may corporally punish students in an emergency situation."

This phrase (which would throw off most beginning legal readers) means: "Even though teachers have to do certain things under this act before they can corporally punish students under most circumstances, all those requirements are thrown out the window in an emergency situation. In an emergency, teachers may corporally punish students." The general rule encapsulated within the "notwithstanding" clause is trumped by the more specific rule stated in the phrase that follows.

Here's another example:

> "Notwithstanding her duty to mow the lawn on Saturdays, Sally can go to the fair on Saturday once a year without mowing the lawn."

In statutory analysis terms, that phrase would mean: "Even though Sally usually has to mow the lawn on Saturday [the phrase encapsulated in the "notwithstanding" clause], she can go to the fair once a year on Saturday without mowing the lawn [the condition that trumps the general Saturday lawn-mowing responsibility].

F. Outside Influences That Reach In and Grab the Statute's Text

As if life weren't complicated enough, merely deciphering the literal meaning of a statute (challenging as that is) is not enough to ensure complete understanding. As with the common law, the flat words of a legislative rule only develop rich meaning in the context of their impact on people's lives. No matter how well drafted, statutes come face to face with unanticipated hidden ambiguities when they are applied to real-life settings.

Imagine the words of an act as if they were displayed in lights on a T.V. quiz show game board or marquee, like on Wheel of Fortune or The Price is Right. As the realities of life interface with the legislative act, certain words light up (come to life), as if touched by the game show host, while others are unaffected. The words that "light up" under specific fact scenarios have special importance only because they are subject to more than one meaning and the choice of meaning dictates the outcome of the conflict that lit the word up in the first place.

For example, let's say we have a rule that says: "Student drivers under the age of seventeen may not drive after dark unless accompanied by a parent." That rule seems clear enough on its face. Now, let's say that John is a student driver who is sixteen. The sun has set and it is after dark. He is driving with a foster parent. Is John allowed to drive? Which word from the rule would "light up" on my quiz show marquee?

The answer to John's question is going to lie in the definition of "parent" (and, hence, I imagine my quiz show board lighting up behind the word "parent"). If the legislature wanted student drivers to be able to drive with foster parents, then John is in compliance with the statute. What if, instead, the facts were different. What if John is a student driver who is under the age of 17 and he is driving alone. It is summer and just about dusk. Some drivers have their lights on, but others do not. The street lights are not yet on. Is John allowed to drive? In this case, the answer to John's question will turn on whether it is "after dark" and, in my mind, the quiz show marquee would light up behind the phrase, “after dark.” The answer to John’s question is going to lie in a determination of what the legislature meant by “after dark.”

G. How Courts Clarify a Statute’s Meaning: The Rules of Statutory Construction

Where a word or phrase in a statute is ambiguous as applied to a specific conflict before a court, the court’s role is to clarify the statute’s meaning. While it is the legislature’s responsibility to draft and pass legislation, it is the responsibility of the courts to interpret and apply the statutes to actual cases (like John’s, above).

In interpreting the meaning of a text, the court’s task is to determine what the legislature *would have intended* the outcome to be when it passed the act. The court is definitely not supposed to substitute its own judgment for that of the legislature. Rather, the court is to determine only the intent of the legislature. Would the legislature have meant for John to be restricted from driving with the foster parent? Would the legislature have meant for John to be restricted from driving at dusk? Such questions, of course, never come up unless someone brings an action in court.[4]

The court determines the legislative intent by following well-established conventions and some common law rules of statutory construction. One of the dominant rules courts follow is that the “plain language” of a statute dictates its meaning. Where there is no ambiguity, there is no room for interpretation. In some jurisdictions, courts can also look to evidence of “legislative history” (records of committee hearings, public hearings, etc.) to determine the spin the legislature intended for a term or phrase.

---

4. There are a few courts that will, on occasion, issue “advisory” opinions. Similarly, some state Attorney General’s offices will issue “advisory” opinions from time to time. For the most part, however, precedent evolves as disputes between parties in controversy are resolved in courts of law.

Evidence of the purpose of the statute can influence a court as well. For example, a purpose section within a statute can clarify what would be the most rational reading of an ambiguous term (where one reading would support the statute's purpose and another would defeat or subvert it). Similarly, in the absence of a purpose section, legislative history can clarify the legislature's purpose in drafting an act. Also, statutes occasionally are followed by "official comments" added by the committee that developed the statute. These comments are not part of the statute itself (they are not "law"), but are included to help others understand what the drafters intended.

One of the things that is ironic about rules of construction is that there are so many that they often seem to contradict one another. For example, some courts have determined that a general statement within an act is trumped by a more concrete, specific statement. On the other hand, specific listings of items can be seen as illustrative of the more general statement (as in the example of our teacher's aide on page 219) and therefore not empowered with the ability to trump the general statement. Other general rules of statutory construction include the following:

- Statutes must be constitutional to stay in force. Therefore, where there is a constitutional or unconstitutional interpretation of an ambiguous term, the statute should be interpreted in a way that is consistent with the constitution;
- Where one reading of an ambiguous term leads to a rational result and another to an irrational result, the rational result should be chosen;
- If a statute contradicts common law, it should be read narrowly to avoid unnecessary conflict between the two;
- Parts of an act should be read together, with the expectation that any one section will be consistent with the others;
- If a statute contains punitive provisions, it should be read narrowly to avoid punishing people or prohibiting acts not clearly included.

Finally, courts may look to common practices within a discipline to determine the meaning of a term within a statute. Thus, if a statute is regulating the food industry and the food industry has a widely understood meaning for the term "flour," the court will assume that is the meaning intended by the legislature when it incorporated the word "flour" in a statute regulating the food industry. Similarly, the courts can look to parallel statutes from other jurisdictions to determine what other meanings have been attributed to a word or phrase in that jurisdiction. Such definitions give the court in this jurisdiction something to consider, but are not determinative of this court's ultimate decision about the meaning of a word or phrase in this jurisdiction.

Once an appellate court has determined the meaning of the text of a statute under circumstances raised by a case that has been brought up on appeal, that meaning sticks (it becomes precedent for subsequent decisions). That word or phrase is no longer ambiguous within that jurisdiction—at least not under similar facts.

Let's look again at John's case. Let's say John had received a citation for driving with a foster parent because a policeman who stopped him did not believe the foster parent was a "parent" within the meaning of the statute. Instead of paying a fine, John and his foster parents took his case to court. The trial judge agreed with the policeman and revoked John's license. John then appealed to the state Supreme Court. At the state Supreme Court level, the court applied the canon of construction that says, "where there's an ambiguous term involving punishment, the statute should be read narrowly to avoid restricting behavior that was not intended to be restricted." The court concluded that John's foster parent was, indeed, a "parent" within the meaning of the statute and reinstated John's license. Now, Margaret has been stopped in a nearby county for driving after dark with her foster mother in the car. There would be no question at this point that Margaret was in compliance with the statute when she drove after dark accompanied by her foster mother. The policeman would have no grounds to cite her and the district court, if things went that far, would dismiss the case.

H. Putting It All Together

When you're reading statutes, then, it is not enough to read just the words of the statute itself—although making sense of the statute's structure and content is a necessary first step in understanding it. You have to also look to case law that may have applied or interpreted the statute to see if there have been any interpretations that clarify the meaning of terms used by the legislature.[5] Similarly, you have to look not only at the statutory section or subsection you are reading, but at related sections and subsections, to see if there are any clues within other sections as to the meaning of terms or phrases when an act is read, as it must be, as a whole.

Finally, if you are reading a statute because you have a real or hypothetical fact scenario in front of you and you need to determine how the statute would be applied, you have to look for special words that may be triggered by the facts before you. If those words have not yet been clarified, you would look to legislative history, to similar statutes in other jurisdictions, or to other sections within the Act to begin to hypothesize how a court might interpret that word or term if faced with your scenario.

I. Statutory Reading Skills with a Big Payoff (E.M.P. O.W.E.R. Works Here, Too)

As with all expert reading, reading of statutes requires you to be able to develop a hypothesis about what the statute probably means. As you read further and find out more about a statute, you may discover that your initial hypothesis is right, or you may find that it is wrong. To develop and modify

---

5. When law students learn to do legal research, they are exposed to "annotated" statutes. Annotated statutes are collections of statutes in which the publisher includes synopses (usually a paragraph summary) of important cases that have applied or interpreted the statute. When using annotated statutes, legal researchers need to be careful to read the cases themselves, rather than relying only on the editor's synopsis of the case, but having the annotations at hand is a good place to start.

your hypothesis, you have to be able to read carefully and closely, paying attention to the drafting conventions set out in Section I of this chapter. You also have to understand the jurisprudential context within which statutes exist, as discussed in Section II of this chapter. Finally, a rich and deep understanding of a statute's meaning is dependent on your willingness to apply strong reading skills to test the outer boundaries of the words that comprise the statute. These outer boundaries can only be tested as individual cases arise (or are imagined or anticipated) that bring into focus conflicting interpretations of the words that comprise the statute itself.

The same reading principles that make for "empowered" reading of cases (explored in Part II of this book) make for powerful reading of statutes as well. To review, these are the seven interactive strategies that you can choose among as you read:

(1) [E]: engaging with energy;
(2) [M]: monitoring your reading and reading for the main idea;
(3) [P]: reading with a clear purpose;
(4) [O]: getting oriented and owning your incoming knowledge;
(5) [W]: knowing the five Ws (the literal content of the statute);
(6) [E]: evaluating the text and impact of the statute; and
(7) [R]: reviewing, rephrasing, and recording notes as you work your way through the statute. As you learn to read statutes effectively and efficiently, you can apply these seven skills as follows:

(1) Read with Energy and Engage with the Text: Think of statutory reading as an investigation or an independent study project. How much can you learn within the four walls of the statute—can you unravel the meaning of the text structure itself? Having successfully taught yourself what the plain language says, can you find latent or patent ambiguities within the text that can be resolved by reading outside the document or by applying canons of construction in the way an appellate court might do?

(2) Monitor Your Reading To Make Sure Your Ideas Are Continuing to Make Sense: Use every reading cue available to you to try to figure out where you're going with your interpretation of the meaning of the statute. The main idea of the reading will shift, depending on the purpose of your reading, and you should be developing a hypothesis about the main idea of the text in light of your purpose as you read. For example, if I'm trying to figure out whether John can drive with his foster parent after dark, the main idea I'm looking for is: "what constitutes a parent?" I may start with the hypothesis that a foster parent, while guardian of the child, is probably endowed with the same rights of supervision as a natural parent. I'll test that hypothesis as I continue to read and as I do more research. If I see a subdivision heading in the act that says something like: "**'Parent' Defined**," I would move quickly to that subdivision of the statute. If "parent" is not defined within the statute, then I'll need to do more research to clarify that term.

(3) Read with a Purpose: Reading never takes place in a vacuum, and effective reading requires the reader to grasp his or her purpose at the conscious level. If I'm reading out of curiosity because I just read an interesting article in the newspaper about John's situation, my main purpose and my strategies would be dramatically different than if I was preparing to represent John at a hearing. The time available for a task markedly effects strategy as well, and strong readers know how much time they have to read and adjust their strategies accordingly.

(4) Get Oriented and Own Your Prior Knowledge: If I don't know much about the regulation of driving, I will want to look over the larger act that this subsection about student drivers is in, just to get a sense of what powers of regulation the government is exercising. If I have a background in foster care, I need to associate my prior experiences with my reading, putting this statute in the context of what I know about other rights and responsibilities foster parents may have. In the spirit of monitoring my reading, I need to also entertain the thought that MY experiences with foster parenting may not generalize to this particular regulation. I need to have some ideas, but I need to be prepared to be surprised. If I don't know anything at all about

foster care and I am surprised by what I am reading, I may want to do some additional reading in other sections of the legislative code or in the common law to see if my present reading of the statute makes sense in light of how foster parents are perceived by the state.

(5) Know the 5 Ws (who, what, when, where, why): In reading statutes, knowing the 5 Ws boils down to understanding the plain language of the statute itself. As discussed in Section I of this chapter, deciphering the plain meaning of complex legislation is not easy. Some of the reading cues you can use to help your comprehension include:

- (a) heading and subheading titles;
- (b) the date the statute was passed (the first date in parentheses at the end of a piece of legislation tells you the date the statute was originally passed; all other dates are dates of amendments. If a statute is old, the language may be unexpected and difficult to understand—especially if you don't put the language in its correct context);
- (c) tabulations;
- (d) definitions sections;
- (e) purpose sections;
- (f) use of critical terms such as connecting words (and, or) and terms of permission or mandate (may, shall, can, must).

(6) Evaluate what you're reading: As with the common law, it's not enough to read statutes passively, assuming they make sense on their face. Rather, exceptional lawyers and law students think about the value of what they're reading. Is the statute well written? Are parts of it confusing (and frustrating to read)? Is the statute going to do what the drafters intended? Did they miss something? Should the statute be amended? Has the statute been misunderstood by the courts?

(7) Review, record notes, rephrase to improve understanding: Statutes, especially older statutes, are not always easy to understand. Parsing out (de-

ciphering) the meaning of statutes requires careful, methodical thinking. Many experienced law students and lawyers find it helpful to rephrase arcane language so it makes sense. Similarly, if a number of ideas are included in one large (incomprehensible) sentence or grouped randomly in a large paragraph, consider circling the parts that could be chunked rationally together and numbering them in an order that makes sense. Alternatively, take out a piece of paper or open your computer and rewrite the statute in outline form using tabulations. Although the particular words used in a statute are critical, words that fail to convey meaning adequately need to be questioned and explored. If you're confused, try to develop a hypothesis about the statute's possible meaning by rephrasing or reorganizing the statute in words that make more sense to you. Be sure, though, that you don't adopt a synonym carelessly, causing you to miss the actual intent of the statute's drafters.

There is nothing in any written statute that can't, eventually, be understood. There is plenty in every statute that can be misunderstood or distorted if read carelessly, too quickly, or naively. The joy and challenge of reading statutes is the same as the joy and challenge of reading cases: the more of yourself you invest in the reading process, and the more open you are to making mistakes and learning from others, the more rewards you will reap.

PRACTICE EXERCISES

These exercises give you the opportunity to practice reading an actual state statute about special education requirements for school-aged children. Remember that you can visit caplaw.com/rll to see some of the responses I thought about as I wrote these practice exercise questions.

1. The excerpt on the next page is from North Carolina General Statute sec. 115C-140.1(a), a statute that appears in North Carolina's Special Education legislation. It is a very difficult statute to read and understand, at least in part because of the long sentences included in the statute and the lack of tabulation.

Try to read this statute exactly as it appears, looking for answers to the following three concrete questions as you read:

(a) A school-aged child whose parents both reside in Durham County has been placed temporarily in a special in-patient program sponsored by the University of North Carolina Hospitals in Orange County. She has left her Durham County school, where she was receiving special services for a visual impairment. What entity is legally responsible for the cost of that child's public education?

(b) Does any other entity or government agency have an obligation to reimburse all or part of those costs to the agency you identified in answer to (a) above? If so, what portion of the costs is this second agency responsible for?

(c) Is the entity that is responsible for the child's free public education while in a group home also responsible for the costs of her care and maintenance?

§ 115C-140.1. Cost of education of children in group homes, foster homes, etc.

Notwithstanding the provisions of any other statute and without regard for the place of domicile of a parent or guardian, the cost of a free appropriate public education for a child with disabilities who is placed in or assigned to a group home or foster home, pursuant to State and federal law, shall be borne by the local board of education in which the group home or foster home is located. However, the local school administrative unit in which a child is domiciled shall transfer to the local school administrative unit in which the institution is located an amount equal to the actual local cost in excess of State and federal funding required to educate that child in the local school administrative unit for the fiscal year after all State and federal funding has been exhausted.

2. On a scale of 1–10, with 10 being the most difficult, how difficult was it to find the answers to these questions? _____

3. On a scale of 1–10, with 10 being the most confident, how confident are you that you have the right answer to these questions? _____

4. Did you have any emotional reactions as you read this statute?

5. Often rewriting a cumbersome statute in simpler form can make a world of difference to your understanding of it, and is well worth the time it takes to do so. I have rewritten N.C. Gen. Stat. sec. 115C-140.1(a) in a more

straightforward way below. Read the statute in its new form, looking for answers to the same questions you responded to above.

Sec. 115C-140.1. Cost of education of children in group homes, foster homes, etc.

Despite any other statutes and regardless of a parent or guardian's place of domicile, the cost of a free public education for a child with special needs who is placed under state or federal law in: (i) a group home, (ii) a foster home, or (iii) a similar facility shall be borne by the local board of education in which that foster home or group facility is located. The local school administrative unit where the child is "domiciled" must reimburse the local board of education where the facility is located for any expenses that local board of education incurs beyond those paid by State and federal funding. The local board of education where the facility is located is not responsible for any care and maintenance costs of the child with special needs.

(a) A school-aged child whose parents both reside in Durham County has been placed temporarily in a special in-patient program sponsored by the University of North Carolina Hospitals in Orange County. She has left her Durham County school, where she was receiving special services for a visual impairment. What entity is legally responsible for the cost of that child's public education?

(b) Does any other entity or government agency have an obligation to reimburse all or part of those costs to the agency you identified in answer to (a) above? If so, what portion of the costs is this second agency responsible for?

(c) Is the entity that is responsible for the child's free public education while in a group home also responsible for the costs of her care and maintenance?

6. Most readers would find this second version of the statute easier to read. Why do you think that is? Can you see other ways you could improve upon this statute to make it even easier to understand?

7. Can you tell by the description provided concerning this child's temporary placement whether her situation is covered by this statute? What additional information would you want to have so you could make that decision?

8. If you knew of a recent N.C. Supreme Court case that had held that an *out*-patient program sponsored by a hospital was not a "group home" within the meaning of this statute, how would that influence your conclusions about who is responsible for this girl's appropriate public education expenses? What words would "light up" for you in this statute as you evaluated its meaning as applied to this girl's educational expenses?

CHAPTER 14

Reading Cases Outside of Casebooks

Reading cases outside the protective confines of a casebook is even more complicated than reading cases within a casebook. The cases in your casebook were carefully pre-selected by your casebook author (an expert) because the author thought they would help you understand something important about a distinct area of law. When you read a case in a casebook, you can rest assured that it is there for a reason—you may not be able to figure out what that reason is at first, and the case (despite editing) may still be difficult to decipher, but each case has had the advantage of plenty of pre-working by a leading authority in the field.

In contrast, when lawyers read cases outside a casebook in practice (or when law students read cases outside a casebook for a legal writing class, a volunteer project, or a summer job), there is no editor helping select useful cases or editing out portions of a case that are not on point. Rather, lawyers have to do more of this work for themselves. To do so effectively requires the use of every one of the advanced reading skills discussed throughout this book.[1]

1. The ability to find applicable law, read it accurately and creatively, and write about it with precision are such critical skills that the American Bar Association requires American law schools to offer mandatory introductory and advanced courses in these areas as a component of accreditation.

A. Background Information You'll Want to Know

Cases outside of casebooks look a little different than they do within the casebooks. The captions (case name, reporter volume and page, court, and date) you have seen at the beginning of cases in your casebooks come from the actual books you will be reading if you are reading from a hard copy printed in a reporter.[2] As has been the tradition in the American legal system for centuries, each jurisdiction has an official "reporter" (collection of cases) in which the court publishes, in chronological order, every case it decides. These reporters are numbered consecutively by volume so that the cases published in them can be easily retrieved by anyone with access to a law library. Today, you can also find almost any published case online.[3]

Below the caption of a case (which also appears as a running header on subsequent pages of the same case), you will often find some editorial tools supplied by the reporter's publisher that can help you skim a case. It's important to note that if you're reading a case online, depending on the company offering the case, these editorial tools may or may not be available.

Where editorial tools are available, they will have varying degrees of usefulness to you, depending on why you're reading the case in the first place. If you use these editorial tools incorrectly, you risk being misled and drawing erroneous conclusions about the case. If you use them correctly, they are an invaluable way to organize your research of a legal question and to save yourself time.

Among the primary editorial tools that can save a legal reader time are "headnotes." A "headnote" is a summary of a key legal point covered in the opinion. Headnotes are categorized and numbered by legal issue (for example, the first headnote in a given opinion might be "Criminal Law sec. 99—comments of trial court"). A short discussion (probably only one or two sentences in length, often quoting directly from the case) appears

---

2. Reporters have been briefly described earlier in Chapter 1 and Chapter 2 of this book. *See supra* Chapter 1, note 5; Chapter 2, notes 1 and 2.

3. Chapter 15, Reading on a Screen, will discuss in further depth how to read cases online.

directly below the headnote number and its caption. This short discussion summarizes (very briefly) what this case says about the headnote topics that the publisher has assigned to the case.

Headnotes, however helpful, should be used with caution and only as an aid to getting oriented, not as a substitute for careful reading of the case itself. Headnotes are not written by the court that wrote the opinion. They are editorial tools added by the publisher. Hence, they are not "law" and cannot be relied on as a statement or summary of law. Moreover, as you have learned in Part II of this book, an experienced legal reader understands that reading an excerpt of a case out of the context of the case as a whole can lead to misconceptions and misreadings. Used with caution, however, headnotes can speed up reading and increase efficiency.

If you are reading cases online using one of the primary paid services that allow you to conduct a document search, you may be able to go quickly to the highlighted portions of an opinion that reflect the search terms you used to find the case online. Using these highlighted words appropriately can speed up your reading by helping you locate where the exact language is that reflects the legal question you are engaged in exploring. The danger of over-using such highlighted text is that the reader can be tempted to "cut and paste" that language from an opinion without becoming engaged with or responsive to the opinion in its richer context. Isolating mere words, while a tempting shortcut, would result in a superficial (and, even worse, downright erroneous) understanding of the case.

Unlike most edited cases in casebooks, unedited cases also contain the names of the attorneys (and firms) on record as well as the names of all judges who helped decide the case. The name of the judge who wrote the opinion (as well as any judges who wrote separate concurring decisions or dissents) appears at the beginning of each opinion.

When law students read cases in a casebook, information about the judges or attorneys is often not relevant to the main purpose of their reading. Practicing attorneys, however, frequently find that they recognize the firms involved in a case or even the names of individual attorneys of record. Similarly, they may know judges or know the reputations of judges involved in the decisions. These types of facts provide important contextual information that can help those lawyers visualize a case more vividly, understand its legal content more accurately, and make wise decisions about its precedential value.

Despite these editorial tools, unedited cases found in reporters are often more challenging to read than are the carefully edited cases included in most casebooks. In an unedited case, multiple issues are likely to have been brought up on appeal. For example, it is perfectly legitimate to argue a case "in the alternative," which means if one theory for why your party should win doesn't work, you want the court to consider another theory. As a result, the issue you may be primarily interested in might be difficult to find among the confusing array of other issues discussed in the case.

The good news, however, is that practicing lawyers generally know what jurisdiction they are working in when exploring an area of law, which means there are fewer rules and principles to uncover—and far less chance of finding irreconcilable results or contradictory rules. In contrast, cases in your casebook (with the exception of U.S. Constitutional Law) have been taken from random state's jurisdictions (partly to get you to think about all the possible rules a court might rationally adopt as precedent). In real life, however, courts are not free to adopt whatever rational rule intrigues them. Rather, they are bound by the doctrine of stare decisis to follow the precedent (decisions) that have been decided by higher courts within that jurisdiction in the past.

Occasionally, for example when a jurisdiction is silent on an issue or when a lawyer wants to challenge the court to change its position on an issue or convince a court *not* to change its position, a lawyer might need to read cases outside of the jurisdiction handling the present conflict. Cases from outside jurisdictions, especially the reasoning in those cases, can influence another jurisdiction—but such outside precedent is not binding. For the most part, the lawyer's reading task will be to figure out what's going on only within the confines of a particular jurisdiction—a much simpler task than learning all the possible perspectives presented in a (jurisdiction-free) casebook.

Policy issues take on a more concrete quality when the jurisdiction is real and known. Rather than being esoteric points of classroom discussion, the real-life policy issues surrounding an area of law in the past and following it into the present are important pieces of personal knowledge that a well-informed attorney can bring to the reading process as he or she engages with the text. Dicta—where policy discussion is often found—can become significant if the lawyer's purpose in reading is to understand the policy behind a court's decision.

Because the present law builds on the principles established in even the earliest cases, experienced lawyers do not dismiss early opinions. Older cases are more challenging to read and more challenging to relate to present-day facts, but set out principles that provide the bedrock upon which all other related cases rest. Experienced legal readers understand that these principles, as applied in case after case over decades and sometimes even centuries, are critical to an accurate and rich understanding of the law today.

B. Reading Skills to Help You Read Unedited Cases Effectively (E.M.P.O.W.E.R. Works Here, Too)

The seven "empowering" reading skills explored in Part II of this book can also help you successfully manage the challenges of reading cases outside of casebooks.

(1) Engage with Energy

It takes a brave soul, and a confident intellect, to engage in a mental debate with the authors of appellate opinions. These authors are, after all, judges and justices, many of whom carry historical status and others of whom may well be in a position to decide the outcome of the lawyer's next case. If a lawyer lacks the intellectual confidence and the courage to engage, reading legal cases can never move beyond the superficial—relegating the reading and thinking to a ministerial function. The best such a timid lawyer could hope to do is to decode the information in a case rather than to interact with the information in the opinion to construct new arguments and new understandings from it.

In addition to having the intellectual courage to engage with an opinion, lawyers who are serious about reading cases effectively have to put aside outside distractions, roll up their sleeves, and take the time to read deeply and thoughtfully. Reading well is not the type of task that can be done alongside other tasks. You can't read a case thoroughly and creatively while also talking on the phone, checking email, or listening to a partner discuss trial strategy. Reading law in a deeply meaningful way requires your undivided attention. It also requires a commitment not to cut corners. Jumping from headnote to headnote in reporters, or from highlighted quote to highlighted quote online, is skimming—not reading—and should be reserved only for times when you consciously decide that skimming will serve your purposes well.

(2) Monitor Your Reading and Read for the Main Idea

Speculation is a key part of good reading in any genre. Reading legal cases as a practitioner is no exception. You are not reading merely to learn information the court is disseminating. You are reading to step inside the world that existed when the decision was made, and to understand from multiple perspectives exactly what occurred. You will begin to understand a case at a richer and deeper level as you move from facts, to the procedural history, through dicta, and to the holding—and back again. As you read, you'll move forward and backwards, guessing at what the court might do, guessing at the court's reasoning, and then—if you're monitoring your reading and thinking well—you'll revise your thoughts as the picture of this case gradually comes into focus.

(3) Read with a Conscious Purpose

Outside of a pure academic inquiry (for example, when a scholar writes a law review article), lawyers generally read cases for one of two reasons: (1) they may be exploring a new area of law, learning a new vocabulary and way of thinking about the rights and responsibilities recognized by courts in this domain; or (2) they may be reading carefully selected cases in great detail in an effort to develop an argument that will support an outcome they desire—or in an effort to anticipate an argument that an opposing party might make in support of an outcome that party desires. As lawyers gain enough experience to become expert readers and practitioners, they often read for both purposes (gathering information and developing strategic arguments) almost simultaneously. Identifying the reading purpose allows the lawyer to consciously choose reading strategies that fit the task at hand.

(4) Get Oriented and Own Your Prior Knowledge

Part of effective reading in the practice of law includes the ability to quickly gain an overview of each case read, and an overview of an area of law as a whole. Familiarity with the editorial cues, such as headnotes and highlighted text, available in hard copy and online speeds up reading. By the same token, proficient readers know that headnotes and highlighted text are the functional equivalent of road signs on a trip—they make the trip easier, but they are not the trip itself.

Headnotes and highlighted text are useful if your reading purpose is to pick up a general vocabulary or to identify cases that warrant a deeper reading. If your reading purpose is to develop a rich understanding of the deeper meaning of that vocabulary and to understand, in living color, actions the court has taken, there is no substitute for taking the time to read the case in its entirety—paying careful attention to the court's treatment of the question of law you are examining. Relying on editor's cues alone (tempting as it is) will undermine your success and mire your reading (and results) in mediocrity.

In addition to getting oriented, knowing what you do know and knowing what you don't yet know are the mark of an expert reader. You will never come to a case with a completely empty mind. Active engagement with the text requires you to think consciously about what you know and the assumptions you may be making and to interact with the author of the case as you make meaning of the court's decision. As you interact with the text, if your brain is engaged, you will also identify questions that will require further reading, further thought, further study.

Finally, it's important to remember that practicing lawyers, just like law students, are not automatons. Lawyers, like all people, have past personal experiences, values, and associations that create feelings—sometimes strong feelings—on many topics. Reading theorists, and all social psychologists, know that emotions intermingle with intellect, causing us to read selectively or with bias. As you read cases in reporters, be alert to the fact that many of the conflicts reflected in appellate opinions may have personal associations for you that can enhance or interfere with your understanding of the legal issues in the case. It is equally important to remember that all cases involve real people with real problems—and that these problems and the people who experienced them deserve our respect as we read.

(5) Know the 5 Ws (Who, What, When, Where, Why)

Just like reading cases in casebooks, finding the "action" in a case that is unedited becomes much easier with time and practice. If you've had experience reading cases in a casebook by the time you read your first unedited case, you will find it's fairly easy to understand the facts of the case and to identify the legal question before the court that is relevant to the legal question you or your client may be investigating.

What becomes more difficult in an unedited case is identification of the procedural history of a case. Identification of procedural history becomes more difficult precisely because it becomes more important at this level of reading. In class, you need to identify the procedural history mostly as a way of getting oriented to the case so you can better visualize the legal facts and the conflict facts. Armed with this knowledge, your discussion in class is better informed and your understanding of the rule that emerges from the case is easier to develop.

In the world of practitioners, however, procedural history takes on critical (really, earth-shattering) importance because the role of the appellate court in hearing the case on appeal is tied directly to what happened to the case below. The details of the possible ways that a case could end up in an appellate court are the subject of weeks, if not months, of heavy reading, thinking, and discussion in first-year Civil Procedure and legal writing classes. It is beyond the scope of this chapter to anticipate those lessons, or to review them if they're in your past. What is important, however, is to recognize that the procedural posture of a case on appeal is an aspect of every case that cannot be ignored if you want to understand the case in any depth.

Take, for example, the real-life case of *Hoffman v. Clinic Hospital*,[4] a North Carolina Supreme Court case that was decided in 1938. In that case, a woman was hospitalized for medical care. When her treatment was finished, she was released by her physicians. A hospital administrator came to her room as she was packing to leave and told her that she could not leave until she paid her bill. She stayed—apparently for several days. Finally, she mustered the courage to leave without paying her bill, but later sued the hospital for false imprisonment.

When her complaint was filed, the hospital asked the trial court below to dismiss the case, reasoning that she had no legal basis to sue for false imprisonment. The trial court agreed with the hospital and dismissed her case. She appealed. On appeal, the North Carolina Supreme Court also agreed with the hospital, affirming the trial court's decision to grant the motion to dismiss. In reaching this result, the court found that a successful suit for false imprisonment requires proof that if a plaintiff was kept where she did not want to be without actual physical restraint, she had to have been afraid that she would have been harmed if she had tried to leave—and, moreover, the court said that a *reasonable person* in the same situation would have had to have been afraid.

Looking at the facts of the plaintiff's case, the court noted that the only evidence Ms. Hoffman put forward was that she, personally, was afraid to leave. The court found that no rational jury could have found that a reasonable person would have been afraid to leave just because a hospital administrator said to wait until the bill was paid. Therefore, the court concluded (as a matter of law) that she had failed to present a case for false imprisonment.

Whether you do or don't agree with the result or the court's reasoning is important information for an engaged reader, but it is not the point here. The point here is that an engaged, experienced legal reader would pay atten-

4. Hoffman v. Clinic Hosp., 213 N.C. 669, 197 S.E. 161 (1938).

tion to the fact that this case came up on a motion to dismiss. Because the case was dismissed below, and affirmed on appeal, the reader now knows that any other case that has facts analogous to this one would not be permitted to get to a jury (as long as the court felt the facts were sufficiently analogous to warrant the same result). Thus, what I would learn from this case is very helpful: I would know that—at least in North Carolina in 1938—a plaintiff in a false imprisonment case had to show evidence of something more than a verbal warning by an unarmed, un-uniformed, fiscal manager in order to support a claim. If no other case has refuted that decision in the meantime, it would still be good law today.

In contrast, what if the "procedural posture" had been different in this case? What if the trial judge had, instead, denied the motion to dismiss and allowed the case to go to the jury? Let's say, then, that the jury felt sorry for the plaintiff and found the defendant hospital liable for false imprisonment. On appeal, let's imagine that the Supreme Court affirmed the decision of the trial court not to grant the dismissal, reasoning that there were enough facts here that a rational jury *might* (but didn't have to) find that a reasonable person might have stayed like the plaintiff did. In that case, the Supreme Court's opinion wouldn't tell me for sure what facts, if proven, would always constitute enough evidence of "reasonable fear of harm" to allow a plaintiff to recover for false imprisonment. It would only tell me that *these* facts provided enough evidence to allow a jury to reach a result one way or the other. Thus, I could surmise that a verbal warning by an unarmed, non-uniformed, fiscal manager *might* be enough evidence to allow a plaintiff to collect damages for false imprisonment—but it wouldn't always have to be. I only know that such facts provide enough evidence for a court to allow a jury to consider the question.

One helpful way to conceptualize why this kind of information is important is to imagine the military gunnery concept of "bracketing." In the Navy, for example, when a gunship is shooting at a target, the initial round may land far to the right of the target. The gun is then wheeled around until a round lands to the left of the target. Whoever is shooting the gun now has a set of "brackets" that establish the outer boundaries on either side of the target. All future shots can be taken between the two boundaries until the target is successfully hit.

Like this kind of artillery "bracketing," a careful reading of cases based on procedural posture can help a lawyer define the outer boundaries of what facts, *if proven*, do or don't satisfy the elements of a particular claim as a matter of law. If a case has been decided by a jury, the jury's decision is a subjective analysis of the facts, so it is difficult to use such a decision to set a legal boundary (one that could be used to predict accurately the outcome of all similar cases). If a court has made a legal decision about the viability of a party's case based on facts alleged or forecast in the pleadings, then you have a case that can give you a "bracket" (outer boundary) for what kinds of analogous facts will always, as a matter of law, support a claim or never, as a matter of law, support a claim.

To a relative beginner in law study or practice, such fine distinctions based on procedural posture may seem overwhelming. If it seems overwhelming to you, don't panic. Take away from this discussion the notion that procedural posture (what happened to the case below) matters a whole lot more when you are reading unedited cases in real life than it matters in a typical classroom (except for the general purpose of learning about the various motions that might have been ruled on below). Over the months and years ahead, start doing as the experts do: pay careful attention to the procedural posture of the case when reading significant unedited cases. Find some experts in the field and pay attention to how they are treating procedural posture in cases. As you learn more about procedural posture, you'll understand your non-casebook cases better (as well as your casebook cases) and you'll be both a better legal reader and a better legal thinker.

(6) Evaluate What You Read

Without question, inexperience hampers your ability to evaluate unedited cases. If you are unfamiliar with the court system, it is hard to know which courts carry the most weight within a given jurisdiction. If you are unfamiliar with the deciding judges, it is difficult to evaluate the weight their decisions may carry with other judges or the way in which their opinions may be influenced by their general beliefs or reasoning abilities. Similarly, lack of familiarity with procedural rules or jurisprudential conventions makes it significantly more difficult to understand whether the court's explanations are sensible and accurate.

The best way to gain experience is to allow yourself to evaluate what you read based on what you *do* know, and ask questions or keep an inquisitive attitude about what you *don't yet* know. We all can read, and so we can form opinions about how well written an opinion might be. We can form opinions about the inherent logic in an opinion—and even more so if we are thinking hard while we're reading. If you can't understand the sense in an opinion, isn't it possible that it simply doesn't make sense? We can also be informed readers, alert to the kinds of writing conventions that a judge might use to distract us from factors in the case that don't support the conclusion reached. For example, has the judge made unsubstantiated statements of law? Is the judge reading precedent broadly or narrowly? Has the judge distorted or dismissed important facts? Has the judge stretched precedent beyond what is reasonable? Has the judge failed to deal adequately with an important line of authority?

It is also possible that you may need to evaluate your own assumptions about the facts or the law in a case if you can't understand a court's action. Try seeing the result of a case through the court's eyes and consider if your personal opinions may not be consistent with that of the court.

As they read actively, these are the kinds of questions experienced lawyers are asking themselves that lead them to sophisticated readings of cases and move their ability to understand the law to new heights.

(7) Review, Rephrase, Record

Reading always goes better if you are willing to go back and recheck yourself, looping a past thought into a present thought, weaving a newly developing idea into one that is more fully formed. One difficulty, in fact, with reading cases online is that this back-and-forth process that characterizes strong reading is more difficult to do when scrolling through a long case, so the tendency is to read in a linear way, letting go of what you read or thought about several pages ago and keeping on moving forward.

Expert readers of law can skim and move forward through cases they are reading for general information, as long as they are taking enough notes about what they are thinking at various points and the new vocabulary they are developing to hold on to the information. Other reading tools such as paraphrasing complex information, creating tabulated lists, and recording synthesized thoughts are a regular part of case law reading often ignored by students hampered by use of library casebooks or hemmed in by online reading. At the risk of felling more trees than any of us would like, there is often no substitute for copying or printing the critical cases, or the critical portions of cases, that are at the core of understanding a legal question so that the reader is free to review, record, and rephrase liberally.[5]

C. In Summary

This chapter has given you an introduction to some of the differences between reading edited cases within the context of a single doctrinal course (like Contracts or Property) and reading unedited cases in the context of a legal writing class, a clinic, or the actual practice of law. Because reading unedited cases is a different (and, hence, new) skill, you may find your reading will be challenging and cumbersome at first, just as your initial reading in a casebook was confusing and uncomfortable. Hang in there. As you gain experience reading unedited cases through legal writing programs, clinical skills and externship courses, summer jobs, and professional employment, your reading (and thinking) will continue to mature and serve as a foundational tool for your long-term professional success.

---

5. But see Chapter 15 re: evolving methods for reading effectively online.

PRACTICE EXERCISES

This was unquestionably a challenging chapter. If you are invested in how lawyers read unedited cases competently, you will probably want to read this chapter more than once. When you're ready, try your hand at the hypothetical attorney assignment below and the accompanying real-life case about two sisters in conflict over the actions of one of the sister's cat. Remember that you can visit caplaw.com/rll to see some of the responses I thought about as I wrote these practice exercise questions.

1. As you've learned, reading for the "main idea" is a critical reading skill. You can't read for the main idea unless you are clear on the purpose for your reading. For this exercise, assume that you are a new associate in a medium-sized law firm, having just graduated from law school and passed the bar. Your purpose for reading the following case is to provide the information that your partner asks you about below.

Your senior partner has approached you to ask you to do some research for one of the firm's long-term corporate clients. The question raised by the client is a personal one this time, and is not about the client's corporate work. Your client lives in a family neighborhood with individual, detached homes and fenced yards, and has lived there for several years. This past year, your client was given a new puppy, a Great Dane, as a gift. The Great Dane, Sandy, is now nine months old and is a good sized dog. Sandy is a happy, playful dog. He has been to obedience school and is reasonably well-trained. Sandy enjoys other animals and occasionally chases squirrels when they come in the yard.

A new neighbor has moved in next door. This new neighbor is afraid of dogs, and is especially afraid of Sandy because of his large size. The neighbor approached our client recently and told our client, "I think you should know that I am concerned about my safety around your dog. If your dog gets out of the yard and hurts me, I will get a lawyer and sue you for damages."

Your senior partner has done some research on statutes and local ordinances and is comfortable that his neighbor would not be in violation of any existing statute or ordinance about leash laws if Sandy were to get out of the yard. Your partner has also found a recent case within your jurisdiction that addresses common law rights and responsibilities of pet owners who may have "dangerous" animals. Your partner does not have time to read the case and has asked you to read it to see, at least from the language of that case, whether your client needs to be concerned about his new neighbor's fear of Sandy. Your partner has specifically asked that you not consider any questions of negligence.

As a new associate with that assignment in mind, please read the following case given to you by your partner:

Ray v. Young No. COA01-1505.

Court of Appeals of North Carolina. Dec. 3, 2002.[1]

Cat owner's sister brought negligence action against owner seeking compensation for injuries inflicted by cat. The Superior Court, Johnston County, Knox V. Jenkins, Jr., J., granted owner's summary judgment motion, and sister appealed. The Court of Appeals, Timmons-Goodson, J., held that sister failed to establish that cat exhibited vicious propensities in the past, or that owner had any reason to suspect that cat would attack sister.

Affirmed.

---

1. Reprinted from West's National Reporter System with permission of Thomson Reuters. This case is properly cited as *Ray v. Young*, 154 N.C. App. 492, 572 S.E.2d 216 (2002).

1. Animals 🔑 70

To recover at common law for injuries inflicted by a domestic animal, a plaintiff must show: (1) that the animal was dangerous, vicious, mischievous, or ferocious, or one termed in law as possessing a vicious propensity, and (2) that the owner or keeper knew or should have known of the animal's vicious propensity, character, and habits.

2. Animals 🔑 67, 70

The gravamen of a cause of action for injuries inflicted by a domestic animal is not negligence, but rather the wrongful keeping of the animal with knowledge of its viciousness.

3. Animals 🔑 70

If the plaintiff establishes that an animal is in fact vicious, the plaintiff must then demonstrate that the owner knew or should have known of the animal's dangerous propensities.

4. Animals 🔑 70

The test of the liability of the owner of an animal is not the motive of the animal, but whether the owner should know from the animal's past conduct that he is likely, if not restrained, to do an act from which a reasonable person, in the position of the owner, could foresee that an injury to the person or property of another would be likely to result.

5. Animals 🔑 67

To determine whether the owner of the animal is negligent, the size, nature, and habits of the animal are taken into account.

6. Animals 🔑 70

Cat owner's sister failed to establish that cat exhibited vicious propensities in the past, or that owner had any reason to suspect that cat would attack sister; although sister presented some evidence tending to show that cat had bitten or scratched people in play, she offered no evidence of any previous behavior by cat that would have indicated his propensity to attack.

7. Animals 🔑 **67**

Absent evidence linking cessation of cat's antidepressant medication or his compulsive disorder, which caused him to ingest foreign objects, with attack on owner's sister, owner had no duty to inform sister that cat was no longer taking his medication.

Appeal by plaintiff from order entered 31 August 2001 by Judge Knox V. Jenkins, Jr., in Johnston County Superior Court. Heard in the Court of Appeals 12 September 2002.

Anderson Korzen Karnersville, & Associates, P.C., by John J. Korzen, and Hardison & Leone, L.L.P., by Elizabeth A. Leone, for plaintiff appellant.

Bailey & Dixon, L.L.P., by Patricia P. Kerner, Raleigh, for defendant appellees.

TIMMONS-GOODSON, Judge.

Sonya Ray ("plaintiff") appeals from an order of the trial court granting summary judgment in favor of plaintiff's sister, Cecelia Whitley Young, and her husband, Randall Young ("defendants"). For the reasons stated herein, we affirm the order of the trial court.

On 15 September 2000, plaintiff filed a complaint in Johnston County Superior Court seeking compensation for injuries inflicted by defendants' cat, "Charlie." The complaint alleged that Charlie exhibited vicious propensities, and that defendants were aware of such propensities. Plaintiff charged defendants with negligence in failing to take adequate precautions to ensure plaintiff's safety while she was a lawful visitor at defendants' residence. Defendants thereafter filed a motion for summary judgment pursuant to Rule 56 of the North Carolina Rules of Civil Procedure, which motion came before the trial court on 13 August 2001.

At the summary judgment hearing, the evidence before the trial court tended to show the following: In early December 1998, plaintiff cared for defendants' dog at her home while defendants were out of town. Defendants did not ask plaintiff to take care of Charlie. On the evening of 6 December 1998, plaintiff returned the dog to defendants' residence. After entering the residence, plaintiff noticed Charlie behind her, "hissing with his back hunched up." Charlie then growled and bit plaintiff on the back of her left ankle. When plaintiff reached down to assess the damage to her ankle, the cat bit her left hand. Because the cat would not release plaintiff's hand, plaintiff "knocked [Charlie] up against the wall with [her] hand in his mouth," whereupon Charlie initially released his grip, but immediately bit plaintiff in the hand once more. Plaintiff knocked the cat against the wall twice more, and Charlie ended his attack. As a result of this attack, plaintiff suffered considerable injury to her left hand.

Plaintiff presented further evidence tending to show that Charlie had bitten both defendants on past occasions, as well as a third individual, Mr. J.D. Denson. Plaintiff also testified that Charlie acted aggressively towards defendants' dog and other large dogs. Finally, plaintiff asserted that Charlie suffered from a "compulsive behavioral disorder" for which he had previously been medicated.

Defendants denied plaintiff's characterization of Charlie as a vicious cat, asserting that his attack upon plaintiff was completely unprecedented and therefore unforeseeable. Defendants presented evidence tending to show that, although Charlie occasionally bit or scratched them while playing, he had never exhibited aggressive behavior of the magnitude experienced by plaintiff. Mr. Denson, the individual identified by plaintiff as having been scratched by Charlie on one occasion, submitted an affidavit asserting that the scratch was superficial and occurred in the course of playing with Charlie.

Defendants also submitted testimony by Charlie's treating veterinarian, Dr. Betsy Sigmon. Dr. Sigmon testified that Charlie's medical records revealed no history of aggression. Dr. Sigmon further described Charlie's history of compulsive behavioral disorder, which had caused him to ingest foreign objects on several occasions, requiring surgery. Dr. Sigmon noted that cats with compulsive disorders "just have to have a lot of attention, a lot of activity. Without that, without [having] constantly something to do, very commonly they're seen for obstructions of their intestines from eating stuff they shouldn't." Dr. Sigmon initially prescribed an antidepressant for Charlie's behavior, but later approved of his removal from the medication because a high-fiber diet appeared to effectively control Charlie's symptoms.

After considering all of the evidence and arguments by counsel, the trial court granted summary judgment in favor of defendants and dismissed plaintiff's action with prejudice. From this order, plaintiff appeals.

The sole issue on appeal is whether the trial court erred in granting summary judgment to defendants. Summary judgment is proper where "the pleadings, depositions, answers to interrogatories, and admissions on file, together with the affidavits, if any, show that there is no genuine issue as to any material fact and that any party is entitled to a judgment as a matter of law." N.C. Gen. Stat. §1A-1, Rule 56(c) (2001); *Joslyn v. Blanchard,* 149 N.C.App. 625, 628, 561 S.E.2d 534, 536 (2002). Summary judgment is properly granted where the pleadings and proof disclose that no cause of action exists. *See Joslyn,* 149 N.C.App. at 628, 561 S.E.2d at 536.

[1, 2] In order to recover at common law for injuries inflicted by a domestic animal, a plaintiff must show "(1) that the animal was dangerous, vicious, mischievous, or ferocious, or one termed in law as possessing a vicious propensity; and (2) that the owner or keeper knew or should have known of the animal's vicious propensity, character, and habits." *Sellers v. Morris,* 233 N.C. 560, 561, 64 S.E.2d 662, 663 (1951). "'The gravamen of the cause of action in this event is not negligence, but rather the wrongful keeping of the animal with knowledge of its viciousness[.]'"

[3–5] If the plaintiff establishes that an animal is in fact vicious, the plaintiff must then demonstrate that the owner knew or should have known of the animal's dangerous propensities. *See Sink v. Moore and Hall v. Moore,* 267 N.C. 344, 350, 148 S.E.2d 265, 270 (1966).

> The test of the liability of the owner of the [animal] is not the motive of the [animal] but whether the owner should know from the [animal's] past conduct that he is likely, if not restrained, to do an act from which a reasonable person, in the position of the owner, could foresee that an injury to the person or property of another would be likely to result.

Id. In order to determine whether the owner of the animal is negligent, the size, nature, and habits of the animal are taken into account. *See id.*

[6] In the instant case, plaintiff failed to establish that Charlie exhibited vicious propensities in the past, or that defendants had any reason to suspect that their cat might attack plaintiff. Although plaintiff presented some evidence tending to show that Charlie had bitten or scratched people in play, plaintiff offered no evidence of any previous behavior by Charlie that would indicate his propensity to attack plaintiff. Regarding a cat's tendency to scratch or bite while playing, Dr. Sigmon verified the common knowledge that, "Cats have claws. Cats have teeth. [The fact that a cat may scratch or bite during play] is one of the possibilities whenever you have a mammal in your possession."

[7] Moreover, although plaintiff argues that defendants had a duty to inform her that Charlie was no longer taking his antidepressant medication at the time he attacked plaintiff, she failed to present any evidence linking the cessation of the medication, or Charlie's compulsive disorder, with the attack. All of the evidence tended to show that the cat's behavioral disorder caused him to ingest foreign objects, and that the medication was aimed at preventing this behavior. There was no credible evidence to suggest that Charlie's disorder made him aggressive, or that ending the medication would cause Charlie to attack someone. Dr. Sigmon furthermore testified that Charlie's condition was being effectively treated through a high-fiber diet.

Because there were no genuine issues of material fact concerning the cat's vicious propensity and defendants' knowledge thereof, the trial court properly granted summary judgment in favor of defendants. The order of the trial court is hereby

Affirmed.

Judges HUDSON and CAMPBELL, concur.

2. Neither you nor your senior partner would want to advise your client based on reading only one common law case. However, assuming that you had done more research and found that *Ray v. Young* is truly representative of the law in your jurisdiction, do you think your client needs to worry at this point about liability for any personal harm Sandy might cause if he gets out of the fence? Are there behaviors from Sandy that you might warn your client to be alert for in the future?

3. A shift in reading *purpose* always causes a shift in reading *focus*. Let's assume, now, that you are not a lawyer but rather are in graduate school studying social work. You are writing a thesis looking at the impact that litigation has on family relations. Go back now and re-read the case again from this point of view. In the space below, explain how this perspective changed your reading strategies:

When we read a case, we can't really know what happened beyond what is reported in the case, at least not without more background information. Nonetheless, part of "expert" reading is being able to speculate about what you're reading and make the text "come alive" by visualizing and engaging personally with the text. In the space below, write a paragraph about how you think the controversy reflected in this case might have changed relations between these family members, recognizing that there is no practical way to externally validate what you're imagining:

If you were reading the case solely from the perspective of the new associate described in Question 1 above, would these speculations be part of the "main idea" of your reading? If not, would that influence how much time and attention you gave to them?

4. About halfway through the case, the court states, "[t]he sole issue on appeal is whether the trial court erred in granting summary judgment to defendants." The Court of Appeals ultimately decided that the trial court was correct, and affirmed the fact that summary judgment should have been granted for the defendants. By granting summary judgment for the defendants, the court decided, based on the pleadings, depositions, etc., that the plaintiff was not entitled to go to trial on the facts and that the defendants had no liability as a matter of law. Do you agree that there were no legally relevant facts in dispute in this case?

Assume that the Court of Appeals had reversed the trial court's grant of summary judgment, allowed a trial, and then (at that trial) the jury had decided that the defendants were not at fault? The result would have been the same—the defendants would not have been liable. Nonetheless, would you be more or less confident about the advice you would give Sandy's owner if this had been the Court's decision?

5. Go back to the last page of *Ray v. Young* and notice that there is a bracketed number ([7]) at the beginning of one of the last paragraphs. That bracketed number refers to Headnote #7 at the beginning of the case. How could you use this headnote (and the others) as a valuable reading tool without shortchanging your understanding of the case?

6. Do you, personally, have strong feelings about animals?

   Did those feelings affect how you visualized the facts in this case?

   Did those feelings affect whether you believe the case was correctly decided?

7. As you read this case, did you have feelings about the human and economic costs that this case may have accrued?

   Despite the poignancy of the probable human and economic costs to the parties in *Ray v. Young*, did the decision of the court help you understand what your client's rights might be concerning Sandy?

CHAPTER 15

Reading on a Screen

Despite the historically glacial pace of change in law schools and the legal profession,[1] electronic media has found its way into the study and practice of law.[2] The vast majority of classes are administered through an electronic learning management system (like Sakai™, Blackboard™, or TWEN™).

---

1. If you are interested in reading more about the history of legal education and about law school reform, a good place to start is with WILLIAM M. SULLIVAN, ANNE COLBY, JUDITH WELCH WEGNER, LLOYD BOND & LEE S. SHULMAN, EDUCATING LAWYERS: PREPARATION FOR THE PROFESSION OF LAW (2007) (often referred to in scholarship about legal education as "The Carnegie Report"); *see also* Judith Welch Wegner, "*Reframing Legal Education's Wicked Problems,*" 61 RUTGERS L. REV. 867 (2009).
2. *See* DAVID I.C. THOMSON, LAW SCHOOL 2.0: LEGAL EDUCATION FOR A DIGITAL AGE (2009)(citing a rich array of books and articles exploring the use of electronic media in law school and law practice); *see also* Sherry L. Leysen, *Brain Plasticity and the Impact of the Electronic Environment in Law and Learning,*" 30 LEGAL REFERENCE RES. Q. 255 (2011); Debra Moss Curtis & Judith R. Karp, "In a Case, On the Screen, Do They Remember What They've Seen?," 30 HAMLINE L. REV. 248 (2007) (describing the authors' integration of technology in their classrooms); Craig T. Smith, *Technology and Legal Education: Negotiating the Shoals of Technocentrism, Technophobia, and Indifference,* 1 J. ASS'N LEGAL WRITING DIRECTORS 247 (2001). The growth of technology in legal education was the subject of a full-day conference sponsored by the Institute for Law Teaching and Learning and hosted by the North Carolina Central University School of Law on March 3, 2012 (conference schedule available at: http://lawteaching.org/conferences/2012technology/).

These learning management systems most often include carefully developed syllabi that are accessed electronically, and, increasingly, professors are creating collaborative learning environments that include mandatory participation in online chat room discussions or wiki-style student writing projects.

Today's students have the luxury of enjoying multimedia presentations in some classes and engaging electronically with students from partnering schools in others. Look to your left and then to your right and you will see many students happily incorporating sophisticated note-taking software into their routine study strategies. Some doctrinal professors enthusiastically record their classes and allow students to access the recordings later. Others not only augment class lectures using PowerPoint™ slides, but make the slides available for students to review after class.

Clinic classes often feature required use of electronic courtroom media and, increasingly, some legal writing teachers are embracing a paperless environment, collecting student assignments and giving feedback online. Even the traditional casebook has been affected by new technologies, with leading law school publishers offering casebooks in increasingly sophisticated electronic formats.[3]

This movement towards integration of electronic media in legal education is consistent with changes in the practice of law as well. Most courts now require or at least offer online filing of documents. Collaborative writing, even among lawyers who are not physically present in the same building, is a frequent occurrence. Electronic discovery is commonplace and some firms have chosen to outsource document review tasks to foreign countries.[4]

Lawyers seamlessly coordinate schedules with clients and associates using a variety of hand-held devices. The most sophisticated of our courtrooms offer opportunities to present evidence in new formats. Researching

---

3. See, for example, the West Interactive Casebook Series™ (offering titles that include both a hard copy and an electronic version with links and helpful reading aids).

4. Aaron Harmon, The Ethics of Legal Process Outsourcing—Is the Practice of Law a 'Noble Profession,' or is it Just Another Business?, 13 J. TECH. L & POL'Y 41 (2008).

in the library has yielded substantially to research conducted online from almost anywhere. The need to store client files (securely) in an electronic format is the current reality.[5] And, increasingly, lawyers draft documents and handle filing from their own computers, without clerical support.

In the end, despite these significant technological innovations, one thing has not changed. The study and practice of law continues to call for an inordinate amount of reading. Increasingly, the material to be read may appear on a screen.

Not surprisingly, reading specialists who study electronic reading (reading on a screen) are clear that reading electronically and reading in print can be very different experiences, and yet—for great readers—they are remarkably the same.[6] Online reading (reading with internet access at hand) lends itself well to information-gathering tasks and is often characterized by "skimming" and "scanning" behaviors that allow the online reader to decide whether to continue reading or move on to a different source.[7] Hypertext and hypermedia links give readers quick access to contextual information,

---

5. Anne Klinefelter & Steve J. Melamut, CLE Presentation at the UNC School of Law's Festival of Legal Learning: How Can I Take My Law Practice to the Clouds? (February 10, 2012).

6. Professor Julie Coiro, a reading specialist at the University of Rhode Island, cautions that we should not assume that people who can read extremely well in print can necessarily transfer that skill to on-screen reading without assistance. She says, "As readers transition to Internet reading environments, emerging work suggests . . . traditional reading and thinking strategies are necessary, but not sufficient, to successfully navigate and make sense of online informational texts [citations omitted]." Julie Coiro, *Talking About Reading as Thinking: Modeling the Hidden Complexities of Online Reading Comprehension*, 50 Theory into Practice 107, 108 (2011).

7. See Leysen, *supra* note 2, for a thorough and engaging exploration of the possible impact of typical web-searching on our ability to read critically. "Scanning is defined as '[to] look quickly but not very thoroughly' while skimming is '[to] read quickly or cursorily so as to note only the important points.' Generally, skimming is only a prereading, preparatory technique. Some of the concerns raised about Internet-style reading is that skimming and scanning are becoming our *primary* means of reading." *Id.* at 261 (emphasis in original)(citations omitted).

but also pose the risk that the reader may be pulled off-task.[8] Online reading allows the reader to, in effect, create his or her own universe of knowledge by deciding what links to follow and what sources to focus on without restrictions imposed externally.[9] And there is no question that having the ability to access expansive amounts of information electronically is both convenient and immediately reinforcing. By the same token, online reading runs the risk of draining the reader's limited energy as he or she tries valiantly to focus on the task at hand, resisting the temptation to check email, a social networking site, or the latest basketball score.

The commonalities among the skills we use to read well, regardless of the media in which information appears, are at least as significant as the differences. Great readers recognize that reading is thinking and that thinking takes energy. They do not try to read in any format if they are too tired to engage with enthusiasm. Great readers have a reading purpose in mind and read for the main idea, monitoring their progress and frequently checking back in with themselves to make sure they are heading in the right direction. They make changes in their goals when necessary. They check their efficiency. They have opinions based on their prior knowledge and take responsibility to pay attention to the source of the text (or other media) they are thinking about. They relate what they are learning about to what they know already, and they fill in critical gaps with additional information. They draw inferences and circle back if they find later they were wrong. They paraphrase. They take notes. They engage (mentally) in a dialogue with the author of a text. Most importantly, they create new knowledge as they read.

Despite the easy accessibility of online information and the potential benefits of integrating new technologies into the law school classroom, all is not smooth sailing as we move from a culture that has read predominantly

---

8. *Id.; see also* Debra Moss Curtis & Judith R. Karp, *supra* note 2, at 256–59.

9. *Id.*; *see also* Julie Coiro, Jill Castek, & Lizabeth Guzniczak, *Uncovering Online Reading Comprehension Processes*, 60th Yearbook of the Online Reading Ass'n 354 (2011).

in print to a culture that accesses much of what it reads electronically.[10] In the early days of computer-based reading, reading online was demonstrably slower than reading in print.[11] Specialists studying the ergonomics of on-screen reading have suggested many reasons why screen reading may be slower than print reading, including poor screen resolution, poor print quality of PDF documents accessed online, line lengths that are too short or too long, the distractions that are rampant in online environments, font size or type, the challenges of scrolling, and general eye fatigue.[12]

---

10. This transition may be especially difficult in the legal field where much of what we read today was written (often many years ago) to be read in print format. New technologies are adding links where authors never imagined they would be, perhaps making online access to cited authority more readily accessible than originally intended. Additionally, as you have learned throughout this book, legal reading requires deep, thoughtful consideration of the stories behind cases and the policies behind statutes. Skimming and scanning are useful (and necessary) strategies to help you find what material to read, but neither are substitutes for the kind of deep reading that is often called for in the study and practice of law.

11. Barry W. Cull, *Reading Revolutions: Online Digital Texts and Implications for Reading in Academe,* First Monday, Vol. 16, Number 6 (June 6, 2011), http://firstmonday.org (citing a 1992 study by Andrew Dillon documenting a thirty percent slower reading rate for subjects reading online in comparison to those reading in print, but also noting that more recent research is seeing that gap narrow or disappear, Jan M. Noyes & Kate J. Garland, *Computer- vs. Paper-Based Tasks: Are They Equivalent?*, 51 Ergonomics, 1352 (2008)). Substantial research in the 1990s and early 2000s documented twenty to thirty percent as a reasonable estimate of how much slower online reading was for most people using technology available up through the first decade of the 21st century. A 2011 study showed that even reading on a tablet or eReader with high screen resolution slowed test subjects down on average of six to ten percent. Jakob Nielsen, *Tablet Readability: iPad and Kindle Reading Speeds,* Alertbox (July 2, 2010), http://useit.com/alertbox/ipad-kindle-reading.html. Some pundits predict that the gap in reading speeds will narrow as technology advances (and as readers develop "new literacies" that make them more proficient online readers).

12. For an interesting look at the science behind eye strain caused by online reading, see Nick Bilton, *Do E-Readers Cause Eye Strain?*, Bits Blog of The New York Times(February 12, 2010), http://bits.blogs.nytimes.com/2010/02/12/do-e-readers-cause-eye-strain/.

One oft-cited early study reports further that our eyes focus more readily on what we hold in our hands than what we look at that we are not touching, accounting at least in part for new studies that show a narrowing gap between print-reading and screen-reading from a tablet or other hand-held device.[13] Additionally, researchers talk about "lean forward" and "lean back" reading, concluding that it is difficult for most readers (even with laptops) to relax when reading from a computer screen.[14] Similarly, engaging physically with text (highlighting, note-taking, paraphrasing) electronically continues to be more cumbersome in many electronic formats than is using a simple paper and pencil to take margin notes.[15] Perhaps because of the physical

---

13. Ziming Liu, "*Reading Behavior in the Digital Environment*," J. of Documentation 700, 707 (2005) (citing P.A. Strassman, Information Payoff (1985)); *see also* Nielsen, *supra* note 11.

14. I am grateful to Pam Siege Chandler, Senior Director, Law School Publishing, Thomson Reuters, for first introducing me to the concept of "lean forward" and "lean back" information-gathering tools. Clearly, hand-held devices are making progress in the "lean back" reading experience, but, interestingly, at least one scholar notes that Steve Jobs, founder of Apple™ computers, side-stepped the lure of creating a pure eReader, favoring a tablet with online accessibility instead. It is reported that Stephen Jobs did not want Apple™ to create a pure eReader and invested in the development of a tablet (with online accessibility) instead because he believed that members of the plugged-in generation would not be willing to stay away from the contacts they maintain through electronic media long enough to read without interruption in any electronic format. Cull, *supra* note 11 (citing John Markoff, *The Passion of Steve Jobs*, The New York Times, January 15, 2008, http://bits.blogs.nytimes.com/2008/01/15/the-passion-of-steve-jobs/).

15. Recognizing that physically engaging with reading (taking thoughtful notes, for example) aids in both comprehension and retention, technology developers are working to incorporate note-taking, highlighting, and organizational features in tablets, electronic textbooks, and software packages. At the time of this writing, those note-taking features were still not as simple to use as pen and paper or highlighters, but, with practice, were helpful. Because the legal profession (and the study of law) requires exceptional deep-reading skills, it is clear that finding and learning to use the most sophisticated online reading tools available is an increasingly wise and necessary investment of time, energy, and economic resources.

challenges of electronic reading, lack of familiarity with reading-enhancing technologies, or lack of confidence in our screen-reading skills, a stunning majority of us (over eighty-two percent in one 2011 study[16]) continue to print out long or important documents when we have the choice.[17]

But there are people out there who read extremely well in electronic formats. You may be one of them. What are these expert on-screen readers doing that sets them apart? Reading specialists agree that, in addition to integrating all the reading skills that make for solid print reading, electronic reading calls for some additional "new literacy"[18] skills. If you are planning on enrolling in law school, it would be wise to explore these new literacies (especially those available to law students) before the school year starts. In

---

16. Liu, *supra* note 13, at 708 (reporting that over eighty-two percent of 1985 study participants reported "always" or "frequently" printing long or important documents to read them); *see also* Channa Herath, *How Do We Read Online: The Effect of the Internet on Reading Behaviour* at 89 (unpublished masters paper, Victoria University of Wellington, 2011) (reporting that over seventy percent of subjects printed material if it was long or important).

17. Interestingly, several studies have indicated that our ability to read details accurately diminishes when we read online, suggesting that we should be careful about proofreading our own work or that of someone else online unless we are confident about our online reading abilities. Curtis & Karp, *supra* note 2, at 259 (citing numerous empirical studies suggesting that subjects not only failed more often to spot errors when working on a screen, but worked slower as well).

18. The term "new literacies" arises from the awareness that online reading is different in significant ways from print reading and requires the development of a collection of additional skills or strategies that reading specialists have come to realize are a necessary component of successful on-screen reading. *See* Kouider Mokhtari, Angel Kymes & Patricia Edwards, *Assessing the New Literacies of Online Reading Comprehension: An Informative Interview with W. Ian O'Bryne, Lisa Zawilinski, J. Greg McVerry, and Donald J. Leu at the University of Connecticut*, 64 THE READING TEACHER, 354 (2008); *see also* Coiro, *supra* note 6. To read more about the "new literacies," explore the website for The New Literacies Research Team at the University of Connecticut: http://www.newliteracies.uconn.edu/.

the law school setting, the most significant of these "new literacy" skills include the following three:

(1) mastering technologies that will make on-screen reading easier and more effective;[19]

(2) making wise decisions about what to read and how deeply to read it; and

(3) managing your energy as you read.

The remainder of this chapter summarizes the best tips I've gleaned from law students and faculty who handle electronic reading exceptionally well.

A. Master Technology[20]

- Your computer is an important learning tool in law school. Arm yourself with one that is reliable and efficient; learn how to use it before school starts. And, if you are purchasing a new computer,

---

19. You've already been exposed to a wide range of technologies in your prior educational and work experiences, and you have developed your own sense of comfort with a technologically rich world. The focus of this chapter is not to provide you with specific technical solutions to the challenges we all face when reading from a screen, but rather to encourage you to recognize that reading on a screen in law school and in law practice is a reality that requires law students and lawyers to develop an interest in and comfort with the technologies through which we access what we read.

20. Since technology changes at the blink of an eye, specific products and tools are not identified by name in the print copy of this chapter. Instead, I hope this chapter will inspire you to think about how you can find the tools necessary to read well on a screen, now and in the future. However, I have included some information about new technologies on the author's webpage that accompanies this book (caplaw.com/rll. If you have discovered a product or tool that has helped enhance your on-screen reading, email information about it to me at ruthannmckinney@coregrammar.com, and I will be happy to post it on the author's site with your recommendation.

pay attention to its screen resolution[21] and whether you can sit with it comfortably as you read and take notes.

- Consider the advantages of using a high-resolution, hand-held device like a tablet when you have substantial on-screen reading to master. Be sure that you have also thought of a way to take notes while you are reading. One student reported reading from the laptop while taking handwritten notes on the iPad.[22]
- There is a learning curve involved in mastering any new technology. If you are using a new tool or are reading in a new medium, take the time to experiment with its features. For example, does your new electronic casebook offer a note-taking function? Does it have a search feature? Is there an electronic Table of Contents that might give you an overview of the subject you'll be studying? If your professor expects you to submit a paper online, learn how to do so well ahead of your submission deadline.
- Lawyers and law students are called on frequently to read material on a screen that was originally designed to be read in print. That kind of document often appears as a protected image-based PDF document that does not allow you to physically engage with the text (not even to take notes or highlight an important passage). You

---

21. "Screen resolution" has to do with technical features regarding the dpi (dots per inch) your screen display offers. In 2012, a professional printing press that used laser technology to create plates for offset printing could print well over 2,000 dpi on paper, but even the best computer screens offered somewhere in the neighborhood of only 90–100 dpi. In 1998, screen usability expert Jakob Nielsen noted that study subjects who used prohibitively expensive computer screens with resolutions of 300 dpi read as fast as those reading in print, and he predicted that the gap in reading speed would disappear as dpi on screen displays approached that number. Jakob Nielsen, "*Electronic Books: A Bad Idea*," ALERTBOX (July 26, 1998), http://www.useit.com/alertbox/980726.html. A 2021 MacBook Air, for example, is reported by Apple to have a print resolution of 227 dpi.

22. I thank my research assistant, Avery Aulds, for this helpful hint.

can make that material easier to read by using available software programs or Apps to convert it to a digital text-based format that allows you to manipulate it as you read.[23]

- Explore annotation applications that will allow you to take margin notes, highlight, record comments, and otherwise engage with digital material in a way that will help you focus and create new knowledge—the key to expert reading.
- Although the ability to take notes without interrupting your reading is an almost indispensable part of effective reading,[24] finding electronic note-taking tools that operate smoothly can be a challenge. If you have the money and space to do so, consider setting up two computer screens: one to read from and one to write your notes with. Maintaining two screens is an easy way to brief when reading cases online, but remember that (with the exception of key terms of art) rewriting information in your own words is a more effective reading tool than simply copying (or cutting and pasting) mindlessly from the text you are reading. Another option is to invest in a tablet and a second computer, reading from the tablet while taking notes on the second computer (or by hand). My 2021 research assistant does a combination of all three: she reads on her laptop and takes handwritten notes on her tablet.[25]

---

23. I am grateful to Dr. Katie Guest Pryal, Clinical Assistant Professor of Law at the University of North Carolina School of Law, for sharing her enthusiasm for on-screen reading and her insights regarding new technologies that enhance the electronic reading experience.

24. *See* Chapter 11, "Review, Rephrase, Record," in Section II of this book to revisit why note-taking is an indispensable critical reading strategy, aiding your ability to focus, your comprehension, and your recall of the material you have read. One study showed that fifty-four percent of readers "always" or "frequently" annotate printed documents but, alarmingly, *only eleven percent* annotate documents they read on a screen. Liu, *supra* note 13, at 708.

25. I thank my research assistant, Avery Aulds, for this helpful hint.

- There are Apps and software that will allow you to change the format of a document to make it easier for you to read. You can change font type and size. You can change background color. You can change the length of lines and convert a two-column format to a one-column format (or vice versa). Taking the time to set up a format that is easy on the eyes will allow you to read more comfortably and for a longer period of time without losing efficiency.[26]
- Consider investing in one of many good software systems and Apps designed to help you organize notes electronically. These programs allow you to not only take notes as you read, but also to organize them in a way that allows you to integrate them with class notes or retrieve them later (even using search features) when you want to review specific information or synthesize your ideas.
- Talk with an ophthalmologist about blue-light glasses and other eyeglass accommodations that will reduce eye strain when reading online.
- Remember that there are many excellent "open source" (free) applications and software packages available. As you explore options to enhance your online reading capabilities, consider the economic costs but don't invest time or energy in a program, regardless of its cost, unless it enhances your electronic reading experience in a way that is comfortable for you. It is helpful to take a "try it and see" attitude with new Apps, but recognize that time is precious in law school. Give yourself a reasonable amount of time to try out a new

---

26. There is a whole "usability" industry that studies how to make accessing information online as seamless and comfortable as possible. Studies by industry experts investigate user preferences on all kinds of dimensions ranging from the benefits of one-, two-, or three-column formats (generally, the shorter the line, the slower the reading) to font style preferences (with Verdana being the online font of choice in more than one study. *See, e.g.*, Sheree Josephson, *Keeping Your Readers' Eyes on the Screen: An Eye-Tracking Study Comparing Sans Serif and Serif* Typefaces, 15 VISUAL COMM. Q. 67 (2008)).

App, but do not let the search for the ideal technologies eat up your study time. Build on what you knew coming into law school and use what is comfortable for you.

- Most law schools have an Information Technology (IT) Department whose members are full of good advice for how to learn about and master technology. Make friends with those individuals and seek their advice. If they offer workshops, attend any that might help you master technology that will enhance your screen reading capabilities.
- Explore printing options at your school. For most of us, there will be times when we want to print a document. Find out if free printing is available and look into whether you can print directly from your tablet using WiFi. Also, especially if you favor printing long documents to read them, find out how to set your printer to print on both sides of the paper (but don't turn in law school papers printed on both sides unless your professor accepts them in that format).
- If your school or professor uses a learning management system, take time before the first day of classes to learn how to use it. Explore each of your classes' course syllabi carefully. Explore the site for each class to see what you can learn about your courses ahead of time.
- If you are technologically averse or inexperienced, find someone who thrives on technology and make friends with that student. Trade some other task (like taking the initiative to form a study group) in exchange for learning new ways to use technology to enhance your reading experiences in law school.

B. Make Wise Choices About What to Read and How Deeply to Read It

- One of the most intriguing advantages of reading online (with internet access) is that so much information is at your fingertips. Online reading has the potential to be one large independent study project of your own making.[27] To take advantage of this wide open format, and avoid being overwhelmed, it is critical to keep your reading purpose squarely in mind, revisiting it frequently to make sure what you are currently reading is really moving the ball forward.[28] One effective strategy is to write your reading purpose down on a piece of paper and review it periodically to make sure you are staying on task.

- Electronic reading materials frequently include tempting hyperlinks to related information. Some of that information can be a valuable way to quickly test an inference you are drawing or to clarify context. But other information may be extraneous and a pure distraction,

---

27. Julie Coiro, Jill Castek & Lizabeth Guzniczak, *Uncovering online reading comprehension processes: Two adolescents reading independently and collaboratively on the Internet*, 60TH Y.B. LITERACY RES. ASS'N, 354, 355 (2011) (theorizing that readers today face an "entirely new category of online reading processes, *realizing and constructing potential texts to read*") *(emphasis in original)*.

28. In his now-famous article, *Is Google Making Us Stupid? What the Internet Is Doing to Our Brains*, ATLANTIC MONTHLY (July–Aug. 2008), Nicholas Carr (not a lawyer) took a personal, hard look at the impact that the internet and other new technologies were having on his ability to think in the kind of sustained way that deep, thoughtful reading calls for. In that article and his widely acclaimed follow-up book, THE SHALLOWS (2010), Carr takes personal ownership of the fact that he feels he can no longer concentrate like he used to, and hence is no longer able to focus on the deeper meaning of the material he reads. He believes he is less creative and less patient when reading. Ultimately, he raises the question of whether extensive online reading and our daily bombardment by electronic media is robbing him (and perhaps all of us) of our ability to think. Mr. Carr is at the center of a growing debate exploring the tensions between the undeniable conveniences of online information-gathering and the risks that we are permanently changing the way we think. *See* Leysen, *supra* note 2(providing an in-depth look at how online reading may actually change the development of synapses in our brains and, further, offering suggestions for effective online reading habits to adopt in a law school setting that calls for deep, thoughtful reading).

drawing your attention away from your actual reading purpose.[29] The only way to know the difference is to read with your brain engaged. If you've made a mistake and have fallen down a rabbit hole, back up quickly and go back to more profitable material. A good rule of thumb to follow is this: do not click on a link unless you know why you are doing so, and be very hesitant to click on a link within the second screen you have opened.

- The cases featured in most electronic casebooks include hyperlinks that can lead you directly to the full text of cases cited within the featured case. Do not just click automatically on those links. Make a decision, considering the following quick tip: Generally (just as in print), if the casebook author had wanted you to focus on a case cited within another case, the cited case would have been included in the main text. Thus, unless your professor indicates otherwise or you are reading a casebook that specifically suggests reading cited cases, do not take the time to click on the link to a case cited within a case you have been assigned.
- Some hypermedia and hypertext links in an electronic casebook can provide interesting background information that can help you relate to the case more easily or could increase your motivation to read the case. If you click on a hypermedia or hypertext link, don't continue to engage unless the link is doing you some good.
- Professors often post reading material on your class learning management system site. At least one study showed that first-year law students tended not to read that material, assuming (wrongly,

29. I am indebted to Professor Aaron Harmon for the following suggestion: "One way to keep from being distracted by hyperlinks that you may want to visit later is to open new links in new tabs in your browser using the CTRL key when you click on a link. The link opens in a new browser, and you can cut and paste the URL into a document or revisit those additional tabs when you choose." Telephone Interview with Aaron Harmon, Clinical Assistant Professor of Law, the University of North Carolina School of Law (April 2012).

it turns out) that the professor would have printed the material if it had been important.[30] Know your professor. Read what is important to your professor and always assume that the course syllabus (even if it is posted only online) is important.

- It is not unusual to be asked to participate in an online discussion or chat room in law school. Most entering law students will have already had experience with such chatroom discussions as undergraduates and maybe even in high school. An online discussion or chat room, in effect, expands the traditional classroom discussion to a to-be-read text format. If you are asked to participate, pay attention to the purpose(s) of your postings and the postings of your fellow students or your professor. Be efficient about learning the law. Know why your professor encourages the discussion, focus on the postings that are enhancing your understanding of the topic, assume that anything you post anywhere on the internet is (or could become) open to the public, and contribute what will be useful to others (and consistent with the etiquette of the site).

C. Manage Your Energy

- Reading on a screen has the potential to be a big boost to your energy. Consider the physical advantages of not carrying around a backpack full of heavy casebooks and notebooks, pens and paper. Finding information online that is easily accessible can save hours of searching in a library—time that you could put to better use synthesizing the information or just relaxing. Search features allow you to move quickly through long documents without even turning pages. But these advantages are only available to you if you have mastered the technology that you need to read online well.
- Reading online lends itself well to information-gathering activities, and reading even long material on a screen is often blessedly

30. Curtis & Karp, *supra* note 2.

convenient. Nonetheless, the benefits of reading online do not outweigh the drain on your energy that can result from a poorly managed online reading experience. Think about what happens to your concentration every time a pop-up surprises you online or every time your eReader reminds you that its battery is low. One way to minimize distractions is to turn-off auditory alerts that visual notifications on all devices. Most law students find it advantageous too deliberately set aside discrete periods of time to unplug without interruption and honor those times.

- If you are studying with your computer, do not open other screens unless you are very confident that you can maintain your focus. For most of us, even if we have minimized extraneous screens, it takes energy to resist the temptation to look at them.
- When you are studying law, the ability to focus squarely (and only) on the task at hand is critical. Thus, avoid multitasking (like reading email during class) when you are trying to learn. You may appear to be juggling many things at once, but your efficiency will be way down,[31] and the extra stress will take a toll on your energy.
- Time management experts suggest checking email, social networking sites, and the internet only once or twice a day, not continuously throughout the day. If this suggestion seems to fit your learning style but you are concerned that you might forget what it is that you intended to check, make a list to remind yourself with later. Also, if your friends and family are used to your checking all messages

---

31. *See* Leyson, *supra* note 2, at 268 ("Research tells us that although we believe we are carrying out multiple tasks at the same time, in reality a decision-making "bottleneck" forms. This bottleneck prevents the brain from executing two decision-making processing at once. Rather, decisions are processed in sequence with time in between tasks.") (citations omitted); *see also* Cull, *supra* note 10 ("Evidence suggests that multitaskers find cognitive focus difficult, that it takes longer to do two tasks simultaneously than it does to complete the same tasks one after the other, and that knowledge gained in dual-task situations can be applied less flexibly in new situations.") (citations omitted).

and responding to phone calls immediately, talk to them about law school and why you have to set up a different pattern when law school starts. Ask them to help you stick to those new patterns.

- Because of the huge demands on your time in law school, many students I spoke with suggested that you should not hesitate to print once you've decided that a document is either important or too long to read comfortably on screen. As you have learned already, time is your most valuable commodity in law school. Do not waste it reading online if you are among the majority of people who read more efficiently in print. But, over the long haul, do consider practicing engaged online reading when you are not under time pressure and see if you can eventually become one of those people who reads as well on the screen as off.[32]
- If you are reading on screen, take more breaks than you might normally take. Reading law well in print is hard work. Reading on a screen is no different and may carry additional physical challenges. You need to rest your eyes and your body to be maximally efficient.[33]

---

32. Aaron Harmon, Clinical Assistant Professor of Law at the University of North Carolina School of Law, shares the following advice: "I recommend students gather information electronically, process for relevance, and then consider what to print and what to process electronically. I also recommend that they try processing information electronically first (instead of printing automatically), then print the key sources and process them a second time in paper." *Supra* note 26.

33. Here's a great gentle yoga tip from Patty Frey, certified yoga instructor and business administrator for The Writing & Learning Resources Center at the University of North Carolina School of Law: Close your eyes. Rub your hands together quickly to warm them, and then cup your hands over your eyes for one minute, breathing deeply. Visualize a restful, peaceful place as you relax. Inhale deeply through your nose. Exhale deeply through your mouth. Return to your work refreshed! *See also* Bilton, *supra* note 12 (quoting Dr. Alan Hedge of Cornell University: "'While you're reading, your eyes make about 10,000 movements an hour. It's important to take a step back every 20 minutes and let your eyes rest. . . .'"); Leyson, *supra* note 6, at 280–81 (suggesting personal habits we can adopt that may counteract the tendency of the internet to "encourage" a "different style of learning" than law school and the practice of law requires).

When you take a break, walk away from the computer. Get up and stretch. Drink some water. Do not switch to another computer-based activity. Doing so is not a legitimate break from screen reading.

- Consider the ergonomics of your on-screen reading experience and don't settle for a reading environment that is physically uncomfortable. Do you feel at ease where you are sitting while you read the screen? Is the lighting adequate? Are you in a quiet area? Can you take notes comfortably in the space you have allotted? Some expert on-screen readers recommend tablets for long reading experiences expressly because tablets lend themselves to a comfortable, "lean-back" (curl-up-with-a-good-book) feeling as you read.
- Reading on the screen, and especially reading online, can be deceptively seductive. We have all had the experience of intending to be online for a short time and suddenly finding that an hour has disappeared. To avoid working longer online than you intended, consider setting a timer that will remind you to take a break. There are good software programs and Apps available to help you set up a time management system that can help you monitor your study time.
- If you have a choice, try not to scroll through a long document. Either print it or format the document so that it has page breaks. Studies show that, unless you have significant short-term memory capacities (which is less likely when you are tired or stressed), scrolling tends to interfere with comprehension and saps your energy.[34]

---

34. *See* Cull, *supra* note 10 (citing Erik Wästlund, Torsten Norlander & Trevor Archer, *The Effect of Page Layout on Mental Workload: A Dual-Task Experiment*, 24 COMPUTERS IN HUM. BEHAV., 1245 (2008) in support of the premise that the act of scrolling and the concentration needed to retain focus when reading long documents on a screen taxes short-term memory and is done more effectively by those with large short-term memory capacities).

- Use the reading tools available to you online to skim or scan material quickly, saving time and energy as you decide what to read more deeply. For example, many legal research search engines highlight your research search terms within the body of the documents you retrieve, allowing you to go directly to the part of a document that includes those key terms. This feature can help you decide if you want to read the document more deeply, but do not assume that finding key phrases is the same as reading the document thoroughly. It is not. Other reading tools that are big time-savers are menus on websites and bookmark features. Once you have identified a document as being worth a deeper read, consider whether you will fare better if you print it or continue to read it online. And one additional tip: maintain a separate document (online or using a pen and paper) that includes the links you have found valuable as you read online. Saving those links (especially if you include a brief summary of the value of the content) gives you an opportunity to return and read the website content more carefully later if you choose to do so. It is also wise to include a notation of the name of the website itself since links are not always available when you return to them at a later date.
- As you learned in Chapter 13, statutes are often written in an outline format to help the reader stay oriented when reading complex legislation. It is easy to lose that helpful visual structure if you are scrolling quickly through a long statute (or if your research takes you directly to the middle of a long statute with many subsections). When you read statutes and related material (like administrative regulations) online, use any available Table of Contents features to get "the big picture." If there are no such features available, scroll up and down, taking the time to understand the physical layout of the legislation and where the part you are reading fits into it. Most experienced lawyers will tell you that reading a statute in print, in the context of their jurisdiction's statute books, is, without question, the safest way to ensure complete comprehension.

- Common law and other case law cannot be separated from the stories of the parties involved in the conflict out of which the published case grows. This principle is fundamental and does not change because a case has been accessed in an on-screen format. Once you decide a case is germane to the legal question you are seeking an answer to, take the time to read the entire case, using the strategies discussed throughout this book. Although electronic search features allow you to move to particular parts of cases with ease (for example, to sections that correspond to a headnote or to sections that contain your key search terms), it is an error in reasoning to draw conclusions based on only a partial reading of the case.
- Whether they read in print or online, great readers read "recursively" (in other words, they don't read straight from the beginning to the end of a document, but rather loop around, going backwards and forwards as they think about what they are learning as they read).[35] In on-screen reading, the search feature is a valuable "recursive" tool that allows you to go back in a text to review where you may have read about a topic before, or to leap forward in a text to see where the topic may appear later.
- When you are working with a document (like an older case or law review article) that was originally intended to be read in print, remember to use the reading cues (like headings and subheadings or chapter titles) that were part of the original document. Also, consider converting the document to a digital format that will accommodate note-taking, allowing you to engage more deeply with the text while reading it more quickly as well.
- If your professor adopts a casebook that can be obtained online or in print, consider your reading style and comfort with technology

35. See Chapter 11 ("Review, Rephrase, Record") in Section II to remind yourself of the value of reading (in print or online) in a "loopy" fashion.

when you decide whether to purchase the hard copy or the electronic copy as your primary text—especially in the beginning stages of law school. Depending on the casebook's publisher, some electronic casebooks include numerous tools (such as internal note-taking systems, search features, electronic Tables of Contents, etc.) that can help you engage with the text effectively. But, if these tools are unfamiliar to you, it will take time to become adept at using them. In addition, until you become confident about your reading purpose,[36] it may be difficult to make informed decisions about what to click on when you are using the electronic version of your book. If you are not completely comfortable with reading long and important information on a screen, stick to reading in the traditional, print text most of the time unless your professor recommends otherwise.[37] Alternatively, consider reading the electronic version on a tablet (or on a separate screen) while taking notes separately. Over time, you can begin to learn to integrate more technology into your online reading strategies, giving you more on-screen reading options.

In the end, expert reading on the screen and expert reading in a book are very different experiences, each offering its own joys and its own challenges. Yet, in fundamental ways, expert reading on the screen and expert reading in a book are remarkably similar as well. Where technology is involved, learn how to use it as a tool to enhance—not distract from—your reading experience. Recognize that technology is ever-changing and that it is here to stay.

---

36. See all of Section I and Chapter 7 ("Always (Always!) Read with a Clear Purpose") in Section II of this book as reminders of the importance of having an accurate sense of what information you need to glean from your reading before blindly decoding (in print) or scrolling (online) through the text.

37. If you make the print copy of an electronic casebook your "go to" version, you can continue to enjoy the electronic version to preview or review material, to visit links that you are curious about, and at times when carrying the bound hard copy is a major inconvenience.

The trick to reading successfully in our technologically rich world is to embrace the idea that you can and must learn to use the tools available (at any point in time) that will allow you to be actively engaged with your reading in a setting that is comfortable for you. Regardless of the medium that carries the message,[38] the kind of thoughtful reading that characterizes the study and practice of law remains a deeply personal experience that calls for you to read with energy and enthusiasm, to make wise choices regarding what to read and how to read it, and, ultimately, to create new knowledge as you engage with the material that is before you.

---

38. Media expert and scholar Marshall McCluhan coined the phrase "the medium is the message" in his 1964 best-seller, UNDERSTANDING MEDIA: THE EXTENSIONS OF MAN. Mr. McCluhan's groundbreaking concept was that the way in which information is communicated is inseparable from the information itself, with each informing the other. Thus, he foreshadowed a world where (for example) the ability to post on social media may, in fact, fundamentally change the nature of what we value in our relationships. Similarly, our ability to follow hyperlinks indefinitely online or our ability to access a PDF document on screen may fundamentally change what we choose to understand from material communicated through the written word.

PRACTICE EXERCISES

The following questions will help you think about the pros and cons of online reading, and they will help you assess your own technology literacy skills in light of the reading tasks you'll face in law school. Remember that you can visit caplaw.com/rll to see some of the responses I thought about as I wrote these practice exercise questions.

1. In the law school setting, in what ways are reading on screen and reading in print similar?

2. Before you came to law school, how often during a typical day would you check email and social networking sites?

   Do you expect to have to change those habits in law school or law practice? Why?

3. This chapter references the fact that most readers prefer to read important or long material in print, even if they could access it online. Why is that?

4. Some people can read long or important documents as effectively on screen as they do in print. Are you one of those people? If so, what is it about your electronic reading that sets you apart? If not, what is one thing you could do to improve your electronic reading?

5. Do you know how to turn off the auditory alert feature on your email and other notifications? Why might you want to turn those features off?

6. Assume you are using a brand-new eBook in lieu of a traditional casebook for your Contracts class.

   (a) You are reading a case about offer. In the first paragraph of that case, the court cites a case in support of its definition of offer. Should you click on the hyperlink to that supporting case? Why or why not? Should your answer always be the same?

   (b) Your electronic casebook contains a link to a site that contains the full, unedited Pepsico ad that is the subject of *Leonard v. Pepsico*, the case you are reading (also appearing in this book in the exercises to Chapter 12). Should you click on the link to that ad? Why or why not?[39]

7. Why might you need to take more frequent breaks if you are reading electronically than if you are reading a printed document?

---

39. If you're curious and would like to see the original "Drink Pepsi: Get Stuff" TV advertisement that was behind *Leonard v. Pepsico, Inc.*, search "harrier jet" and "Pepsico" to check out a clip online.

CHAPTER 16

Conclusion

In 1930, more than seven decades ago, Professor Karl Llewellyn admonished his students:

> "I have hinted before [in earlier lectures] at what can be gotten . . . from the cases. I know no more fascinating record of the human tribe if you have the wit to read it. The wit to read it! Within a hair we have lost the art of reading. There was a time when men [and, presumably, women] read by putting all of themselves and their experience into what they have read. Reading was active, reading was creation. . . . Now, reading is different. The author does your thinking for you—as your instructors, you sometimes hope, will do your thinking for you. . . . Go, then, and read. Go, then, and look, and *see*."[1]

If Professor Llewellyn was concerned about the lost art of reading in 1930, it is hard to imagine what he would think about reading today.[2]

---

1. K.N. Llewellyn, The Bramble Bush 151–53 (3d ed. 1960) (emphasis in original).

2. Laura P. Graham, *Generation Z Goes to Law School: Teaching and Reaching Law Students in the Post-Millenial Generation*, 21 UALR L Rev 29 (2018) (documenting changes in reading habits and advocating for teaching critical reading skills to Generation Z law students); Maryanne Wolf, Reader Come Home (2018)(presenting a compelling, well-researched picture of the universal changes digital reading is causing in all readers' brains, including in those of us who read law).

In 2004, a study conducted by the Research Division of the National Endowment for the Arts was released indicating an alarming drop in literary reading.[3] Measuring sheer volume of reading in objective numbers, the study highlights a staggering decrease in the amount of reading we do.[4] In 1992, 54% of the population read at least one book of literature. Just ten years later, in 2002, only 46.7% of the population reported reading even

---

3. Nat'l Endowment for the Arts, Reading at Risk: A Survey of Literary Reading in America (2004), available at https://www.arts.gov/sites/default/files/ReadingAtRisk.pdf. This study was cited by Cathaleen Roach and Carol McCrehan Parker in their presentation, *Is the Sky Falling: Ruminations on Incoming Law Student Preparedness (and Implications for the Profession) in the Wake of Recent National and Other Reports,* and by Ian Gallacher in his presentation, *Keeping Books on the Horizon: Teaching Legal Research to the Google Generation,* both presented at the 2004 Conference for the Legal Writing Institute (Seattle 2004)). Interestingly, at least three additional presentations at that conference targeted reading as a neglected fundamental skill for incoming law students. *See* Debra Moss Curtis & Judith R. Karp, *In a Case, In a Book, They will Not Take a Second Look! Critical Reading in the Legal Writing Classroom,* presented at the 2004 Conference for the Legal Writing Institute (July 22, 2004); Dorie Evenson, James Stratman, and Laurel Currie Oates, *Research on Legal Reading,* presented at the 2004 Conference for the Legal Writing Institute (July 22, 2004); Laurel Currie Oates, *Teaching Students to Read, Analyze, and Synthesize Statutes and Cases,* presented at the 2004 Conference for the Legal Writing Institute (July 23, 2004). The latest study from the NEA, conducted in 2017, confirms the need for concern: https://www.lrs.org/2019/08/21/national-endowment-of-the-arts-survey-finds-that-53-of-american-adults-read-a-book-for-pleasure-in-the-past-year/.
4. Nat'l Endowment For the Arts, *supra* note 1. Recent studies forecast good news for those of us who love reading. The National Endowment for the Arts conducted a follow-up study in 2009 that shows a marked increase in literature reading among young people aged 18–24, reversing a two-decade trend of declining reading reported in its 2004 study. http://www.nea.gov/research/ReadingonRise.pdf. Also, in a study released in April of 2012, the Pew Internet & American Life Project noted, "43% of Americans aged 16 and older say they have either read an e-book in the past year or have reader other long-format content . . . in digital format. . . ." The project also documented the fact that "[f]ully 42% of readers of e-books said they are reading more now that long-format reading material is available in digital format." http://libraries.pewinternet.org/2012/04/04/the-rise-of-e-reading.

one book of literature. In the 18–24 year old age group, only 42.8% of the survey's subjects reported engaging in literary reading—a drop of 28% in that age bracket in twenty years.[5]

Despite the omnipresence of internet searches, video communications, and sound bites, the lifeblood of exceptional lawyering continues to be exceptional reading. Not for the faint of heart, exceptional reading requires energy, intellectual confidence, personal humility, and a commitment to the value of what you are doing.

The discourse of law thrives on the written word and the ability of those who read the law to make sense of what has been written in the past. Careful, close reading in law reaches beyond mere words into the reality behind the cases and statutes recorded for posterity in the written word. The responsibility placed on lawyers as protectors of people, institutions, and governments is awesome. The ability to meet that responsibility begins for each of us as we read law with our hearts as well as our minds, with thoughts anchored in the past as well as thoughts reaching forward to the future, and—above all—with a humble awareness that the development of just and fair results begins with careful, close, and critical reading.

---

5. *But see* Ian Gallacher, *"Who Are Those Guys?": The Results of a Survey Studying the Information Literacy of Incoming Law Students*, 44 Cal. W. L. Rev. 151 (2017) (finding that incoming law students in 2017 read far more than the national average but, nonetheless, needed to further develop some literacy skills that are prerequisites for success in the legal profession).

APPENDIX A

Test Your Reading Speed[1]

Before I started doing research about reading, I held the common misconception that reading speed—in and of itself—was necessarily the key to success as a reader. As I've learned more about the discipline of reading, I've come to understand that people who read slowly and methodically aren't necessarily the "best" readers, but people who race through their reading like it's the Indianapolis 500 aren't necessarily the "best" readers either.

Reading well occurs when the reader acquires the ability to use a number of inter-related skills when he or she reads, and when the reader chooses among these skills wisely in light of the purpose of the reading being tackled. The main body of this book explores how expert readers approach a reading task and, specifically, how expert law readers approach reading law. This addendum is here to help you figure out your baseline reading speed so you can determine if you have any kind of unusual problem with your reading that might be getting in the way of reading efficiently and effectively in law.

1. I am grateful to Frank S. Kessler, Reading Instructor at the Learning Center for the University of North Carolina at Chapel Hill, for generously sharing his insights about reading speed, as well as many other aspects of effective reading, with me and with the students at the University of North Carolina School of Law.

To figure out your average reading speed, choose anything you have around the house that you'd like to read. Try to avoid picking up a highly technical journal full of vocabulary you're not used to or one that is full of numbers. Also, try to avoid picking up a newspaper article or magazine where the text is printed in columns. Something that has writing from one margin of the page to the other will be ideal. Read something you haven't read before.

You are going to read for five minutes. Get a stopwatch with a timer or work with a friend who has a watch with a second hand.

Choose a place in the text to start and then begin reading. Read until your time is up. Mark where you started and where you stopped in the text.

Go back and calculate how many average words are on a line by counting three or four lines and dividing the number you get by the number of lines you counted. Next, count how many lines you read (you should count a partially completed line as a full line).

Finally, multiply your total number of lines read by the figure you got for the average number of words per line. Divide by five (assuming you read for exactly five minutes). This final number is the average number of words per minute (more or less) that you're reading per page.

On average, a college student with good reading skills will read about 250 words per minute. An exceptionally fast college reader can cover more. True speedsters can read upwards of 500 words per minute without losing comprehension. If you are reading less than 250 words per minute, try taking the test again to see if the first one was right. If it was, and you really are reading significantly slower than 250 words per minute, you would be wise to figure out how to speed up your reading in general.

Most university campuses have a reading center available to their students. In all probability, a reading specialist at that center would be willing to work with a professional student interested in picking up his or her reading speed. If your campus doesn't have such a center, or if the specialists there can't work with post-graduates, you can use any number of good books to improve your own reading speed. Many are available routinely online or at most bookstores.

I have seen law students improve markedly in their reading speed by doing simple exercises over a period of only a few months—bringing a reading speed of 150 words per minute up to over 250 words per minute in one or two semesters. Think how much more free time (and how much more time to think about other study tasks) such a student would have. All else being equal, the 250-word/minute student could read a 100-page college assignment in a little over three hours. The 150-word/minute student would be reading that same assignment for five and a half hours. Thus, in that one assignment alone, the faster student could save almost two and a half hours of reading!

Of course, as the rest of this book demonstrates, there is far more to being an expert reader than simply finishing an assignment quickly. Especially in an area of reading as complex as law, the real issue is one of effectiveness and efficiency. Expert readers read selectively—so they're not reading every word or every sentence anyway. They know what to pay attention to and what to let go of, not as a trick of the eyes, but because they have a cognitive understanding of what the "main idea" is that they're looking for when they read. Similarly, issues such as fatigue affect all performance and a tired reader is never as effective or efficient as he or she might have otherwise been.

Nonetheless, knowing your speed is useful information. Use this information to your advantage.

APPENDIX B

Getting in a Good Reading Groove

Developing new habits takes conscious effort. The best way to develop healthy reading habits in law is to force yourself to think consciously about what you are reading and how you are reading it. This addendum introduces you to a beginning checklist you can reproduce (copies available online at caplaw.com/rll) and use for the next several weeks as you read cases. This beginning checklist is long—too long to use forever or on every case you are reading. However, as you learn to read law like an expert law student, you should use it on at least one case a day in each of your classes for the first two or three weeks of school.

After you have integrated the questions raised in this checklist into your daily reading habits (so that the questions come up in your mind automatically and you are reading with these questions in the back of your head), you can (and should) shift to the second Checklist ("Focus and Enjoy") found in Appendix C. That checklist is designed to condense the questions raised in the beginner's checklist into four succinct and efficient questions that you should ask yourself *each and every time* you read a case throughout law school. By chunking the questions raised in the first checklist into the broader questions raised in the second, you will be moving from a beginner stage to an expert stage of casebook reading. If you try to use the second checklist (Appendix C) first, it won't do the same thing for you. Instead, you may find that you miss information altogether (instead of including it automatically) because you won't have developed the right "reading groove" through practice.

Beginning Case-Reading Checklist

(Developing the Right Reading Habits)

A. Before You Read the Case

My purpose for reading this case today is:

I have the following amount of time to complete my reading:

I have looked at many of the following external cues:

____ Course Title
____ Table of Contents
____ Course Syllabus
____ Background Reading in Text
____ Section Heading & Sub-heading
____ Running Header
____ Other cases in this cluster
____ Notes & Problems
____ Case Name & Citation
____ Judge's Name & Stature

I am aware of the following internal cues/thoughts:

____ I have prior knowledge about this area of the law
____ I have prior knowledge about the era or geographical location of decision
____ I have prior knowledge about these facts
____ I have some emotional reactions to this topic or the area or date of decision

I have the following hypothesis about what this case will show and how it will fit in my professor's overall plan for this course:

I am *guessing* that the following words *might* be key "magic" words (see Chapter 11) that will characterize rules & principles in this area of the law:

B. As You Read the Case

____ I marked sections that made no sense and decided whether to figure them out or move on. If I decided to figure them out, I did the following:

- ____ made an inference from the content
- ____ looked up a word in a legal dictionary
- ____ asked a peer, an upper-class student, or my professor
- ____ reread the section more carefully
- ____ read ahead to see if there were cues later in the case
- ____ paraphrased in my own words, using Plain English
- ____ other

____ I asked questions of the opinion's author (the judge) and/or responded to thoughts the judge expressed in the opinion.

____ I visualized the operative conflict facts in living color (see Chapter 9).

____ I can explain accurately to a layperson how this case wound through the courts and got here (see Chapter 9).

____ I have modified or affirmed my original hypothesis about the case at various points.

____ I have made up at least one hypothetical to test what I think the rule is in this case.

____ I am still confused about:

____ I feel satisfied about:

____ If there were related "Notes & Problems," I read them and they caused me to also think about:

C. After Reading the Case

I believe the main point of reading this case in the context of this course is to learn:

The main point this case contributes to my coursework is based on the following broader policy considerations or big-picture rationales (why is this result "fair" or a good idea):

If the decision had been mine to make *at the time this case was decided*, I would:

____ agree

____ disagree

Because:

If the decision were mine to make *today* (not when the case was decided), I (personally) would:

____ reach a similar result under similar facts

____ reach a different result

Because:

D. After Reading a Cluster of Related Cases and Text

In addition to the author's choice of cases themselves, the author's background information and related Notes & Problems caused me to speculate that the following are common themes in this area of law:

The specific issues/factors/elements are the kind of things a judge would consider if faced with a new conflict arising in this area of law:

Stated succinctly, the majority rule appears to be:

Stated succinctly, alternative rules (if applicable) appear to be:

Stated succinctly, the following exceptions or defenses appear to exist to this rule:

The big-picture policy/fairness reasons for the development of these rules appears to be:

These policy reasons should be balanced against the following potentially conflicting policy/fairness concerns:

The key ("magic") words that hold special meaning (beyond a layperson's meaning) in this area of law are:

E. When You Are Reading Online

This is an acceptable screen on which to read because:

I am comfortable reading the document in its present format or could change it by doing the following:

I am able to take notes in the following manner:

Some electronic reading tools that I am taking advantage of are:

I have considered (or am) printing this document because:

APPENDIX C

Advanced Reading Checklist

(Focus & Enjoy)

This addendum introduces you to an advanced reading checklist you can reproduce (copies available at caplaw.com/rll) and use whenever you read cases once you've integrated the kinds of questions raised in the Beginning Reading Checklist (Appendix B) into your daily reading. As a supplement to briefing, you can use this checklist (or think about the questions it contains) to help advance your reading. Eventually you should strive to integrate these questions into your daily reading habits (so that the questions come up in your mind automatically and you are reading with these questions in the back of your head).

1. What is the exact legal question in front of the court (that pertains to the sub-topic of the course in this section of the casebook)?

2. What is the court's exact answer to this question?

3. In the court's mind, why does this answer make sense?

4. Keeping the importance of deductive reasoning in mind (Major Premise, Minor Premise, Conclusion) what would you personally have decided if you'd been the judge? Why? What other decisions could have been rationally made?

5. What does this case add to your understanding of this section of the course?

APPENDIX D

Resources for Further Reading

The following resources, among others, strongly influenced me as I developed the ideas for this book. If you enjoy thinking about reading, especially in the context of law, you might enjoy exploring these resources as well.

A. Resources Focusing on Legal Reasoning

BENJAMIN N. CARDOZO, THE NATURE OF THE JUDICIAL PROCESS (1921)

EVA H. HANKS ET AL., ELEMENTS OF LAW (1994)

KENNEY HEGLAND, INTRODUCTION TO THE STUDY AND PRACTICE OF LAW (2d ed. 1995)

OLIVER WENDELL HOLMES, THE COMMON LAW (Mark De Wolfe Howe, ed., Harvard University Press 1963) (1881)

EDWARD H. LEVI, AN INTRODUCTION TO LEGAL REASONING (1949)

K.N. LLEWELLYN, THE BRAMBLE BUSH (3d ed. 1960)

JOHN MAKDISI, INTRODUCTION TO THE STUDY OF LAW (2d ed. 2000)

DAVID S. ROMANTZ & KATHLEEN ELLIOTT VINSON, LEGAL ANALYSIS (1998)

B. Resources Focusing on Reading Theory and Related Intellectual Skills

Mortimer J. Adler & Charles Van Doren, How to Read a Book (1972)

Kenneth L. Higbee, Your Memory (2d ed. 1996)

The Nature of Expertise (Michelene T. H. Chi et al., eds., 1988)

Michael Pressley & Peter Afflerbach, Verbal Protocols of Reading (1995)

Jeffrey D. Wilhelm, Improving Comprehension with Think-Aloud Strategies (2001)

C. Resources for Learning about Effective Electronic Reading Strategies

Barry W. Cull, *Reading Revolutions: Online Digital Texts and Implications for Reading in Academe*, First Monday, Vol. 16, Number 6 (June 6, 2011), http://firstmonday.org

Nicholas Carr, The Shallows (2010)

Debra Moss Curtis & Judith R. Karp, *In a Case, On the Screen, Do They Remember What They've Seen?*, 30 Hamline L. Rev. 248 (2007)

Sherry L. Leysen, *Brain Plasticity and the Impact of the Electronic Environment in Law and Learning*, 30 Legal Reference Res. Q. 255 (2011)

The website for the University of Connecticut New Literacies Research Lab: http://www.newliteracies.uconn.edu/

D. Scholarly Work Expressly Addressing Aspects of Reading in Law

Linda L. Berger, *Applying New Rhetoric to Legal Discourse: The Ebb and Flow of Reader and Writer, Text and Context,* 49 J. LEG. ED. 155 (1999)

Hugh Brayne, *Learning to Think Like a Lawyer—One Law Teacher's Exploration of the Relevance of Evolutionary Psychology,* 9 INT'L J. LEGAL PROF. 283 (2002)

Scott Burnham, *Critical Reading of Contracts,* 23 LEG. STUDIES FORUM 391 (1999)

Dorothy H. Deegan, *Exploring Individual Differences Among Novices Reading in a Specific Domain: The Case of Law,* 30 READING RES. Q. 154 (1995)

Peter Dewitz, *Reading Law: Three Suggestions for Legal Education,* 27 U. TOL. L. REV. 657 (1997)

Elizabeth Fajans & Mary Falk, *Against the Tyranny of Paraphrase: Talking Back to Texts,* 78 CORNELL L. REV. 163 (1993)

Ian Gallacher, *"Who Are Those Guys?": The Results of a Survey Studying the Information Literacy of Incoming Law Students,* 44 CAL. W.L. REV. 151 (2007)

Christina L. Kunz, *Teaching First-Year Contracts Students How to Read and Edit Contract Clauses,* 34 U. TOL. L. REV. 705 (2003)

Mary A. Lundeberg, *Metacognitive Aspects of Reading Comprehension: Studying Understanding in Legal Case Analysis,* 22 READING RES. Q. 407 (1987)

Laurel Currie Oates, *Beating the Odds: Reading Strategies of Law Students Admitted Through Alternative Admissions Programs,* 83 IOWA L. REV. 139 (1997)

Michael Hunter Schwartz, *Teaching Law Students to be Self-Regulated Learners,* 2003 MICH. ST. DCL L. REV. 447

James F. Stratman, *The Emergence of Legal Composition as a Field of Inquiry: Evaluating the Prospects,* 60 REV. EDUC. RES. 153 (1990)

E. Scholarly Work Expressly Addressing Reading Online in Law[1]

Katherine J. Cameron, *In the Eyes of the Law Student: Determining Reading Patterns with Eye-Tracking Technology,* 45 CAP. U. L. REV. 433 (2017)

Kari Mercer Dalton, *Their Brains on Google: How Digital Technologies Are Altring the Millenial Generation's Brain and Impacting Legal Education,* 16 SMU SCI. & TECH. L. REV., 409 (2013)

David Hricik & Karen Sneddon, *Screen Time: Legal Documents in the Digital Age,* 38 SUM DEL. LAW 14 (2020).

Laura P. Graham, *Generation Z Goes to Law School: Teaching and Reaching Law Students in the Post-Millenial Generation,* 41 UALR L. REV. 29 (2018) (including an exhaustive review of related literature)

Shailini Jandial George, *Teaching the Smartphone Generation: How Cognitive Science Can Improve Learning in Law School,* 66 ME. L. REV. 163 (2013)

Patrick Meyer, *The Google Effect, Multitasking, and Lost Linearity: What We Should Do,* 42 OHIO N.U. L. REV. 705 (2016)

Robert Minarcin, *OK Boomer—The Approaching Dizruption of Legal Education by Generation Z,* 39 QUINNIPIAC L. REV. 29 (2020)

1. I am grateful to Daniel Sifredo (UNC Class of 2023) for his research skills and commitment to compiling this list of articles related to reading online in law school and the legal profession. This list is not exhaustive, but each contributes important contributions to the field. Additional articles and books are cited within each article.

Kristen E. Murray, *Take Note: Teaching Law Students to Be Responsible Stewards of Technology*, 70 CATH. U.L. RV. 201 (2021)

Lauren A Newell, *Redefining Attention (and Revamping the Legal Profession) for the Digital Generation*, 15 NEV. L.J. 754 (2015)

Carolyn V. Williams, *#Critical Reading #Wicked Problem*, 44 S. ILL U. L.J. 179 (2020)

F. Significant Resources Outside the Field of Law

If the global impact of online reading is of interest to you, consider reading the work of these two scholars:

Dr. Naomi Baron, Professor Emerita of World Languages and Culture at American University, is widely recognized for her research in digital reading. She is the author of nine books, including THE FATE OF READING IN A DIGITAL WORLD (2015) and HOW WE READ NOW (2021).

Dr. Maryanne Wolf, Director of the Center for Dyslexia, Diverse Learners, and Social Justice at the University of California, Los Angeles, is the author of a number of important works related to reading education, including READER, COME HOME: THE READING BRAIN IN A DIGITAL WORLD (2018). Dr. Wolf's engaging book raises an important question—and offers some intriguing answers: how can we, as a culture, maintain our ability to think deeply, critically, and thoughtfully (an ability developed through traditional print reading) while also benefiting from the ability to gather and process data quickly from multiple sources that is the hallmark of digital reading? This is a particularly compelling question for those of us in the legal profession to consider given the enormous amount of legal information we access and the responsibility we carry to maintain the collective (and individual) ability to think deeply, critically, and thoughtfully about its import.

ACKNOWLEDGMENTS

Writing this book has reminded me that writing, thinking, and reading are integrated, collaborative activities. Without the substantial help of many colleagues, students, friends, and family members, my initial ideas about reading and law could not have evolved into this text. I hope all those who touched this project know how grateful I am for their thoughts and encouragement.

At the risk of leaving someone important out, I'd like to first thank the students at the University of North Carolina School of Law for sharing their reading experiences with me over many years and also for sharing concrete suggestions as I worked my way through this book. Specifically, I'd like to thank Atinuke Akintola (Class of 2006), Tamika Jenkins (Class of 2005), and Jennifer Neuhauser (Class of 2005) for their concrete writing and content suggestions, and the members of my fall 2004 writing section as well as the entire LEAP class of 2007 for their input and encouragement. I would like to especially acknowledge the irreplaceable help of my Research Assistants, Chrystal Lee (Class of 2005) and Ed Eldred (Class of 2006), for their background research, editing suggestions, and collaborative support. In addition, I am indebted to Jeremy Franklin (Class of 2008) and Saurabh Ashvin Desai (Class of 2009) for invaluable suggestions for the second printing, and to Emily Roscoe, from the University of North Carolina School of Library Science, for remarkable research about electronic reading. Finally, a heartfelt thanks to my Research Assistant, Carmen Hoyme (Class of 2005), for her initial research, thoughtful editing comments, and unerring attention to the many details involved in the final production of the first edition of this book. Avery Aulds (Class of 2023) and Daniel Sifreto (Class of 2023) offered invaluable advice and research assistance as I wrote this third edition, and each reminded me, in retirement, of what a joy and privilege it is to work with tomorrow's lawyers.

One of the further joys of teaching in a law school is having the opportunity to maintain ongoing contact with highly competent alumni. I gratefully acknowledge the significant assistance of our alumni, Mr. Jeff W. Hudson and Mr. Neal Ramee, who generously shared their areas of expertise with me as I thought through the content of this book.

Numerous colleagues from the University of North Carolina School of Law helped identify illustrative cases and shared thoughts about the reading process, including Professor Scott Baker, Professor Jack Boger, Professor Ken Broun, Professor Charles Daye, Professor Maxine Eichner, Professor Joe Kalo, Professor Eric Muller, and Visiting Professor Wilson Freyermuth. Professor Bobbi Boyd, now on the faculty at the Campbell University School of Law, gave invaluable advice concerning both content and editing, and offered an abundance of moral support as well. Ms. Patty Frey, our program administrator, offered critical support services and creative ideas throughout the writing process. I am indebted to the Law School's Information Technology Department and to at least the following faculty colleagues who provided important support for the second edition: Aaron Harmon, Anne Klinefelter, Jon McClanahan, Katie Guest Pryal, and Leslie Street. Finally, I am particularly grateful for the consistent encouragement of the Deans under whom I served at the University of North Carolina School of Law: Professor Judith Wegner, Professor Gene Nichol, Professor Gail Agrawal, Professor Jack Boger, and Professor Martin H. Brinkley.

Colleagues outside of the law school shared their thoughts and offered input from across disciplines. Dr. John Edgerly, Dr. Glen Martin, and Dr. Dan Darnell of the University of North Carolina's office of Counseling and Psychological Services, Dr. Rod Dishman and Dr. Patrick O'Connor of the University of Georgia, and Dr. Amy Rountree shared ideas and statistics from their respective professions about healthy student behavior. Early in my work, Dr. Karah Rempe of UNC's Department of English and Comparative Literature shared her enthusiasm and expertise in reading with me, inspiring me to think about creative ways to engage law students in their reading assignments, and, for the second edition, Dr. Jill Fitzgerald, Professor Emeritus at the University of North Carolina School of Education, launched my foray into research about on-screen reading. I am also grateful to Dr. Dorie Evensen of Penn State University for her significant insights about reading and theories of adult education. I am indebted to my long-term friend, Ms. Polly Hochwalt Wolfe, for sharing her understanding, gleaned from many years as a teacher, of how the use of think-aloud reading protocols can improve reading skills. Mr. Frank Kessler of the University of North Carolina's Learning Center has given his time generously and effectively over many years to help me and to help our students develop an understanding of reading in the legal context.

I am grateful for the support and encouragement of colleagues throughout the legal academy, including Dr. Marty Peters of the University of Iowa College of Law, Professor Suzanne Rowe of the University of Oregon School of Law, Professor Ian Gallacher of Syracuse University College of Law, Ms. Cathaleen Roach of DePaul University College of Law, Professor Laurel Currie Oates of the Seattle University School of Law, Professor Leah Christensen of the Thomas Jefferson School of Law, Professor Nancy A. Wanderer of the University of Maine School of Law, and Dean Michael Hunter Schwartz of McGeorge Law School, whose creative work on engaged learning in law school heavily influenced my approach to this book. Professors Elizabeth Fajans and Mary R. Falk, through their foundational work in this area, have had an enormous impact on my ideas about reading and law. I also offer my heartfelt thanks to Scott Sipe at Carolina Academic Press, as well as Ryland Bowman, Jennifer Hill, Jessica Curtis, Arthur Iannacone, Rachael Meier, Tim Colton, Linda Lacy, Keith Sipe, and Bob Conrow, for their enthusiasm, encouragement, and creativity. I owe gratitude to our colleagues at Thomson-Reuters, Pam Siege Chandler, Kelly Mickelson, and Trina Tinglum, for their generous copyright assistance and shared interest in the increasing use of technology in legal education.

No writing project can go forward without the explicit support of family and friends, and I am especially grateful to my husband, Ray E. West, my parents, George and Lucy McKinney, my sister, Dr. Mary Schweitzer, my brother, Dr. George McKinney III, and my sister-in-law, Dr. Marie McKinney. I appreciate the assistance of my adult offspring, Bret Gerbe, Lynda Gerbe, Matt West, and Ashlie West, who offered their usual insights and encouragement along the way.

Finally, I would like to thank Dr. Mary Lundeberg, Professor and Chair of the Department of Teacher Education at Michigan State University, whose seminal dissertation work in the area of case law reading was inspirational. Her generosity in sharing her reading expertise motivated me to pursue my interest in reading and my conviction that reading well is the key to success in the study and practice of law.

INDEX